CW00552469

Rivers of Wales

Rivers of Wales

JIM PERRIN

with an introduction by ROB MIMPRISS

GWASG CARREG GWALCH

First published in 2022 by
Gwasg Carreg Gwalch, 12 Iard yr Orsaf, Llanrwst, Wales LL26 0EH

ISBN: 978-1-84527839-7

This book is published with the financial support of the
Welsh Book Council.

Printed and bound in Wales at
Gwasg Gomer, Llandysul, Ceredigion

For my youngest son Lewis Perrin Williams

Cymro, dringwr, ecolegydd

"It is the feminine principle and the waters of life that hold the key to wholeness in a patriarchal society."

Roselle Angwin

"The life in me is like the water in the river."

Henry David Thoreau

"The essence of life is flow, not fix."

Thomas Wolfe

"...unto the place from whence the rivers come, thither they return again."

Ecclesiastes 1.7

Contents

Foreword

There is an earlier book by Jim Perrin on a river theme. Called *River Map*, and published with work by the photographer, John Beatty (Gomer, 2001), it follows the Dee from its industrialised mouth to its source, a journey taken by the narrator at a time of personal crisis, when his relationships, like the river, have been polluted and befouled, and his inner life cries out for the cleanliness and purity, the self-knowledge and the redemption, which the clear waters at the source of the Dee represent. The book is out of print, and I am glad to have a copy, but it has much in common with this newer material. The same writers are mentioned in both; there is the same awareness of history and cultural heritage; the same dramatic encounters with wildlife, and the same enjoyment of physical comforts which conclude a day's walk.

While *River Map* reflects a time of personal crisis, and offers a deeply personal response, in *Rivers of Wales* the crisis is shared. Jim describes the arrogance and carelessness with which Afon Teifi has been polluted, almost annihilating fish stocks. His description of the mouth of Afon Dwyryd aches with longing for the wealth of bird-life once found there. Jim aligns these environmental concerns with the transcendentalist spirit which he finds at work in Kate Roberts and D. J. Williams, as well as Waldo Williams and Henry David Thoreau. Thoreau's first book, *A Week on the Concord and Merrimack Rivers* (pub. 1849) is a celebration of solitude, of long, lonely hikes, and of nights spent alone in the mountains under the stars. But it is also written in memory of the brother with whom he spent a river trip, in a relationship of such perfect amity that there is no need to tell us which of the two gathered wood for the fire and which put up the tent, which brother was troubled by nightmares and which of them gave him comfort.

In *Snowdon* (Gomer, 2012) Jim's prose is erudite and purposeful. In *The Hills of Wales* (Gomer, 2016) it vividly reflects the sparseness of a landscape of 'startling geometries' (p. 150), 'elegant, sharply defined' (p. 99), which speaks to us most clearly when we are alone (p. 133). His descriptions of the hill-slopes above Llanllechid at dusk, hill-slopes I have known since childhood, convince me that his writing will not lead us astray. Yet in contrast to the focus of the other books, *Rivers of Wales* gives us Jim at his most companionable. It is filled with books he admires, folk-tales and anecdotes that will entertain us, people with whom he has shared the landscapes he describes, and it is a delight to be led through the book as though by a long-familiar walking partner, knowledgeable, observant and funny. It is a cliché to say that Seneca is more readable than the other Stoics because he is more fleshly and fallibly human. Jim differs from Thoreau in part because he lacks his po-facedness and pomposity.

If one is taken aback by the range and ferocity of his views, one will contrast them with those of the bigoted, who in fact have few opinions because they have few interests, and who express those few with the meanness and fearfulness which have polluted their capacity for joy. Jim condemns 'that spiteful, stiff and self-regarding crew' of the book world and of academia, condemns authoritarianism in wilderness management and self-righteousness in the arts; yet the far greater part of this book is given over to praise. He will celebrate a good ale, a hearty meal, a lively conversation; he shows an affectionate enjoyment of the eccentricities of those he meets; yet the quality of which he speaks most is generosity. This habit in his thought reminds me of the earlier writer of landscape and heritage, Glasynys (Owen Wynne Jones, 1828-1870). A short story by Glasynys, "Noson yn yr Hafod"', describes an evening spent as a guest with cottagers in the mountains. A neighbour comes, there is story-telling, music and dancing, and the narrator compares the simple happiness of this family, who will open their home to anyone and share freely with those in need, with the pride of the industrialists and the Nonconformists who would condemn their innocent pleasures as frivolous or sinful or wasteful.

Where there is anger in *Rivers of Wales*, it expresses Jim's moral purpose. Environmental destructiveness is a consequence of blindness and heedlessness, of which the opposite is connection, not only with the natural world but with each other and with ourselves. It is distance and a sense of otherness that allows a government based in England to use Welsh land to enrich its own followers, or, in *The Hills of Wales*, to requisition a whole district for the purposes of training for war (p. 246). With that same indifference to human need, 'punitive, mean-spirited and often callous' (Philip Alston, *United Nations Human Rights: Office of the High Commissioner*, 16th November 2018 online), the U.K. government has driven hundreds of thousands of our fellow citizens to hunger, homelessness and death (Toby Helm, *The Observer*, 1st June 2019 online). As I write, *The Independent* tells us that businesses are dumping untreated sewage in Welsh rivers as a result of chemical shortages occasioned by Brexit (Jon Stone, 7th September 2021 online), *The National* describes an ecological crisis of the Wye as a microcosm of global catastrophes (Rebecca Wilks, 18th & 20th September 2021 online), *The Conversation* describes the American military's massive impact on global pollution (Benjamin Neimark et al, 24th June 2019 online), and *The Guardian* warns us of failing harvests, stalling economic growth and a breakdown of international order in our lifetimes unless our destruction of the environment can be brought to an end (Edward Helmore, 25th July 2021 online). It is tempting to turn away from the natural world, to hide from its increasingly uncomfortable summers and its disconcertingly quiet springs, to lose oneself in work and the human world, including the activism we might hope will save it.

A little while after being invited to write this foreword, I sat above my village among the ragwort and the thistles, and some of the children greeted me as they walked into the dusk. They were going to their place by the oakwood and the stream where they are in the habit of sleeping under the stars. They were in trouble a while ago when they took firewood to their camp that was not theirs to take. I cannot think of Thoreau's 'great ocean of solitude, into which all the rivers of society run' without thinking also of William James's 'great mother sea of consciousness,' containing all that has or will be thought and felt, which, if we do not share James's confidence of immortality, off-sets the sense of isolation and helplessness that can chill our hearts. At some point, the waters of ocean, sea and river must surely merge, and we are not required to build connections ourselves, but only to take cognisance of the connections that are in and about us. I suspect Jim would think kindly of those children, despite the theft, since they are not very much younger than he was when he began wilderness camping in Wales. And seeing them gave me a momentary sense of connection with him, linking Arfon with Ariège – one of many in Wales who feel connection with Jim as countryman, colleague and friend.

Rob Mimpriss
Bangor, 2021

INTRODUCTION:

Loops, Meanders,
and Thoreauvian Digressions

"...the speed, the swiftness, walking into clarity,
Like last year's bryony are gone."
Ivor Gurney, "The High Hills"

To open with an epigraph from the Severnside poet and composer Ivor Gurney (1890-1937) seems entirely fitting. If we accept nationality as dependent on country of birth (though I'd rather it were elective), then Afon Hafren is a Welsh river, though for some of its course it has to find its way through western shires of England. But the Severn's not a river I'm writing on at length here. What's important in Gurney's lines is their profound sense of loss – something we'll encounter recurrently throughout this book. How, then, could I find a better way of beginning a sketchbook of Welsh rivers than with impressions from over seventy years ago by the finest of all writers on the natural history of Wales?

William Moreton Condry – "Bill" as he was generally known – was one of those rare people whose life's work was to pass on to others with unassuming eloquence his own astonishing breadth of knowledge about nature and the Welsh environment, and to use his capacity as a modestly brilliant teacher to help people see. There is a threnodic aspect now to what he enables us to see so clearly in excerpts quoted below from a long letter written by him to a friend, Reg Perry, early in 1946. The Clywedog valley is no longer as it was in that hopeful time in the 1940s when Nazism had been defeated and the neo-fascism of our time would have been unimaginable. Woodlarks then poured out exquisite cadences of their song – quite unlike, and immeasurably finer than, those of its close relative the skylark – on Bill as he walked up the Clywedog in that post-war year. They no longer do so in our day. The hard winter of 1963 ended the woodlark's long tenure in Wales. As for the Clywedog, that too is a sad story of detrimental change.

We'll find the same malevolent fate has affected other rivers. Despite intense local opposition, in 1963 work began on a towering grey concrete dam by the old Bryntail lead-mine workings five miles up-valley from the former weaving town of Llanidloes. Read David Constantine's fine stories in his collection *Under the Dam* from 2005 and feel the terror in this earth-tremulous land; or ponder the cataclysmic event that concludes D.H. Lawrence's novella *The Virgin and the Gipsy,* posthumously published in 1930. Here's a passage from its penultimate page:

> *The flood was caused by the sudden bursting of the great reservoir …*
> *It was found out later that an ancient, perhaps even a Roman mine*
> *tunnel, unsuspected, undreamed of, beneath the reservoir dam had*
> *collapsed, undermining the whole dam … And then the dam had burst.*

The dam's purpose is the regulation of flooding along the Severn[1] that was Ivor Gurney's muse. There were attempts to sabotage construction work on it by militant nationalist groups in Wales, which briefly delayed its completion, but it was finished in 1967. Since then it has reared ominous and threatening above the quietly beautiful valley of the formerly free river. So many valleys

---

[1] At the time of writing the national headlines are again full of reports of flooding in Shrewsbury, Ironbridge, Bewdley, Upton, Tewkesbury – looks like the planners need to don their thinking caps again?

in Wales have been thus dammed, their water channelled away to supply the needs of English populations and industries. Many more reservoirs were planned, and only averted by concerted local opposition – without which might have been lost Croesor, Cwm Penamnen, perhaps even Pennant Melangell (itself now blighted – in this of all places – by shooters of driven birds, their shots echoing round the enclosed valley and discharged right up to the boundary of Melangell's sanctuary itself.)

Wales exports its surplus rain, and rather than being paid for, the Welsh landscape itself pays in the dire affective cost of reservoir-construction on Welsh rivers, communities and wildlife. These are themes that will re-surface here and there throughout this book. For now, let's indulge ourselves in the prelapsarian vision expressed in Bill Condry's limpid prose from immediately after the Second World War, when the world once again, for however brief a time, seemed hopeful and young:

An altogether blue, cloud-sailing, beckoning April morning as I go off to revisit an old haunt – the stretch of country that shelters to the east of Plynlimon. Leaving my car at Llanidloes where two rivers meet, I walk not up the Severn which is the natural and ancient pathway to the west, but up the deep and wooded valley of the Clywedog which, like the Severn, has its source on Plynlimon. Everywhere the delights of the upland spring: shining, green river pools, leafing hazels, sunlight shafting deep and bright into leafless oakwoods, dippers singing on midstream rocks, a glistening white plume of black-headed gulls streaming behind a tractor ploughing down an impossible slope on a far hill.

The effortless simplicity of evocation here is characteristic of Condry's writing: the leafing hazels; the tractor edging down its impossible slope; the black-headed gulls chasing the plough. We come then to a passage that is essence of Condry, apotheosis of his *A River Sutra* outlook:

> *The valley narrows. Steep, unploughable, rock-broken slopes close in*
> *on me. Abruptly the trees become sparse. I come to a long-abandoned*
> *lead mine and watch a hen wheatear carrying straws into its ruined*
> *walls. A long-tailed tit steers a huge white feather into a blackthorn.*

So much of what Bill writes is gone now, in its place an ugliness of concrete and artificially restrained water – all very expedient for those seeking to alleviate the problems created over decades by building on the flood-plains of rivers. I'd be more in favour of a propitiatory approach to the Celtic goddess Aerfen, whose little-known shrine is over the source of Afon Dyfrdwy. Rivers, remember, are the feminine principle of landscape. Consider how many have names derived from the Anglo-Saxon word for the female sexual organ: the River Kent in Cumbria; the Kennet in North Wessex (that runs, appropriately, past Greenham Common); the Quinny Brook in Shropshire? As with women themselves, it's better to honour and praise than attempt to restrain. That's certainly an approach that Bill – a wise man highly supportive and appreciative of the way women are in this world – would have approved. Meanwhile, two important matters for our consideration. The first is the way in which rivers act as wildlife corridors into the heart of the land. Here's how the unpublished epistle to Reg Perry continues:

> *As you say we must be where the buds of the spirit find the easiest*
> *unfolding. We must find the spring each in our own way. At Ponterwyd*
> *a month ago the spring looked far behind as I wandered the silent hills*
> *with never a bird or living thing in miles. Yet even then there was a*
> *magic day when the snow blew right out of the sky for a few precious*
> *hours, and the three lakes stretched away blue before me and I slept*
> *half an hour on a patch of dry stones at the water's edge…*
>
> *That was one of the great days when we walked the iron-bound*

marshes and knew the real joy of winter, and were congratulating ourselves about the beauty of winter in the hills. … a passing raven destroyed all our illusions by passing straight across to the crag called Craig y Pistyll with a mass of sheepswool in her bill. Her mate of course flew with her close, and their purposefulness – there was none of the wing antics – reminded us of the Season, its nearness and the heavy responsibilities lying just ahead! These days and days of a bitter slow cold thaw, depressing days, rain sleet snow… under a warm rain and a fitful moon, curlews were fanning out to the warm soaking hills all the night through. Oh goodbye beloved estuary-flats and the ebb and flow of the quiet tide and the succulent lug-worm harvest and the great winter flocks on the saltings and the flooded water-meads!

Where has that sense of peace and plenitude gone? How can we have betrayed those who went before, to whom it was supremely valuable, by letting it pass away? Even in the course of a desultory trip into the town of Aberystwyth, the bird-life among the harbour mud still uplifts his spirit before he heads back towards the animating encounters with nature for which he lived even then.

Up to Ffrwd Myherin where no ravens are nesting this year; but I looked down on a lovely tawny fox curled in sleep just below me on a grassy ledge. Through the glass I admired his very red mane and velvet black ears and was tempted to drop a pebble on his nose for the joy of seeing him move on the crags. But no. Rather let him dream his foxy dreams in the warm spring sun and the roar roar roar of the ffrwd. If only my life could be like that; sleep in the sun where the Welsh waters whisper the way down into the valleys.

The ever-alert naturalist in Bill soon rouses him from somnambulistic romanticism to acute interest and observation.

Skirting the birdless lakes on to my lovely Rhuddnant where I crept and slithered as near as I could to some eighteen watchful duck. Oh creep down the marsh brother Condry, get your feet in the muck and your knees; let your hot soft belly feel the thrill of oozing water. Let your senses claw out the blood and bone knowledge from the heart of life! The mallard – one pair – curse them, saw me first and were off, followed soon by a pair of unknowns, big duck with much white on the wing, then a flock of small brown whistlers, presumably teal – I don't know teal – leaving six faithful widgeon, who never go away, are always the last to move, and who merely retire to the other side of the pool.

You can see in these jottings the making of the pre-eminent recorder of the natural history of Wales that Bill became. These next few paragraphs scan across the landscape he would in coming decades make unforgettably, indissociably his own.

…the hills and the air and the sing, sing, singing of the larks on a spring morning! I exulted, I was free, within my limits. I wanted to be much freer, I wanted to discard all things and go as naked as the bare brown hills so quiet there, so eternal in the ancientness of sunlight and time. It is surprising how many of the delicate moor sounds we lose even in the rush-rush of a soft wind past the ear as we walk and the swish of boots in the stiff white grass. When I stopped I could still get glimpses of the woodlark song far back. Down the forestry … the songs of many hedge-sparrows, goldcrests, wrens, blackbirds but no thrushes or ouzels. A single peacock butterfly sunning itself on the grasses, but none of big brown fox-moth caterpillars that are supposed to walk about on warm days in spring before pupating … in the immediate foreground I looked for golden plover and found none.

The plaintive call of the golden plover still sounds as distinctive redolence of this spacious country, from which so much else has departed. Ahead of him, from old lead-mine settling lagoons, came another of the identifying calls of this country – the soft whistling of widgeon. He ends this remarkable letter – just imagine what pleasure receiving it would have brought to the war-oppressed consciousness of that time, what hope and sense of renewal! – with more encounters: short-eared owl, woodcock, and the hope of woodlark singing in the dark as he approaches the hostel that's to be his shelter for the night. After all the discipline, confinement, and focus of wartime service, to receive a letter of that degree of liberty and close, joyful observation! With Penny Condry's blessing, I pass it on to you as an example of what to look for along the rivers, among the wetlands, of Wales.

This book does not, nor indeed could, present a comprehensive gazetteer of all the rivers and streams of Wales. What it seeks to do is give an appreciation of the individuality of seven Welsh rivers. Rivers are texts by which are expressed the land's folklore, its mythology, the culture of the people, the character of each region, even the harm done to our landscapes by uncontrolled, profligate or unthinking use. They are agents of landscape evolution, ever-changing, immensely powerful, capricious, demanding of respect. They're also alluring, playful, affording infinite recreational opportunity. Fishermen, swimmers and canoeists love them. Their vital threads braid the landscapes for the creation of which they have in part frequently been responsible. What I offer you in this book is not a geographical study of Welsh rivers. You'll find little here on epigenesis, transported loads, river-capture or long profiles. Look for those specialized terms in the established authorities (F.J. Monkhouse and E.G. Bowen are the foundation scholars here) who describe them more knowledgeably than I can. What I am concerned with is the tradition of topographical writing: what will interest the general reader with a love of Welsh culture and landscape and the forces that have contributed to its formation. Where my text impinges on the geographers' sphere of interest is in the point of land structure. This is a westerly country, mostly comprising high plateau, much of it above the 500-metre contour. As every Welsh would-be colonist or holidaymaker from time immemorial can testify, it rains here – rains a great deal, in fact. In some places the annual rainfall can reach 200 inches a year. The upland terrain acts as a great sponge, soaking up precipitation, acting as midwife to the birth of many rivers. Mynydd Hiraethog, Y Migneint, Waunygriafolen, Y Berwyn, Pumlumon Fawr, Cilfaesty Hill, Radnor Forest, The Black Mountains, Fforest Fawr, Bannau Brycheiniog, Preseli – all these have their river-children. I hope you enjoy these observations, memories, riparian wanderings as much as I have done throughout the greater part of a life spent in the outdoors and in Wales. Be careful, though, for these are changeable presences – the deaths of four "paddle-boarders" on Afon Cleddau in November 2021 acted as timely reminder of that truth. Keep your focus on appreciation of their variety and beauty, and on preserving them from all pollution, which will take much work, and unremitting pressure applied to politicians to sharpen their environmental will where there's little profit other than the vital legacy to our children of a cleaner and healthier environment.

The book is organized into individual essays, covering my seven choices from among the great river systems of Wales. They are more beautiful than those of any other area of Britain to my Welsh-chauvinist consciousness. Dip a toe in, immerse yourself, watch out for the depths, the whirlpools, the estuarine quicksands. Above all, appreciate, protect and enjoy! I take my definition of a Welsh river as one that has its source in Wales. As far as I know, there's only one river that rises in England and for most of its course flows through Wales, and even with this – Afon Camlad, quite a minor tributary of Afon Hafren – comes from Shropshire, a county D.H. Lawrence, in his novella St. Mawr, considered to be imbued with the aboriginal spirit of Britain, and one that I regard as essentially Welsh in character (consider the name of that marvellous Shropshire hill Caer Caradog, for example). There are major causes of environmental concern brought up throughout the book. I should mention the 2019 figures from the Environment Agency that awarded "Good" ecological status to a mere ten per cent of Afon Dyfrdwy, five per cent of Afon Hafren. Other rivers – Afon Teifi in particular, and Afon Gwy downstream from Glasbury – have been similarly affected by "accidental" releases, by agricultural run-off, by pollution from intensive poultry-rearing units and pig farms. On the vexed issue of shooting badgers to control the spread of bovine tuberculosis, an authoritative study in November 2021 concluded that "few badgers are even infected, let alone infectious, a fact that points us squarely back in the direction of the real issues. Namely an ineffective cattle test [for bovine TB] that leaves infected cattle in the herd, and a complete lack of emphasis by DEFRA and the APHA [Animal and Plant Health Agency – an executive arm of the Department of the Environment] on any number of other potential factors, from a lack of biosecurity measures to infected slurry in watercourses." Take careful note of that final sentence! The position nationwide is not one that gives room for complacency. As the United Kingdom distances itself from European Union environmental standards, under a Conservative government little interested in anything other than English nationalism and the profit motive, the situation is unlikely to improve and the fish stocks will continue to decline, the streams flow turbid and brown, the banks bear chemical tidelines, the "accidental" discharges of raw sewage proliferate, the birdlife diminish. That some of this has come about through "green" energy technology, used and presented by governments whose "libertarian" ethos fails to insist on even minimal standards of inspection and competence on the part of eco-scheme installers, has resulted in grave damage being done to some of the most valuable and widely loved of all Welsh river eco-systems. We have to bring pressure to force change here, so that something pure is left for the survival of our wildlife and the enjoyment of generations who come after us.

This is right too because rivers are traditionally viewed as feminine. Mythology defines them as such, sees them as flowing, cleansing, healing, nourishing, even capricious and destructive at times where their essential natural purpose has been polluted and abused. I like that *frisson*, and the richness and resonance it might bring to the finished text. I've experienced Welsh rivers in many perspectives. I've swum in underground pools and stream passages deep beneath the Swansea Valley in the course of caving adventures; have canoed and rafted down the flooding Wye from Builth to Glasbury; have sought out on foot mysterious chasms and sources in the Ordovician and other landscapes and marvelled at what I've found there: Pwll Uffern Cothi, Ogof y Gŵr Blewog, Waunygriafolen and its unrecorded chapel over the first water of Afon Dyfrdwy. I've studied the accounts of earlier writers – Coleridge on the Tanat, Hazlitt on the Dee, Wordsworth on the lower Wye, Eifion Wyn on the Dwyfor – and smiled at George Borrow's pet word "disemboguement" for the place at which a river flows into the sea. I've lingered along estuaries, waded across Traeth Bach at the mouth of the Dwyryd from Aber Iâ to Llanfihangel-y-traethau. In my mis-spent youth I gaffed salmon out of Afon Lledr and tickled sea trout from Afon Dwyfor. I've observed otters and goosanders on Afon Teifi, Barnacle geese and herons along Afon Dwyryd. I've traversed deep gorges of Ystwyth and Rheidol, leapt the Llam y Lleidr above Llangollen (albeit in 1976, at a time of extreme drought, when my legs still had youthful spring in them), camped alongside Afon Hengwm looking across to Cerrig Cyfamod Owain Glyndŵr under Pumlumon, on a night of full and eerie moonlight that called up mind-phantoms from across the battlefield of Hyddgen. And next morning bathed in the pool below the footbridge straight from my tent.

Welsh rivers have provided many of the most memorable experiences in my life. Their allure, variety, range of interest, and intoxicating beauty, I take as a given, even after sad centuries of despoliation. In the last few years agrochemical pollution has taken its toll of Teifi and Dyfrdwy, leaving shoals of dead and dying fish and a harsh, white, phosphate tideline here and there along their once-lovely, once-thronging banks. The wildfowling fraternity, the activities of which have been actively promoted in recent years by a highly organized representative body and by corporate interest, has had a markedly deleterious effect on the rich avian life that formerly existed on Cardigan Bay estuaries, which saddens me. Comment on it elicits waspish co-ordinated criticism from vested interests whose barbaric recreational opportunities are thus threatened with curtailment. In a time of worldwide species loss, so they should be! In a sense, this will be an environmental book passionately pleading the cause of riverine monitoring and protection. It will also primarily be a book in the old tradition in which writers like Pennant, Borrow, Bradley, Massingham, Condry, worked – a book of journeys, for rivers have long lent themselves to that theme. I take as its model one of the two works that Henry David Thoreau – perhaps the finest of all nature writers – wrote during his stay of two years and two months during the 1840s in a wooden cabin built by himself on land belonging to Ralph Waldo Emerson close to Walden Pond near Concord, Massachusets. The two masterpieces he wrote here were *Walden*, or *Life in the Woods* (published in 1854), and his *A Week on the Concord* and *Merrimack Rivers*, which was published in 1849 and recorded a fortnight's trip he and his elder brother John had made ten years earlier, in 1839. The most exhaustively detailed of Thoreau's biographers, Robert D. Richardson jr., has the following to say of this erratic and wonderful book:

> *It is an example, as is Walden, of the Coleridgean idea of organic form: it grew like a pear on its branch, not like a bowl on the potter's wheel. It is the first of the many American books shaped along a river trip, the first in which the river becomes a stream, not just of water or even of time, but of consciousness itself.*
>
> (Robert D. Richardson Jr., Henry Thoreau: *A Life of the Mind*, U.C.P. Berkeley, 1986)

The present book takes from Thoreau's example (and I can feel my own mentor Bill Condry nodding his approval at this) permission to digress, to expatiate, to diverge from the narrow channel in order to examine reflections that may illuminate, or at the very least create a more complete and compound impression. A last point on method – throughout the book, and as in several earlier ones I've written, I've used the footnote as a means of creating alternative and parallel discourse. A literary critic, the late Al Alvarez, picked up on my purpose here when he wrote about their function in my 2006 biography of the mountaineer Don Whillans, that I'd used them to write a social history in footnotes of British climbing in the latter half of the twentieth century. You may discern a parallel purpose here in the representation of our attitude towards some Welsh rivers.

PART ONE

"Most lovely…
which the world can boast of": Afon Gwy

If the River Wye were a film, metropolitan reviewers would give it a unanimous five-star billing. Landscape and travel writers have been doing just that since the eighteenth century. "The fairest of English rivers by a practically indisputable title" is how A.G. Bradley[1] rated it in 1909, with the typically arrogant English colonialism of the time. George Borrow, ever the enthusiast for all things Welsh, raised the stakes with his assessment of the Wye as "the most lovely river probably, which the world can boast of"! I rack my brain in response to that, and am hard put to come up with a convincing alternative (even though, once the river leaves Wales, it's no longer quite the sparkling wonder it is west of the border). Nearer our own time, George Peterken, in his outstanding New Naturalist volume, *Wye Valley* (which restricts itself, unfortunately, to the lower Wye beyond Hereford), comments that *"the Wye* [is] *arguably the finest and least spoiled of all the major rivers of Britain. It is also the 'unknown' river, for, despite its qualities, it has attracted relatively little attention."[2]* There certainly isn't an "English" river that can compare, and if you're going to tell me that for some of its course the Wye *is* an English river, I'll respond that the sections of which that's true are neither the most distinguished in terms of landscape nor the most environmentally outstanding in their

---

[1] Arthur George Bradley (1850-1943) was the most prolific English topographical writer of his day, and a highly knowledgable and cultured one too, whose dozens of books can still be read with pleasure for the instruction they afford and information they impart.
[2] George Peterken, *Wye Valley*, (Collins 2008), p. 2.

wildlife, their lack of pollution. If the Wye were human and Wales had independence, this marvellous river, through accident of birth and long residence for the greater part of its 154-mile course, would certainly be possessed of a Welsh passport. But Bradley was of his overweening and colonial time, so let's just send him on his spectral way with the gentlest of slaps on the wrist, appreciate his enthusiasm for this most glorious of *Welsh* rivers. And then do what another overbearing and alarmingly eccentric Englishman did in 1854, and visit the source of the Wye.

George Borrow made the purpose of his visits to the three major rivers that rise on Pumlumon Fawr disarmingly plain in what is to my mind still the finest of all British travel books[3]: his *Wild Wales: Its People, Language and Scenery* – the account of a summer and autumn he spent with his wife and step-daughter in Wales during 1854, which was first published by John Murray in 1862 and has, despite dips in Borrow's reputation, been consistently in print ever since. Here's how he explains to his guide from Castell Dyffryn his need to visit the sources of the Rheidol, Severn and Wye during the wet October of 1854:

"It is not only necessary for me to see the sources of the rivers, but to drink of them, in order that in after times I may be able to harangue about them with a tone of confidence and authority."

Borrow in a nutshell! His particular blend of idiosyncracy, bluster, religious prejudice, sly humour, partiality for good ale, extensive knowledge and ingenuous curiosity tends either to alienate him from or endear him to such few of his readers as remain today. I'm firmly of the endeared persuasion, having first encountered *Wild Wales* in the form of a copy bought at Easter 1960 from a little bookshop that used to exist by the northern end of the Dee

---

[3] I deliberated long and hard over this claim, and should add that if there were a shortlist, the accounts by Johnson and Boswell of their shared Scottish journeys would certainly be on it, as would Thomas Pennant's *Tour in Wales* and perhaps his *Tour in Scotland*.

bridge in Llangollen on my first solo walking tour of Wales. It served as my exclusive reading matter (it is a long, dense book) for the whole of the next fortnight as I made my way up the Dee, over from Bala to Trawsfynydd, across to Harlech by way of Bwlch Tyddiad, and up to Snowdon in the incessant rain, which had the positive side of showing Welsh rivers to best advantage in all their fullness and fury. Most Welsh topographical books allow Borrow to conduct you to the sources of Pumlumon's rivers. Perhaps it's time for a change of guide? I could offer the duty myself, but acerbity might cloud commentary on the habitual approaches? The most popular is from the south, and takes you through an unspeakable long morass on a slope with an irredeemably dull outlook over a vista encompassing wind-turbines and all their brutally marring associated works on or around every hill ridge (except for those in National Parks, of which there are not nearly enough) between here and Severn Sea. If you choose to follow Borrow's route to Pumlumon's trio of sources, on your own head be it, and if you don't look out, you'll be over your head in it. A.G. Bradley gives a good impression of the nature of this country:

> *"Of its great lonely heart, tuneful only with the noise of waters, the bleat of sheep, and the plovers' cry, of its romantic girdle of crag and wood, of little white-washed sycamore shaded homesteads and rude hoary shrines of British saints through which these bog-fed torrents break, the outer world knows absolutely nothing at all."*

Following Borrow's route will take you to the long moorland gable of Pumlumon, with its extensive views north and west, its vast sense of space, and these days the considerable expanse of Llyn Nant y Moch immediately to the west – reservoirs to supply English communities with water are a recurrent and distressing theme of this book which I'll not pursue in detail. Instead I'll leave you in the hands of another eccentric guide to the Wye's source, who deserved to remain far better known. He was Robert Gibbings (1889-1958), an artist and author, son of a Cork clergyman, and perhaps the pre-eminent wood engraver of the twentieth century. Gibbings studied medicine at University College, Cork for three years, but had an eye for female beauty and persuaded his clergyman father to let him go to the Slade School of Art in London, where he found his vocation and pursued it – with a gap during the Great War when he served with the Munster Fusiliers and was wounded at Gallipoli – for the rest of his life. He ran the Golden Cockerel Press, was associated with Eric Gill, and produced work as crisp, evocative and elegant today as when the blocks for it were first cut decades ago. His illustrations adorn his books, many of them on riverine themes (he wrote on the Thames, the Seine, the Irish Lea that flows through Cork City), all of which are enchanting blends of acute natural history, a close ear for human conversation and humour, and delicious stylized illustration. A blond, bearded giant, six feet two inches tall and twenty stone in weight, he's long overdue a revival. Equally at home propping up a Welsh bar corner or observing the symbiotic relationship between a goosander and a curlew on the lake in front of a cottage near Llangurig where he lived during the war years, his professional milieu was the print room of the Golden Cockerel Press. He supervised production of fine editions that nowadays fetch enormous prices on the rare occasions they come up for sale. The best of his books published in a more commercial, mundane and wartime utility fashion is his *Coming Down the Wye* of 1942. Gibbings belongs with the best of nature writers in English. Here's his account of being at the source of the Wye, to give you something of the flavour of the writing:

> "*I was at the source of the Wye. After a gentle murmuring underground the water welled up, brushing aside the young spring grass, to form a*

pool no bigger than a bowler hat. Then gently it glided between rich tussocks of moss and rushes, still bent from their load of winter snow, until it tumbled like a shower of sequins over the black velvet of a peat face. The pool below this was wider and deeper, and with every yard of its flow the strength of the rivulet increased. Small streams from successive dells and dingles joined in, and so, between thick felts of sphagnum moss starred with cotton grass, and over rocks long since worn smooth, it frisked and dived towards its first main tributary a thousand feet below.[4]

Gibbings' life during the writing of *Coming Down the Wye* was in a relatively stable and peaceful phase. He lectured – very well, by all accounts, his students reportedly loving his anecdotalism, attention to their work, and avuncular presence – in typography and book illustration at Reading University. This was a man who, despite being strongly attracted to women and as an artist passionately appreciative of the female form, was not ideally equipped psychologically for marriage, he having experienced the Augustus John milieu of the Slade, with its intense sexuality and pronounced fragility of connubial bonds. His second wife and children had been evacuated to Canada for the duration of the war in 1940, leaving Gibbings to live a bachelor existence during term-time at Reading, and to spend most of his leisure and vacation time in the tiny primitive cottage by a small lake near Llangurig, the first settlement of any size on the upper course of the Wye, and one with enough pubs to satisfy his cravings for conviviality (two of them, *The Black Lion* and *The Bluebell*, are still there, and still inviting). We should join Gibbings again by the source of the Wye, to gain a fuller sense of one of the most interesting and talented characters we'll encounter in this journey down the most beautiful of all rivers:

---

[4] Robert Gibbings, *Coming Down the Wye* (J.M. Dent, 1942).

"...a north-east wind in March is a poor help to meditation, and it was not till midsummer that I realized the full glory of the mountains. Then it was ecstasy, ecstasy unbelievable. I was one with the earth, one with the shale and the shingle washed clean by the winter springs. A warm wind swept over the hills, combing the short grasses, caressing everything it touched. I was alone, utterly alone, and for as long as I wished. A gull soaring in the valley was the only moving creature, a sheep bleating from the shadow of a rock the only sound except for the wind, the wind in the grasses. Purple and silver the grasses, as they bent in the breeze. And the great mountains heaved and swelled; and the river, a thin silver stream, sprang from gigantic thighs."

There we have it again! A Celtic goddess, kin to *"great-bladdered Emer"*, from the *Táin Bó Cúailnge "by whose pissing armies were drowned"*! The river as feminine principle of landscape, and who better than an artist to express its eternal and ever-flowing power and presence. Gibbings was a major influence on a national icon, the young David Attenborough. The expressive delicacy of his woodcuts is a marvel. In his river books he is among the most closely observant of nature writers in English. Here he is, giving a description of goosanders – now an increasingly common bird on the Wye, incidentally, much to the chagrin of the trout fishermen who can only look on as this magnificent sawbill duck pillages the stock in "their" river. But we can deduce from Gibbings' account that it was also numerous along the Wye eighty years ago:

"Of all our ducks these must be among the handsomest, the drake with his dark green head, black back and ivory breast and sides suffused with tints of salmon, the ducks with chestnut heads, grey backs, and the same flushed breast; both of them with crimson bill."

There's the artist in that precise and scrupulous description of their appearance. He's even better when he comes to describing their behaviour:

"It is a wonderful sight to see a dozen of them, in a great phalanx, swimming at full speed down the lake [in front of his cottage by the lake above the Afon Marteg], throwing out long silver ripples to some thirty yards behind them. Their speed and the ease with which they dive recall the activities of dolphins, and there is the same joyous expression on their faces. It seems that for the most part they swallow the smaller of their prey as they catch them under the water, but often they bring a larger one to the surface before disposing of it. Then with it well down in the gullet the bird rises on its tail in the water, and flaps its wings violently as if to shake it further down. Next moment it has dived again." ·

I know of no better account of a bird fishing than that! And the observation becomes even more acute when a heron appears on the scene and a mutually assistant hunting relationship establishes between them:

"When the ducks are present in numbers they pay little attention to their neighbour, but when one of them is there alone it seems glad of companionship. The duck will then fish close in to where the heron is standing, while the tall bird stands motionless, with neck outstretched, on the alert for anything that might be disturbed. I have seen this go on for nearly an hour, the duck sometimes sitting close up to the heron, almost touching it, as though the two were happy to be in each other's company."

This is nature writing of a very high order – simply expressed, sharply observant, absolutely honest and accurate in every detail. It's devoid of affectation and ego too, which are the besetting sins of much contemporary nature writing, obscuring its subjects in a frenzy of euphuistic style and tortured language. I've seen this exact symbiosis between heron and goosander take place at the beautiful pool below the Rhinogydd, Llyn Tecwyn Isaf, and can vouch for the precise truth of Gibbings' description – and truth is what the writer-naturalist must aim for. Meanwhile, our beautiful Welsh river is rushing headlong from its mountain birthing-pool, and within its first few miles has taken in a substantial tributary, the Tarenig, of quite different character to itself. The Tarenig has cut deep into the Ordovician slates, is rocky and clean, its pools bottomed with the kind of clean silt into which the hen salmon gouges the furrow in which she'll lay her eggs, for this is one of the headwaters of the Wye, to which, in the autumn, the salmon come to spawn. They make their way into many of the streams which join the Wye high up in its course, and the life-cycle of the salmon is one of the most interesting stories[5] in the whole of natural history, perhaps only trumped by that of the eel's arduous journeyings from European rivers to the Sargasso Sea and back[6].

If this book has a model, it comes from Henry Thoreau, doyen of all nature writers, whose first book, *A Week on the Concord and Merrimack Rivers* (1849), was about the fortnight (!) of journeying in a home-made canoe that he and his elder brother John had made in 1839 from their Concord home. John had died at New Year, 1842, of tetanus after cutting his finger whilst stropping a razor. Henry's book is widely discursive, constantly digressive ("my opera omnia", he called it, and it is precisely that – ninety per cent of it is composed of digressive essays on topics aside from that of the journey the two brothers made together) act of homage to his admired elder brother. It was little read at the time and is still the least popular, as well as the longest, of all Henry's major works. But it's a river book, and its meanders, whirlpools, tributaries, and digressions are the essence of that genre. Read *Huckleberry Finn*

---

[5] Two fascinating books written on this are Henry Williamson's *Salar the Salmon* (1935) – a kindlier and more interesting book, in my view, than his earlier and better-known *Tarka the Otter* – and Richard Shelton's *To Sea and Back* (2009) which is thorough, scientific, and excellent on the physiological side of salmon's homing instincts.

[6] See Tom Fort's classic *The Book of Eels* (Harper Collins 2002) for the definitive account of the eel's mysterious life cycle.

again if you doubt me. Or ponder this extract from Thoreau's book:

"[The poet] *should be as vigorous as a sugar maple, with sap enough to maintain his own verdure, beside what runs into the troughs, and not like a vine, which being cut in the spring bears no fruit, but bleeds to death in the endeavor to heal its wounds. The poet is he that hath fat enough, like bears and marmots, to suck his claws all winter. He hibernates in this world, and feeds on his own marrow. We love to think in winter, as we walk over the snowy pastures, of those happy dreamers that lie under the sod, of dormice and all that race of dormant creatures, which have such a superfluity of life enveloped in thick folds of fur, impervious to cold. Alas, the poet too is, in one sense, a sort of dormouse gone into winter quarters of deep and serene thoughts, insensible to surrounding circumstances: his words are the relation of his oldest and finest memory, a wisdom drawn from the remotest experience. Other men lead a starved existence, meanwhile, like hawks, that would fain keep on the wing, and trust to pick up a sparrow now and then.*"

Alas, that advice, in our current world of readers' groups, media-promoted literary fashions, self-endorsing social media commentary, Amazon reviewers, doctorates awarded for twenty-thousand-word dissertations (in more stringent times before the onset of the Thatcherite Diseducation Project theses of 100,000 words were required) on modish themes in the contorted syntax approved by present-day tertiary education, is unlikely to gain much approval even at a notional level. Therefore I recommend Thoreau's rivers book (as well as those of Robert Gibbings, which are similarly cast) to you. Its method is my own in the present volume, and parallels that of Borrow in *Wild Wales*. It's the Autolycan one of story-telling, snapping up of unconsidered trifles, chasing after escaping themes, ox-bow wanderings, musings, ponderings and rapids-running, all strung on the threads of hither-and-yon journeyings. I hope you picked up on the phrase expressive of Thoreau's intense personal agony about his brother's death in the passage above ("bleeds to death")? We tune these travels to our own emotional pitch. And now, before we rejoin the enjoyable, well-informed and challenging company of our good friend Robert Gibbings and his cronies in the convivial atmosphere of the *Black Lion* or the *Bluebell Inn*, let's enjoy our first long digression and consider the necessary theme of the basis of nature writing in English – a genre in which Thoreau is so distinguished an exemplar. Let me begin this crucially relevant (and no doubt exasperating to all the non-dormice among you) digression with a consideration, of which I'm sure Mr. Gibbings, good Cork man and Blarney Stone kisser that he was, would approve, of everyday country habits of a previous age, and how they inculcated a sense of harmony, belonging and order into rural existence through proximity to the cycle of nature.

> *"Out of all these circumstances – the pride of skill in handicrafts, the detailed understanding of the soil and its materials, the general effect of the well-known landscape, and the faint sense of something venerable in its associations ...there proceeded an influence which acted upon the village people as an unperceived guide to their conduct, so that they observed the seasons proper for their varied pursuits almost as if they were going through some ritual. Thus, ...when, on an auspicious evening of spring, a man and wife went out far across the common to get rushes for the wife's hop-tying, of course it was a consideration of thrift that sent them off; but an idea of doing the right piece of country routine at the right time gave value to the little expedition. The moment, the evening, became enriched by suggestion of the seasons into which it fitted, and by memories of years gone by."*

That's from George Sturt's *Change in the Village* (1912). It's hardly a recognizable description of life in a present-day Home Counties parish, and I doubt if many now read George Sturt (1863-1927); which is a pity, because this Surrey-born wheelwright and author, in books like *Change in the Village* and *The Wheelwright's Shop* (1923), posed a crucial question with which contemporary society still struggles; and to which – despite increasing cultural signs of a yearning for the renewal of a close relationship with nature – we have yet to find an adequate answer: what measure of compensation can be found in contemporary life for the loss of connection with process and the natural cycle which was woven through the whole human life-fabric in a pre-industrial world, the disappearance of which has left us with a kind of psychic insubstantiality by comparison with those who, in the marvelling and resonant phrase of the American author Barry Lopez, *"radiate the authority of first-hand encounters"*? This is the problem with which our Irish drinking-companion of *The Bluebell* and *The Black Lion* wrestles in his amused and knowledgable way. It's something that's troubled me throughout the years in which I've written on outdoor themes.

Recent British nature writing with varying degrees of success has attempted to give us as if by proxy, and also to urge us into our own experience of, those animating encounters. I would rather (bearing in mind T.S. Eliot's insights into the vitalizing role of historical precedent from his essay "Tradition and the Individual Talent") drop from the outset the misconception that this is "new" in the sense of marking a radical departure from the practice and preoccupations of its antecedents. However much our culture may insist on novelty, we should acknowledge the living influence of what has gone before. That point of view appears to have been anathema to the editor of the infamous *Issue 102* of the journal *Granta*, which was a kind of manifesto for what had become known, particularly in *The Guardian* newspaper, as

The New Nature Writing – a tag that *Granta* bolted firmly into place through endless repetitions. The "Editor's Letter" in Issue 102 begins thus:

> *"When I used to think of nature writing, or indeed the nature writer, I would picture a certain kind of man, and it would always be a man: bearded, badly dressed, ascetic, misanthropic. He would often be alone on some blasted moor, with a notebook in one hand and binoculars in the other, seeking meaning and purpose through a larger communion with nature: a loner and an outcast."*

Jason Cowley[7]'s need to genuflect before contemporary gender-issues aside – and a glimpse at the contents of issue 102 and the sex of their authors confirms the mere gesturalism – this sneering caricature is interesting. It roots in a set of perceptions dimly recollected from Evelyn Waugh's supercilious novel *Scoop*. The *"badly dressed"* is particularly odd. I had not realized that attention to nature demands study of the looking-glass to see if we pass muster with the *metro litterati*'s style-police; nor that negative values attach to a *"blasted moor"*, to asceticism, to wearing a beard, possession of notebook and binoculars or seeking a *"larger communion with nature"*. (Larger than what, I wonder?)

Cowley's remarks are, of course, pure tosh and the disrepute they engender is compounded by his ignorant misrepresentation of the entire tradition of nature writing in English, the only three works of which he seems able to cite being Barry Lopez's *Arctic Dreams*, Jon Krakauer's *Into the Wild*, and Erich Maria Remarque's *All Quiet on the Western Front* (the two latter most definitely not being in any way categorisable as nature writing). Puzzle that out for yourselves. And whilst you do so, here are some relevant thoughts on the "new nature writing "of seventy years ago from a truly

---

[7] Later the editor of *The New Statesman* – a periodical affectionately known as The Staggers, on account of its frequent canvassing for subscriptions and changes in political stance.

authoritative writer on nature. James Fisher[8], in the third issue of a journal which accompanied the launch of Collins' masterful publishing project, the New Naturalist series, wrote:

> *"Others are… by authors whose excessive consciousness of the exquisite nature of their prose, and the distinction conferred on the reader by a peep at their personalities, are so grotesque as to baffle description."*

Application of that formula pins most of our so-called "new nature writers" firmly to the specimen-board. Fisher again, with perfect rigour:

> *"Do these people really believe that the search for truth is less important than the search for poetry or art or aesthetic satisfaction or 'happiness'? Do they not understand that the purest source of these imponderables is in the realms of fact, and that the establishment of facts is most simply done by the ancient methods of logical science? Once facts are despised, fancies replace them; and fancies are poisonous companions to the enjoyment and appreciation of nature."*

Good nature-writing, then, is founded on two crucial principles – applied knowledge and close attention. These are what made the late Barry Lopez's writing so frequently outstanding. Our current British writing on nature borrows from two main sources. From across the Atlantic, clue, breadth of subject-matter and methodology are provided by an influential roll-call of late-twentieth-century American and Canadian nature, wilderness, fiction and natural-history writers working in a tradition the origins of which lead back through Aldo Leopold and John Muir to Thoreau and the Transcendentalists. Ed Abbey, Edwin Way

---

[8] James Fisher (1912-1970) was a founding editor of Collins New Naturalist series, to which he made several distinguished contributions, including a definitive monograph on *The Fulmar* (1952), acclaimed at the time of its publication as a milestone of ornithological research and the most important single-species study ever published.

Teale[9], Annie Dillard, Cormac MacCarthy, Peter Matthiessen, Barry Lopez, Mary Oliver, George Schaller, Bernd Heinrich are prominent among them. This very strong body of work from North America has had an unfortunate recent shading effect on the British origins of the genre (if a subject-area that subsumes topographical writing, natural history, nature-poetry, ornithology, hill-going and mountaineering narratives, some travel and even the rural novel can truly be called a genre). Here it has flowed limpid and uninterrupted from the elegiac lyricism of the Anglo-Saxon *Seafarer* and *Wanderer*, from early Welsh gnomic poetry, from Dafydd ap Gwilym and the middle-English alliterative verse of the Gawain Poet to the present day. For over six hundred years, under the pervasive influence of Virgil's *Georgics* and in long-loved and culturally complex classics like *The Compleat Angler*, *The Seasons* and *The Natural History of Selborne*, the energy and relevance of nature-writing and its social, symbolic and valuative dimensions have been maintained. The latter half of the twentieth century has added prolifically to the tradition. I think of the delectable prose-texture and visionary insight of Nan Shepherd's Scottish ecological essay, *The Living Mountain*, and of the work of other Scots about their native hills and wild: Sorley Maclean, Jim Crumley, Cameron McNeish. Much of Seamus Heaney's work (shocked recoil of his "Death of a Naturalist" poem notwithstanding) is rooted in the landscape of his Irish boyhood. From Wales, William Condry's work is lucid model for any aspiring field-naturalist; Angharad Price revivifies familial land-connectedness with the surest touch in her beautiful neo-classic *O! tyn y gorchudd*; Robert Minhinnick, the late Nigel Jenkins, Gwyneth Lewis, Christine Evans – they have all placed natural themes at the centre of accomplished poetry; in their differing

---

[9] Teale's monumental *American Seasons* tetralogy is one of the masterworks of nature writing in English. Long out of print, and little known in Britain, it has been neglected whilst many inferior works are fêted by factional audiences.

ways the novelists Niall Griffiths in *Sheepshagger* and Owen Sheers in *Resistance* achieve perfect natural pitch, and the crises of faith central to the fine religious novels of Emyr Humphreys are played out against the constancy-in-change of the Welsh countryside.

There is an entire body of work in the Welsh language: Waldo Williams' poetry places him alongside Richard Jefferies and Thomas Traherne as nature-mystic; D.J. Williams' short stories, his memoir of childhood *Hen Dŷ Ffarm*, and the Eryri fictions of Kate Roberts, are outstanding in their bodying-forth of the interplay between social and natural setting, as is Siân Melangell Dafydd's *Y Trydydd Peth* – 2009 prose medal winner at Yr Eisteddfod Genedlaethol in her home town of Y Bala – which takes as its subject Afon Dyfrdwy. In England, Ted Hughes, Alice Oswald, David Thomson, George Ewart Evans, Ronald Blythe, Colin Tudge, Richard Mabey, Roger Deakin, Paul Evans, Mark Cocker and Tom Fort – the list is by no means exhaustive – have all produced work of distinction within the broad spectrum of rural-writing genres. Buxton's *The Redstart*, Baker's *The Peregrine* and Desmond Nethersole-Thompson's *The Greenshank* are works of literature as well as ornithological monographs. Derek Ratcliffe's writing is remarkable not just for the closeness and encyclopaedic knowledge of his bird-observations but also for the deft economy with which he conveys spirit of place. If we had to define a *"New Nature Writing"*, this and much more would be the extent of it, drawing from the past as future writers will draw from it and inform its project with their own crafted and informed perceptions in coming time. There is no break here, only a loving and subject-focused continuity, a rich continuing thread within a literature still mostly resistant to the ego-infused hothouse-lexis and rent-a-sentence syntax of the creative-writing industry. That aside, the public appetite for this writing surely points up the implied question of George Sturt's from almost a century ago.

How do we reconnect?

The direction in which to look for an answer is clear enough, and our relict wild country and natural landscapes (each of which are of value though they are not one and the same, as the rural writer H.J. Massingham was at pains to point out even in the first half of the twentieth century) which are its providers become ever more attractive as we hold to the view. What's less certain as we look there is what's left, and what the fate will be even in our time of that scant remainder. That uncertainty begs a further question: the vital everyday connection to the land which was available to our forebears gone, how aetiolated for us has become the capacity to see which was its concomitant? It may seem a romantic foible to do so, or even Cobbett-like counter-progressive crankishness, but the argument can soundly be made that we have paid for the undoubted progress of the last two centuries with the loss of our relationship to things in themselves small, unquantifiable in material worth, fragile for certain, clearly unfashionable, their given value now only notional and tokenist, but in sum and in their contribution to our existing in harmony on this planet effectively beyond price:

> *"Talk of mysteries! Think of our life in nature, – daily to be shown matter, to come in contact with it, – rocks, trees, wind on our cheeks! The solid earth! The actual world! The common sense! Contact! Contact! Who are we? Where are we?"*

Thoreau again – if you're a writer on nature you cannot escape his influence – from his essay on an ascent of Mount Katahdin posthumously published in 1864. Like my own mentor in writing about nature, Bill Condry, who wrote an excellent short biography of him, I stand in thrall to Thoreau, regard him as one of the profound voices in any wilderness philosophy and aesthetic. What comes through from the broken syntax and ecstatic utterance in the passage quoted above is its insistence on connection – that thrice-repeated word *contact*, the crucial questions to which it leads. Contrast their directness, their foundation-significance, with our present-day culture's insistence on the oxymoronic phrase *virtual reality*, and the importance of this elemental space into which Thoreau disorientatingly ventured then becomes self-evident. The key vocabulary here is contact, connection, relationship. When we do not position ourselves thus in regard to the natural world – when our relationship there has become distant or slight, that of an occasional visitor or of one sent out as though by Evelyn Waugh's Lord Copper, proprietor of *The Beast*, to comment and report on a country as alien to the inhabitants of Metroland as Ishmaelia or the moon – then a depression and a poverty sets into our psyches. There is a very interesting dialogue on just this point in a passage from George Borrow's uncategorizable masterpiece *Lavengro* of 1851. It occurs in the form of a conversation between a narrator newly out of the city – a character who may or may not have a good deal in common with Borrow himself – and his gipsy friend Jasper Petulengro:

> *"There's night and day, brother, both sweet things; sun, moon and stars, brother, all sweet things; there's likewise a wind on the heath. Life is very sweet, brother; who would wish to die?"*
>
> *"I would wish to die –"*
>
> *"You talk like a gorgio – which is the same as talking like a fool – were you a Rommany Chal you would talk wiser. Wish to die, indeed! A Rommany Chal would wish to live for ever!"*
>
> *"In sickness, Jasper?"*
>
> *"There's the sun and stars, brother."*
>
> *"In blindness, Jasper?"*
>
> *"There's the wind on the heath, brother; if I could only feel that, I would gladly live for ever."*

As with Thoreau on Mount Katahdin, as with the peppery-pragmatic William Cobbett, as with each of that significant group of "nature" writers – Richard Jefferies, George Sturt, W.H. Hudson, Edward Thomas, Henry Williamson, H.J. Massingham (most of them surely due for re-appraisal though Edward Thomas as a prose writer has been receiving rather more than his due in the last decade) – who were working in Britain in the decades around the turn and up to the middle of the last century, what you catch at in the Borrow extract is a writer working against the temper of the time, bodying forth his own views in brilliantly evocative simple images, his social criticisms in so slyly elliptical and attractive a way that, having once read them, they become a part of our habit of thought. In presenting the fictive as the literally true he is an early precursor to W.G. Sebald, whose ruminations on landscape in *The Rings of Saturn* go right to the heart of the matter:

> "...*Sir Thomas Browne, who was the son of a silk merchant and may well have had an eye for these things, remarks in a passage of the Pseudodoxia Epidemica that I can no longer find that in the Holland of his time it was customary, in a home where there had been a death, to drape black mourning ribbons over all the mirrors and all canvasses depicting landscapes or people or the fruits of the field, so that the soul, as it left the body, would not be distracted on its final journey, either by a reflection of itself or by a last glimpse of the land now being lost for ever.*"

There is an echo here, surely purposive from the polymath Sebald, of Paulinus of Nola's fifth-century stricture, "*Not only pagan literature, but the whole appearance of things as apprehended by the senses is the lotus flower; so men forget their own land, which is God, the country of us all.*" Be under no illusion about how deliberate, suggestive and counter to that view is Sebald's collocation of landscape and soul; nor how literally we are meant to interpret his final, chilling dependent clause. Our landscape is being taken from us, still and in accelerated manner. Modern living mostly disallows that close relationship to land which would fret awareness of its destruction into our continual thought. The Welsh phrase, *dyn ei filltir sgwâr* – a man of his own square mile (re-gender for yourselves as appropriate) is apposite here. It is necessary to be that if you are to write authentically on nature. *"Tradition… cannot be inherited, and if you want it you must obtain it by great labour"*, wrote Eliot. The amiable founding-father of British natural history, Gilbert White, fleshed out the point with force and clarity in a letter to his Welsh friend Thomas Pennant dated August 1st, 1771:

> *"Faunists, as you observe, are too apt to acquiesce in bare descriptions, and a few synonyms: the reason is plain; because all that may be done at home in a man's study, but the investigation of the life and conversation of animals is a concern of much trouble and difficulty, and it is not to be attained but by the active and inquisitive, and by those that reside much in the country."*

The Country and the City – title of one of Raymond Williams' late books of incisive social commentary – what does the former really ever know about the latter? Metroland enthusiasts for the *New Nature* fad take note here– there is rigour, rurality, discomfort, patience, application necessary to be on close terms with nature. Dipping in and out of scenery or tarns, striking poses for the photographer sent along by *The Guardian* newspaper, imposing patterns of attention-deficit culture, re-invoking familiar worn sources from the libraries – these are not enough, lack depth and habitual opportunity for radiance-bringing first-hand encounters that only come when we put ourselves without design in the natural environment. The same point is re-iterated by Andrew MacNeillie, son of Ian Niall – long knowledge hence his birthright. We'll meet Ian again when we encounter the Afon

Serw, wildest of tributaries to the Afon Conwy, by Cefn Garw, the most remote house in Eryri, in the chapter on *Cynfal, Dwyryd, Glaslyn*. In a fine volume of autobiography entitled *Once: A Memoir,* Andrew writes:

> *"You'll become a naturalist without study, by nature, first nature, second nature. Nature is rude and incomprehensible at first, said Whitman, but don't be discouraged; it holds divinity enveloped in it. Divine it. It holds you, and you only knew it, bare-forked as a divining rod as you step into the religion of landscape.."*

The answer to Sturt's implied question is perfectly plain. A loving relationship to nature is more than ever essential as our everyday sense of its reality fades, as we sit in front of our screens or walk along with attention riveted to the smartphone, the natural environment entirely occluded from view and focus centred not on the wide perspective but instead on a few centimetres of perspex. Forego the vapid egotisms that characterize our society and culture; make contact with nature; lose yourself there; go into the wild not as day-tripper, sight-seer or literary career-enhancer but delightedly bearing the visceral sense of its importance in our lives, and the ardent desire to protect it at all costs; attune to oneness; be still; attend; observe. It may be, as Richard Jefferies wrote over a century ago in his unbearably poignant final essay, that *"No one else seems to have seen the sparkle on the brook, or heard the music at the hatch, or to have felt back through the centuries"*; but through going into nature these are assimilated into individual consciousness. Surely the task of a truly new nature writing will be adequately to express affect, value and symbolic significance of these holy things? Having thus established a few Thoreauvian ground-rules, let's take ourselves back to Llangurig, to the company of a true exponent of them in Robert Gibbings, and to the early course of the River Wye, with a few meanders straightened out and parameters established for our accompanying it on its seaward journey. We re-find our artistic *roué*, pint before him, in the bar of Llangurig's *Blue Bell Inn*:

> *"That man in the corner with the two dogs has trained one of them to answer to Welsh and the other to English. In that way they never mistake orders and there's no confusion. That old man in the corner is nearly eighty. His wife is dead and his children married. He lives alone, and gets up at five o'clock in the morning just to hear the birds sing. That chap with the rosy cheeks and the bushy eyebrows, lighting his pipe with the red-hot poker, is talking about the old cobble-stone floors or 'pitched' floors as they are called. His father's house had one till the inspectors came and made them take it up and put down concrete instead…"*

There may not be not quite the same tenor of conversation in Llangurig pubs these days (though get them on to the *Health & Safety Executive* and conversations can heat up considerably). But nor is there the old indigenous population now. The desirable old cottages have been sold as second homes or holiday lets and subjected to television-programme-provoked, homogenising "makeovers". BMWs, Range Rovers and Mercedes park outside. The old community's broken up and dispersed, the rural skills that I still encountered in isolated communities fifty years ago, have been lost. Here's Gibbings again, game for any adventure, sauntering by the river one fine July afternoon and bumping into a friend of his from the *Blue Bell* (try this at your own risk – it's highly illegal and Water Board bailiffs are more likely to waterboard you these days than accept what you're doing as traditional sport as they did in Gibbings' day, or mine not long thereafter, when there was always someone stationed at the entrance to the valley to follow the bailiff's van upstream, blaring his horn in warning to us as he went):

"Coming for a swim?" [Dai] *asked.*

Of course I'd met him before; in fact, we'd been out on one or two private expeditions...

"Anything you like," I replied, for the day was too hot for walking, and I was being devoured by horse-flies which abound in the valley.

"Seen any fish?" he inquired, as he led the way downstream.

"I saw a couple with dark backs, in among those weedy stones at the corner."

"Ground feeders," he said. "Surface feeders are always brighter."

"Fish can change colour quickly," I told him. "I've seen a blue fish change to brown in three seconds in the tropics."

"Trout can't change their habits," he replied. "You look at their heads. The mouth of a surface feeder is cocked upwards: a ground feeder's lower jaw is in a straight line with his belly. I'll tell you another thing, the flesh of the ground feeder is a deeper colour from feeding on shrimp, more like the salmon."

Enough of poaching, and enough too about the community of Llangurig as it was eighty years ago, and irrevocably is no longer. It's still a charming village amid these high, bare hills. Its pubs are still worth visiting, and its church in the round churchyard is peculiarly grand and quirkily restored, with its shingled steeple rising from a sturdy turreted tower. Inside it has an angel choir, a screen reconstructed from early drawings, and stained glass that pursues in unusual fashion themes from the Celtic Christian church. It's a gem of a building, Grade Two listed, well worth a visit, and its restoration in the 1870s at a cost of £10,000 – a huge sum at the time – was paid for by a remarkable local character generally known as the Chevalier Lloyd[10]. There's much in

[10] Jacob Youde William Lloyd (1816-1887) was ordained in 1839, converted to Catholicism, served in the Pontifical Zouaves, and was made a Knight of the Order of St. Gregory. He was also an historian, genealogist, and antiquarian – certainly one of the more colourful Welsh parish priests of his time!

Llangurig to detain us, but it's time for us to bid it a regretful
farewell and head on down the section between Llangurig and
Glasbury where the Wye gains its maturity and becomes the finest
of Welsh rivers in terms of landscape beauty and cultural interest.
It also starts to take itself seriously along the reaches leading to
Rhaeadr Gwy. By the time of its arrival at this important upland
market town it's been augmented by some considerable streams.
Afon Marteg joins in above Rhayader, flowing down through Pant
-y-dŵr from St. Harmon, where Francis Kilvert – a name
indissociably connected with the Wye – had his first incumbency
(and didn't much like it – the church there he thought hideous
and cold.) We'll hear much more of Kilvert when we arrive at
Clyro. For the moment, we can appreciate the sight of the force
of water flowing through Rhayader, and the impressive cataract
within a very short walk of the crossroads at the town centre
where, if you arrive at the right time of year, you can watch
herculean efforts of salmon leaping the falls on their way to the
spawning grounds in the headwaters. Salmon poaching here was
particularly open and unrestrained during the construction of the
Elan Valley dams. The navvies and natives of the town, faces
blackened, torches flaring, spear and *tryfar*[11] at the ready, reputedly
hauled out two hundred fish a night in this period – a kind of re-
enactment of the Rebecca Riots that had begun in the summer

---

[11] A trident, the favoured implement for salmon-poaching in Wales. Though the more
skilful preferred a shark hook lashed to a straight pole cut from the hedge as being easier
to conceal. I remember going into the old ironmongers on Cricieth High Street during
my Cwm Pennant years and asking for a large gaff hook. The old chap in the brown work-
coat behind the counter looked puzzled in that amused way that actually says "We've got
a right one here!" and showed me a few items that clearly were not fit for the covert purpose
I had in mind. Eventually, seeing the disappointment beginning to register on my face, he
stopped the elaborate tease and said, "Maybe what you're looking for are shark hooks?"
then reached in a draw under the counter, brought out a handful of very large and sturdy
barbed hooks, which he spread across the counter. "You'd better take half a dozen," he
advised. "You always lose a few before you get the hang of it." Good salesman, that! And
of course there are plenty of sharks in Wales (Sais business people for the most part)!

of 1839, ostensibly in protest against the effect on rural communities of the new toll-gates by which the ruling classes were imposing heavy taxation on the Welsh population. But perhaps it was also as the manifestation of a breakdown in the traditional social structures of rural Wales? Whatever the cause, the revolt was expressed in the most dramatic fashion in 1839, and flared up again with considerable violence, which continued for the next year, in the winter of 1842[12]. The navvies and Rhayader residents who brazenly gaffed and speared the salmon at the town falls would certainly have remembered the "Hosts of Rebecca" and their taunting of authority, just as, in the 1970s, the people of the Welsh countryside kept a discreet and unanimous silence about the identity of Meibion Glyndŵr throughout the long duration of a campaign against second-home owners who were pricing local residents out of the rural Welsh housing market and hence destroying and deracinating long-established indigenous communities – a campaign which was notably endorsed by the poet-priest R.S. Thomas.

You can turn off in Rhayader for Elan Village and the mighty dams and reservoirs in the valleys of the Claerwen and Elan rivers, but I won't be joining you. These huge reservoirs put the fear of God into me. I feel much the same as the protagonist in David Constantine's disturbing short story, *Under the Dam*, about a man who lives with all that weight of water, all that pent-up and restrained energy, just above his house. There's a kind of terror for me in such places. I imagine an earthquake shaking the dam to its foundations, and the flood then tearing it apart and sweeping it downriver with appalling force and destructive power. The vengeance of the Goddess Aerfen! Don't imagine this is entirely far-fetched. There are earthquakes in Wales from time to time.

---

[12] For an authoritative and serious study of this period of Welsh history, see David Williams, *The Rebecca Riots: A Study in Agrarian Dissent* (University of Wales Press, 1955, revised 1986).

One I remember, on 19th July 1984, measured 5.4 on the Richter Scale, had its epicentre at Llithfaen in the Llŷn peninsula. It was strong enough to wake me at seven o'clock one morning by shaking books off the shelves in my bedroom, and caused considerable damage to property throughout North-west Wales.

As well as his support from Meibion Glyndŵr, I'm also absolutely at one with R.S. Thomas on this antipathy towards reservoirs. He wrote in a poem on the subject that *"The serenity of their expression/Revolts me, it is a pose/For strangers, a watercolour's appeal/To the mass, instead of the poem's/Harsher conditions."* The times when I've been in valleys below reservoir dams – that appalling 237 ft. high wall of grey concrete, for example, above the old Bryntail lead mine, three miles from the populous little town of Llanidloes on the Afon Hafren that holds in the waters of the Clywedog reservoir – have filled me with loathing and dread. The same with the dam at Llyn Brianne in Elenydd, which would sweep away Llandovery and probably Llandeilo too if ever it were to fail. As to what lies drowned under the waters, I cannot pass the site of Capel Celyn, its chapel and houses now lying underneath Llyn Celyn above Y Bala without muttering *"Cofiwch Dryweryn"*[13] to myself, and repeating the phrase from R.S.'s poem about these reservoirs imposed on remote and long-established Welsh communities being *"the subconscious/Of a people, troubled far down/With gravestones, chapels, villages even."*

Another major poet is indelibly associated with Cwm Elan. Percy Bysshe Shelley, the great radical among the Romantic Poets[14], and his young first wife Harriet came to live here in 1810,

---

[13] *"Remember Tryweryn!"* (also written as "Cofia Dryweryn!") You'll find this as roadside graffiti throughout Wales, even fifty years on from the drowning of a significant place in Welsh culture to service the needs of English urban populations. Listen to the Pembrokeshire singer Meic Stevens's poignant lament *Tryweryn* – you can find it on YouTube – to gauge something of the feeling this atrocity still arouses among the indigenous population of Wales.

[14] William Wordsworth aspired to this role in his youth, but quickly became apostate from

having discovered and leased the house, Nantgwillt, and paradise of an estate that Thomas Groves, a Wiltshire gentleman, had created here on *"10,000 almost worthless acres"*. You can still see the remains of its garden wall in exceptionally dry summers, near the mouth of the Nantgwyllt just before the site of the old saw-mill on the west bank of the Caban Coch reservoir. Harriet's illnesses, the remoteness of the location, difficulties over the lease, reaction to the ill-timed publication of his *Declaration of Rights* pamphlet during the Napoleonic Wars, and lack of financial support from his shrewd and concerned father put paid to Shelley's plans to found a radical community here. The young couple, under government surveillance, hopes dashed, Harriet in continuing poor health, left for Chepstow in June, and by the 28th of that month had arrived in Lynmouth on the north Devon coast, hoping to realize their Elan valley radical community plan in what immediately seemed to them a more congenial environment. So the Elan valley was left to its louring clouds and water-gathering cycles, that in the last two decades of the nineteenth century attracted Birmingham's water engineers, who corralled in five reservoirs 22,000 million gallons of pure Welsh water, incessantly replenished by the clouds above, and sent it cascading through pipelines to supply the needs Birmingham a hundred miles away, from which city it ultimately drains as waste water not into the Irish Sea but into the River Humber and the North Sea.

Shelley didn't quit Cwm Elan, however, without bidding it farewell in a little-known poem written within a year of leaving that's not generally included in collected editions of his poetry. For all the criticisms you can level against Shelley as man and poet – and they are many – I remain an admirer of his work and of his brave and forthright character. *"The Retrospect – Cwm Elan"* is

---

the cause. By the time he attained old age and was producing matter like the abysmal sequence of sonnets on capital punishment, he could more accurately be described as an ossified arch-conservative with a sclerotic blood supply to his withered brain.

not to be dismissed as mere juvenilia. *"Epipsychidion"* or *"The Mask of Anarchy"* it is not, but nor can you brand it with Thomas Groves' jibe against his own acres at Nantgwillt as being "almost worthless". As a cultural measure of how far taking the subject of landscape for poetry had progressed in the fifty-five years since the 1757 publication of Edmund Burke's pivotal text *A Philosophical Enquiry into the Origin of Our Ideas of the Sublime and Beautiful*, the value of Shelley's youthful poem is immeasurable. Here's an extract so that you may judge for yourselves:

> *The moonlight was my dearer day;*
> *Then would I wander far away,*
> *And, lingering on the wild brook's shore*
> *To hear its unremitting roar,*
> *Would lose in the ideal flow*
> *All sense of overwhelming woe;*
> *Or at the noiseless noon of night*
> *Would climb some heathy mountain's height,*
> *And listen to the mystic sound*
> *That stole in fitful gasps around.*
> *I joyed to see the streaks of day*
> *Above the purple peaks decay,*
> *And watch the latest line of light*
> *Just mingling with the shades of night;*

The interplay here between Shelley's poetic imagination and the specific landscape from which it seeks its inspiration is both instructive and fascinating. *The Retrospect: Cwm Elan* deserves to be better known as one of the important methodological and thematic texts of the Romantic Period in Britain. Shelley expressed himself more prosaically in a letter to Elizabeth Hitchener written at much the same time, that gives a fascinating glimpse into the questioning cast of mind that produced *A Defence of Poetry[15]:*

> *"This country of Wales is excessively grand; rocks piled on each other to tremendous heights, rivers formed into cataracts by their projections, and valleys clothed with woods, present an appearance of enchantment – but why do they enchant, why is it more affecting than a plain, it cannot be innate, is it acquired?"*

Abstruse philosophical and literary-critical historical considerations aside, we've left Rhayader and its salmon-spearing inhabitants well behind us, hastened on past the yellow-brick road that's Newbridge-on-Wye, noted the arrival of a considerable tributary on the eastern bank, the Afon Ithon, that winds its way down from the heaven-on-earth[16] that's Llandrindod Wells (if the Ithon's in flood, and you're fishing or canoeing, you'll probably be roundly cursing it! It flows through a region of thick grey clay around Disserth, and brings that tint with it to obscure the clarity of the Wye), and where it flows over the strata of Builth Rocks, it froths up into great rafts of foam like those I remember from my Manchester childhood beneath the weirs of the River Irwell in

Salford. To come back to the Wye around the disemboguement[17] of the Irfon, the Reverend Francis Kilvert was here in April 1875,

---

[15] Written in 1821, posthumously published in 1840. As an undergraduate studying English and Welsh Language and Literature rather more years ago than I care to recall, this essay was both mocked and admired by us students in equal measure. "Poets are the unacknowledged legislators of the world"? Not sure how much I'd like to see that put into practice..!

[16] ...or so I was told many years ago by an old lady called Joan, who I met in a café on Middleton Street in Llandod (as it's fondly known) and who informed me that she came here for day trips out at every possible opportunity. Bless her! It also has an active cell of the Communist Party, who meet in The Herb Garden Café (of course!) to pursue their enquiries into the diamat. I like the place well enough to live there these days, even though, to its shame, it now has a tory M.P. – an error I ascribe to angloid incomers.

[17] Pure mischief, including this word! For me, it's one of those that sums up George Borrow, who uses it regularly in describing his Welsh journeys. It simply means 'to flow out at the mouth'.

and left the following description:

> *"A little below Aber Ithon we saw Colonel Pearson salmon-fishing across the river and Charlie waiting upon him. So we sat down upon a little green sunny knoll of the little promontory that runs out between the meeting of the waters of the Ithon and the Wye and talked and watched the fisherman.*
>
> *"Presently a fish rose at him, he struck it, and within a quarter of an hour the salmon was gasping on the bank, an 8lb. fish. We crossed the river[18] to him, and there was a consultation whether the salmon was a clean fish. He was not in first rate order, and had probably been in the river for some time but he had the 'travelling mark' raw under his throat and so sentence was given that he was a good fish and he was knocked on the head. 'If that is a kilt[19] I never see a kilt,' said old Davies, the lean and hungry-looking tailor, withal one of the keenest and deadliest fisherman on the Wye.*
>
> *"Soon after we left him, Col. Pearson killed another salmon in beautiful order, 11 lbs., and Mr. Venables[20] brought it up to my room in triumph to show me, whilst I was dressing for dinner."*

The fishing aside (if you recoil at the bloodthirstiness here, I'd like to point out that Kilvert thoroughly despised shooting as a sport, and the bloodlust of its practitioners), Kilvert also left a memorable description of this reach of the Wye:

> *"As we glided up the valley, sweeping round bend after bend we saw new prospects and beauties still opening and unfolding before us, distant azure mountains, green sunny bursts and dark blue wooded hollows of the nearer hills with gentle dips and dimpling swells on the hillsides softly bosoming. Then suddenly came a vivid flash, dazzling with a blaze of diamond*

---

[18] By way of one of the fords used by the Welsh drovers and their herds, coming down from Epynt on their way to the English smithfields.

[19] A kelt (not kilt) is a hen salmon after spawning, when she will spend time recovering in the river before making her way back to the sea and going through the whole cycle again.

[20] Kilvert was curate to the Reverend Venables when the latter was incumbent at Clyro.

sparks thrown off as if by a firework, on the stream suddenly caught and tangled amongst broken rocks, swept roaring in a sheet of white foam through the narrowing channel, or with a stately and gracious bend the river broadened, peaceful and calm, to a majestic reach, long and silver shining, veiled here and there by fringing, overhanging woods and broken by the larch spires dawning a thickening green."

We're now, in this following of the Wye, almost at Builth Wells, where the Wye receives another very attractive tributary, the Irfon, which flows down from the hamlet of Abergwesyn, home of a remarkable Anglo-Welsh poet, Ruth Bidgood. Daughter of a Welsh-speaking minister, she was born in Glyn Neath and died in March 2022 at the age of 99. Her work is as good as any religious poetry from the last century. She moved to a bungalow at Abergwesyn during the 1970s, and campaigned against the siting of huge new reservoirs in Elenydd ("the Cambrian Mountains"), as well as opposing the spread of enormous mono-culture conifer plantations throughout Wales, which for her drastically changed the character of the country and destroyed much of its good land and many of its communities[21]. These are both major themes in her fine 1970 poetry collection, *The Zombie-Makers*. Hers is a voice we should long be at pains to heed. I've read with her at the

Wyeside Arts Centre in Builth Wells, at Theatr Hafren (as it then was) in Newtown, and in Machynlleth. On each occasion, the affection for her from local audiences was palpable – hers one of the clear voices of post-war rural Wales.

---

[21] I'm entirely in sympathy with her resistance to both of these blights on the landscapes of Elenydd. I remember supervising and assessing Duke of Edinburgh Awards Scheme students on expeditions through tracts of upland newly acquired for conifer plantations. What had previously been viable upland grazing had been turned, through a regular grid of drainage ditches scored across it, into something resembling a war zone complete with trenches, mud, and barbed wire, to cross which became an exhaustion to the body and the spirit, driving home the message reiterated time and again that English governments at Westminster have scant regard for Welsh landscapes.

Builth Wells itself is a curious little town. If you ask where the wells are, and of what kind, well, you might well ask! Sulphurous, saline and chalybeate is the answer to the second part of that question, and as to where you'll find them, your Bath Chair had better be in good order and you'd better not be too ill or infirm. They're some way out of this odd little town crowded around its now-vanished castle. Most of the works of Edward I's chief castle-builder, Master James of St. George, have survived rather better than that at Builth – think of Caernarfon, Harlech, Conwy, Beaumaris. Of Builth, there are just a few traces of masonry around a steep motte up a narrow back street – certainly worth looking out, but far from imposing. Various Welsh princes over the centuries took exception to its presence among their hills, and with supply chains being lengthy, garrisons small and nervous, and wild land all around, its non-survival was guaranteed. The chief attraction of Builth is the annual Royal Welsh Show at Llanelwedd across the river, held every July and the great event in the Welsh agricultural calendar. I went once with a group of Owen John Owen's friends from Cwm Pennant. I've still scarcely recovered from the hangover, nor from the rally-style race back late at night in highly tuned Ford Escort Mexicos – car of choice for most Welsh farm boys in that period, and offering little in the way of comfort or suspension for their passengers. My advice to anyone thinking of repeating the experience would be the same I'd give to those (only Welsh speakers need apply!) heading for Y Maes at Welsh culture's great annual moveable feast, *Yr Eisteddfod Genedlaethol*. In both cases, make sure you take your wellingtons. Welsh mud can be as deep and clinging as the Welsh peoples' bond with their home country. There are several ways of getting out of Builth. I was speaking once at a literary festival in Scotland with my late friend, literary critic and fellow climber, Al Alvarez. He probed me, late at night after several glasses of whiskey in the house where we'd been housed, about the state of a relationship in which I was then involved. When he'd heard enough, he came out with a piece of advice that I still treasure:

"There's only one way out of a bad relationship, and that's fast..!"

I don't have a bad relationship with Builth, and know of at least four good ways out of the town. But the best of them is one we often used to take fifty years ago when I was an outdoor pursuits instructor at the City of Oxford Outdoor Pursuits Centre – The Woodlands in Glasbury on Wye. On wet days when the river was high, we used to don wet-suits and buoyancy aids, load two substantial rubber dinghies onto the roof rack of one of the centre's minibuses, head for Builth, and from The Groe car-park just upstream of the six-arched bridge we launched the dinghies, six students in each of them and one instructor, with another instructor in a kayak paddling alongside. The students whooped and screamed at the top of their voices as the current raced us towards the bridge and the instructors sat comfortably wielding the steering paddle to keep the craft clear of the gravel spits. Once clear of town we bobbed along, keeping to the swift deep channel. Herons that we passed closely by as they fished from the bank were not the least concerned by our presence. I'd initially been concerned that, with those dagger-beaks, they might try to puncture our inflatable craft. If we'd been walkers along the bank or fishermen, they'd have taken to their huge and ponderous wings and glided away. As it is, a gimlet eye fixed upon us, they concluded we were neither threat nor source of food, and returned to their intense study of the river. You can get so close to wildlife when you're on the water. The vast quarries above the A481 junction at Llanelwedd – this is where the facing stone for the Elan Valley dams came from, thus marring two formerly pristine landscapes – glower down behind your straining shoulders as you paddle on, and the current carries you rapidly along.

To shake you out of your reveries as you bobble along peacefully out of Builth, the river curves round to the south and an odd little tributary, the Duhonw, that drains the eastern end of Epynt, surges in beyond the bend. Thus augmented, the stretch of river that follows is changing in character. For the next half-mile there are rapids, concluding in the sudden jolt of a natural weir. The boat rears up on the standing wave, crashes back down into troubled water, and bucks onward having given us forewarning of the shape of things to come. On the eastern bank, another river bounces in. This is the Afon Edw, coming down from Llanbadarn-y-garreg, Rhulen and Glascwm, wonderfully clear, alder-lined, perhaps the prettiest of all the Wye's many tributaries. Kilvert mentions that on 20th May 1871 he was told by the Reverend Russell, Vicar of Aberedw, that the Hawkstone pack of otter hounds had killed three otters in the Edw that morning. The gentlemen didn't like their salmon fishing interfered with! It was formerly a river of some repute among poachers, many of the stories about whom have entered Wyeside mythology. What their fate would have been if caught can be well imagined. The Reverend Powell of Dorstone, a local clergyman-squire whose father was a close associate of Kilvert, was a keen preserver of fishing on the Wye. H.J. Massingham recounts how Powell once apprehended a group of poachers and confiscated their equipment of *tryfar* and net, but was unable to press charges of poaching against them because they were not in possession of any fish. Years later, bones of the fish were discovered under a moveable tombstone in Aberedw churchyard where the resourceful miscreants had hidden them – the general faint whiff of putrescence around churchyards in regular use ensuring that no-one would look too closely.

This little area is rich in ecclesiastical interest, and we'll be coming to the most eccentric of the region's more recent incumbents quite soon. Aberedw church is well worth seeing. It's at the head of a cluster of houses grouped around the *Seven Stars Inn*, a yew tree of exceptional girth dominating the site of the ancient *clas*. The dedication of the church is to Cewydd, a sixth-century saint who also founded the fine mother church at Disserth in Radnorshire, and whose traditions as a patron saint of rain were taken over by the Saxon saint Swithun. Giraldus Cambrensis in his usual tart fashion explains the process of appropriation thus:

> *"All the monasteries in Wales are involved in one and the same vice ... for they are wont to occupy the parish of mother and baptismal church, and either in large measure diminish their extent or obtain complete control over them, expelling the parishioners and leaving the churches empty and deserted."*

Cewydd also bore the epithet *Hen Gewydd y Gwlaw*[22]. He was well-known in Brittany as well as in Wales, where the rain saint was obviously a very important figure. His original saints' day was on 2nd July. When the Saxon Swithun's relics were transferred to Winchester Cathedral on 15th July, AD 971, the day was one of torrential rain that resulted in widespread flooding, and it was this event, allied to the older Welsh name, that has given rise to the modern beliefs about St. Swithun's Day. As you stand in the churchyard at Aberedw and look across the river at the craggy bulwark of Llandeilo Hill, rearing up above the confluence of Edw and Wye, you can pick out the dark square entrance of the rock shelter that was Cewydd's hermitage. These early saints placed little premium on comfort. I remember traversing across the lakeside cliff and crawling into the narrow entrance to St. Kevin's Bed by the upper lake in Glendalough, County Wicklow. There was barely room to lie down in it, and the access was

---

[22] "Old Cewydd of the rain".

distinctly tricky and polished. St. Cewydd's cave is less obvious, more commodious, but it's still a dank, unendearing shelter, shadowy, north-easterly in aspect, its walls covered in carved graffiti, rather in the manner of Ogof Twm Shon Cati at the summit of Dinas above Abergwesyn. In the matter of its name, this Aberedw rock-shelter mirrored the process Giraldus describes above. What had been Cell Cewydd became Llywelyn's Cave. *Ein Llyw Olaf* reputedly spent his last night here, *"heb dân, heb wely"*[23], before riding on next day to seek and be refused shelter at Builth Castle. So he continued on to Cilmeri, where he met his death by the sword of an English soldier, who did not initially recognise him. His head was hacked off and sent to Longshanks in London, who ordered it to be impaled on a pikestaff at the Tower of London.

The valley of the Wye itself has narrowed here by the confluence with the Edw, and taken on a more dramatic aspect. All around the shoulder of Llandeilo Hill are craggy outcrops of the local Silurian rocks. When I worked in this area, I used to wonder if they had rock-climbing potential. The short answer is no, but they look alluring nonetheless. Of more interest is the conical bracken hill on the east bank before you reach the confluence with the next major tributary, the Bach Howey. Twyn y Garth is its name, known locally as Gun Hill. It's barely 1,000 feet high, and is a magnificent viewpoint. Look closely at the summit and you'll see the reason for its local name. Up there, its wooden-spoked wheels rotted away within their rims, the barrel and shield red and fretted with rust, is a 25-pounder field gun from the Great War. How it came to be there tells you something about the rivalries that have always sprung up between small Welsh rural communities. The two nearest villages of Erwood and Llanstephan bought it jointly from the Ministry of Defence after

---

[23] "…without fire, without bed". Cf. "Ystafell Cynddylan" in Canu Aneirin.

the war (still in working order at that time, apparently, though coming by the appropriate munitions might have presented problems). It was initially installed on the village green at Erwood. A small war over it started between the youths of the two villages. It was regularly removed from one to the other in the dead of night until a truce was declared and a post-war settlement agreed. Hence the re-naming of Twyn y Garth and the gun's present location on its summit, having been towed up there by a team of heavy horses. All this is to mark time as the river rushes us relentlessly onward towards the most dramatic event in its course between Builth and Hay. Here's the description from an old edition of a canoeists' guide to the Welsh rivers:

> *"Below Erwood the adrenaline starts to flow and the mouth dries as the paddler reaches the infamous "Hell Hole" rapids. Hard in their day, they can still provide a shock in high water with a poor line of descent! Warning is given as soon as the chain bridge at Llanstephan comes into view. The line lies far right [and] is tough; in higher water options over the central rock steps exist. In full spate the stopper middle and left takes on a vicious character – care should be exercised (IV). Below the bridge is a perfect surfing hole at low to medium conditions. Easier rapids follow, until a final flurry over a steep drop occurs about a kilometre above Boughrood/Llyswen bridge."*

That should give you a good insight into the mentality and practice of white water canoeists. As far as white water rafting goes, the noise and power of the water here when the river's in spate, the hectic nature of steering through that maze of channels, drops and standing waves, that throw the dinghy and its seven occupants about as though it were a child's toy, is exhilarating and deafening. The students, screaming all the while, frantically wield their Canadian-style paddles. The boat bucks and kicks its way through, spray drenches across it, causing the students to shriek ever louder, the course down the successive steps in the strata is difficult and complex. Twenty yards away my fellow instructor Eric Hoole in his orange KW7 kayak, double-bladed paddle flashing aloft as he rides the watery rodeo, glasses covered in spray, face set into an ecstatic grin, tries to exchange the occasional glance to point to the best line of descent. But the truth of the matter is that you have given yourself up to the power of the river, and your ability to control events is limited more or less to guiding the pliant, cumbersome craft into roughly the best line downriver, whilst urging your crew on to intense efforts in keeping to that and from pitching head over heels at the huge standing waves that lie in wait below every drop, where the hissing water curves round and round on itself and could trap any discrafted person in that recurring circle until the breath's gone from their body and they float away lifeless downstream. I look back and am amazed at the risks we were allowed to take with children not much younger than ourselves at this and other activities. But a series of tragic accidents that occurred in the mountains and on water throughout the last decades of the twentieth century – particularly the 1971 Cairngorms and 1993 Lyme Bay disasters – changed all that and brought in much tighter regulations, rigorous certification, and a change to the entire nature of the outdoor pursuits industry (as it became).

I have a sense that in the older approach – planned and led by those who, through their own long participation in canoeing, caving, climbing, mountain adventuring, had acquired the survival instincts required in those environments – was latitude for exercise of a developed instinct for risk, an awareness of all its deadly dimensions, that was far more acute and more truly safe than one that depended on set rules and procedures mechanically learned and followed by rote rather than contingency. Safety, to my mind, comes primarily from within. But in this, as in so many other things, the mask of anarchy that aids individual growth has long been cast aside in favour of more rigid social forms, and the notion of adventure as an educational medium – somewhat tarnished by a catalogue of fatal incidents – is no longer as inspiring an ideal as it was in my youth, before it was supplanted by the learning of skills and the belief that they alone could safeguard and see the individual through all situations.

There was another factor operating in the decline of the adventure centres from their 1970s heyday, and that was the simple one of cost. These places were expensive to run and to equip, and could only take limited numbers of students. The educational value of adventure was hard both to define and to justify. Beyond all that, shortly after I took up my post at The Woodlands, Ted Heath won a majority for the Conservative Party at the 1970 General Election. He appointed Margaret Thatcher as his Secretary of State for Education. Very shortly thereafter the foundations were being laid for the all-consuming Thatcherite Diseducation Project with its relentless and draconian budgetary cuts and syllabus-trimming, the tragic results of which we can observe in the current state of the nation. Now those who wish to raft through Hell Hole must have funds to buy their own equipment and transport to get to it. Or they must seek out the insured, regulated and certified private service providers who operate on the river, and pay the large fees they charge for lesser adventures than those we gave the schoolchildren of Oxford for minimal charge and with maximum enjoyment. And so is the continuing embourgeoisement of society assured, and its divisions enforced...

After the thrills of Hell Hole the Wye changes in character. Another substantial tributary, the Bach Howey, spills in on the east bank, having made its way down from Painscastle. This used to give another of our frequent outings from The Woodlands for an activity described on our fortnightly programmes as "gorge-walking". Under its older name of "ghyll-scrambling" it had been practised in the English Lake District since the nineteenth century. You simply donned boots and waterproof clothing, headed for the nearest gorge – the Bach Howey was that for The Woodlands – and made your way up it by a combination of wading, traversing across rock walls (with much laughter-inducing plunges into the pools below), and occasionally, in the more exciting gorges on the Ystwyth and Rheidol gorges in the vicinity of Pontarfynach, by way of lassoes and rope-manoeuvres which were complex, precarious and very time-consuming if the group was large (sea-cliff traversing on the Gower Peninsula or the Castlemartin cliffs in Pembrokeshire, using the same techniques, was an associated activity).

There was no need for ropes in the Bach Howey gorge, though it was an impressive place in its way. You'd often see dying salmon being washed down after spawning here, sometimes with ravens, carrion crows, or even otters feasting on them. There was one highly impressive section of the Bach Howey, strangely well known for a place so remote and well-concealed. It's called Craig Pwll Du, and is off to the right from the section of gorge we mostly used. You peered up a mossy-walled cleft towards a thunderous sound of falling water, ventured closer, and saw a whiteness of spray in stygian gloom roaring into a pool once deemed bottomless. Kilvert in his diary mentions the brave and enterprising Mr. Foulkes, who was unprepared to take gossip and rumour at face value (nor should any of us – all too often they have their roots in calumny and Kleinian Envy). Mr. Foulkes made his way to Craig Pwll Du, stripped off, dived in, and found himself in serious trouble by becoming entangled in underwater tree roots. But he survived to tell the tale. The place is one of those secretive, affecting places you come at unexpectedly on these rivers that cut down through the Ordovician strata to create their own mysterious ante-chambers to other worlds. I was always aware of the way this stole upon the minds of my students as we approached Craig Pwll Du and its spouting tumble over resistant strata into black and somehow threatening water. "The glen of Craig Pwll Du... has its own loveliness to halt the wanderer", wrote W.H. Howse in the classic topographical book on Wales's forgotten county of Radnorshire[24]. Bill Condry also admired this beautiful gorge that joins the Wye by way of a beautiful, flower-rich riparian meadow just above Llanstephan.

The last time I was here was on a bright May morning after sharing an event at Hay Festival with Mark Cocker. We waited on the old viaduct over the river, its parapets adorned with notices forbidding abseiling. This was built to carry "Scapa Specials" laden with prime Welsh steam-coal from The Valleys to the British fleet in Orkney. On the bridge we were met by expert local bryologist Ray Woods. At the fundraising event for Builth's Wyeside Theatre that I shared with Ruth Bidgood a few months before, Ray had agreed to take Mark and myself for a walk, and expound on his speciality of lichens. I blame Ray entirely for our not having reached the waterfall in its spray-pearled, mossy cauldron deep within the gorge that day – a site around which Bill Condry had enticingly described impatient bittercress, Solomon's seal, perennial knawel, red catchfly, "and both the hellebores". Never walk with a botanical enthusiast if you seek to arrive at a destination! Bill's wife Penny, who has a wicked sense of humour, memorably describes them as "the bottoms-up brigade"! (This is observation, not complaint, and certainly not an injunction to finish your drink.) Afterwards, brains reeling from imparted information, Mark and I agreed that we had seldom spent a more intellectually exciting four hours, or been in the company of a

---

[24] W.H. Howse, *Radnorshire* (Hereford, 1949)

better naturalist and communicator. We covered a bare half-mile of riparian woodland; heard of the traditional usage of a crusted grey lichen, crottle, in dyeing; peered through an illuminated magnifier at minuscule growths on trees and rocks; marvelled at the extraordinary structural beauty and strangeness of these combinations of fungus and alga growing together in symbiotic relationship to produce an organism – the thallus – differing entirely from its constituent parts. Through Ray's lucid enthusiasm and encyclopaedic knowledge, mitochondria within these complex cells seemed to contain the secret of life itself. I've seldom experienced a greater sense of wonder in nature – the symbiotic gift of an exceptional communicator and a tiny organism that seems quite insignificant. Until you learn to look. You can look up Ray Woods' conducted botanical walks in deepest Radnorshire for yourself, and be well rewarded for your efforts. Here's a brief excerpt from an informative address Ray gave in Machynlleth as the William Condry Memorial Lecture for 2012:

> *"Acid rain still dogs the lichens of most of Wales. We have learned that just here and there by a combination of local topography, usually in the shape of high ground to the east and with a somewhat basic soil and the naturally basic bark of trees such as ash and willow a fragment of what would have been the lichen cover of a lot of Wales survives. In these deep sheltered ravines the trees are covered with enormous growths of tree lungworts, jelly lichens, fish-smelling Stictas and other specklebelly lichens as the Americans call them. A recovery might just be possible if we can get rid of acid rain."*

Craig Pwll Du is now designated as a Site of Special Scientific Interest. On the gate into the gorge from the Wyeside meadow at the entrance to the gorge, notices strictly warn you against trespassing here. The world has grown significantly smaller since

I first entered this rarest of botanical domains. Here's Bill Condry:

"Wye tributaries such as Edw and Bach Howey (Bachawy) ... go dropping down ravines and dingles in cool shade and the spray of waterfalls. ... Plant-seeker or not you will enjoy the falls of the Bach Howey under Craig Pwll-du. ...

He then discloses the species list I've given above – all the plants still there, as they were in Bill's day several decades ago now. Let's leave the little Wye with that nod to his memory and re-join the main river. The ten miles from Boughrood to Hay are, by comparison with what's encountered above, quite placid. I remember being with Bill Bowker, who was Chief Instructor for many years at another outdoor centre down the road from the one I worked at in Glasbury-on-Wye. (Bill's centre was Glasbury House, owned by the London borough of Redbridge, and run for many years by a fine old local countryman called Norman Pugh, who imparted to it a character entirely distinct from The Woodlands, where I worked.) It was a wet morning and Bill and I were standing on the bank just below Llyswen bridge, where the Wye begins its great curve eastwards to make an exit from the Welsh hills. The shallow rapids below the bridge were in front of us. Bill picked up a stone from a pool in the river, examined it, showed it to me. It was limestone. There were fossils in it. "I don't think it came from anywhere along the Wye," Bill said. Then he drew my attention to the slopes of the Black Mountains which had dominated the view in our rafting descent; digressed into a brief explanation of the subject of river capture; and then recounted the experience of a crisp, blue-skied morning when he'd looked down from the Ordnance Survey pillar on Pen Rhos Dirion to see beneath cloud-filled valleys and all the former courses of the rivers full and flowing again with frothing vapours. As he talked, I was experiencing the same epiphany that must have come to him in that moment, which he now, in profoundly educative fashion, offered to me, unforgettably:

"A complex mind cannot find out the truth of anything, it cannot find out what is real – and that is our difficulty. From childhood we are trained to conform, and we do not know how to reduce complexity to simplicity. It is only the very simple and direct mind that can find the real, the true. We know more and more, but our minds are never simple; and it is only the simple mind that is creative."[25]

On a July morning in 1872, the Reverend Francis Kilvert, with his fellow clergyman Tom Williams, incumbent of Llowes, made his way up the valley of the Bach Howey above its gorge, with the intention of paying "a visit to the eccentric solitary, the Vicar". They carried on along the greensward tracks of Llanbedr Hill, heading for a place that still retains its apartness and sense of quietude. There was a simple, primitive dwelling place among the heather, the Cuckoo Rocks sentinel above. Few come here even now, though its long-time resident is well worthy of remembrance and respectful pilgrimage.

As we turned the corner of the little grey hut and came in sight of the closed door we gave up all hope of seeing the Solitary and believed that our pilgrimage had been in vain. Then what was my relief when I knocked upon the door to hear a strange deep voice from within saying 'Ho! Ho!' There was a slight stir within and then the cabin door opened and a strange figure came out.

So The Solitary was in residence! Kilvert gives us a memorable description of his physical appearance:

The figure of a man rather below middle height, about 60 years of age, his head covered with a luxuriant growth of light brown or chestnut hair and his face made remarkable by a mild thoughtful

---

[25] Jiddu Krishnamurti (1895-1986), *Freedom from the Known*.

melancholy blue eye and red moustache and white beard. The hermit was dressed in a seedy faded greasy suit of black, a dress coat and a large untidy white cravat, or a cravat that had once been white, lashed round his neck with a loose knot and flying ends. Upon his feet he wore broken low shoes and in his hands he carried a tall hat. There was something in the whole appearance of the Solitary singularly dilapidated and forlorn and he had a distant absent look and a preoccupied air as if the soul were entirely unconscious of the rags in which the body was clothed.

As naturally as though he were accustomed to receiving visitors every day, he ventured out to greet his fellow clergymen, and to involve them in his planned business for the day. Kilvert makes clear the poverty, disorder and squalor in the cabin, yet though shocked, there is a warmth in his account towards the man of the cloth who chose to live in this place and this manner:

No table cloth. No grate. The hearth foul with cold peat ashes, broken bricks and dust, under the great wide open chimney through which stole down a faint ghastly sickly light. In heaps and piles upon the floor were old books, large Bibles, commentaries, old-fashioned religious disputations, CMS Reports and odd books of all sorts, Luther on the Galatians, etc. The floor was further encumbered with beams and logs of wood, flour pans covered over, and old chests. All the other articles of food were hung up on pot hooks some from the ceiling, some in the chimney out of the way of the rats. The squalor, the dirt, the dust, the foulness and wretchedness of the place were indescribable, almost inconceivable. And in this cabin this lives the Solitary of Llanbedr, the Revd John Price, Master of Arts of Cambridge University and Vicar of Llanbedr Painscastle.

Williams soon returns to join them, and the Reverend Price tells something of how he came to live in a place which still has the quiet sense of divinity lingering around it. A cart loaded with peat had been sent down to be unloaded, whilst the three clergyman walked on up the hill to see Pen Cwm rocks, *"the last place where the little people* [i.e. the fairies] *were seen."* To the west the pool of Llanbwchllyn was gleaming silver in its cup of the hills, curlews were pitching up to their lovely crescendos, the poignant call of the golden plover sounded all around, and the two young clergymen lounged in the dry heather at the feet of this poor, dishevelled, charismatic holy man who would in earlier days surely have been proclaimed one of the saints of the Celtic Church in Wales. He told them how pleased he was that the rocks around his home had been observed by others than himself. *"I said to myself,"* he observed, *"that those were very beautiful rocks."* They returned to his cabin for refreshment:

> *"Looking round his habitation it seemed suddenly to occur to him that it was not just like other people's. 'I am afraid', he said, 'that I am not very tidy today.' A little girl, he told us, came to make his bed and tidy up, four days a week. Going to a dark corner he routed out three wine glasses which he washed carefully at the door. Then he rummaged out a bottle of wine and drawing up his flour pan to the table and taking his seat upon it he filled our glasses with some black mixture which he called I suppose port and bade us drink."*

When Kilvert and Williams made to leave, he went with them to show the way down to the church: *"The people who met him touched their hats to his reverence with great respect. They recognized him as a very holy man and if the Solitary had lived a thousand years before he would have been revered as a hermit and perhaps canonised as a saint. At a gate leading into a lane we parted. There was a resigned look in his quiet melancholy blue eyes. The last I saw of him was that he was leaning on a gate looking after us. Then I saw him no more. He had gone back I suppose to his grey hut in the green cwm."*

The three having gone their separate ways, Kilvert infuses his description of his own walk back to Clyro with an ecstatic sense of the benediction he felt from having been in The Solitary's presence:

> *The evening became lovely with a heavenly loveliness. The sinking sun shot along the green pastures with a vivid golden light and striking through the hedges here and there tipped a leaf or a foxglove head with a beam of brilliant green or purple. …. I crossed the Bach Wye by the short cut at Trewilad … stood on the stepping stones to watch the little herd of cows undriven coming lazily through the brook home to Trewilad to be milked. The water, darkly bright, came flowing down and filling the cool shadowy lane, and the red and white cows loitered slowly down to the brook, standing still often in the shallow water as they forded the stream, and the air was full of sunshine and the honey scent of the charlock, and the hedges were luxuriant with the luscious sweetness of woodbine and the beauty of the stars of the deep red rose."*

If that doesn't make you want to visit the valley of the Bach Howey, and read more of Kilvert's diary, what will? John Price was born in the small upland Carmarthenshire village of Bethlehem in Dyffryn Ceidrych. His father Thomas was a farmer at Llwynymendy Uchaf, where the ground falls away into Dyffryn Tywi. His intellectual grasp in his youth impressed those who knew him, and through patronage he was enabled to matriculate at Queens' College, Cambridge, from which institution he gained an M.A. in Classics. After his ordination in 1834, he was appointed curate in a Lancashire parish. A love affair with a beautiful young woman there ended in his rejection when she decided in favour of another suitor. With a securely packed sequence of letters which recounted the history of their relationship, he returned to Wales, and after several years of marginal existence, through the influence of a clerical cousin he was preferred to the incumbency at Llanbedr-Painscastle – an exceedingly poor and scattered parish that had been without a priest for some decades. Its church was in ruins, its population more likely to attend the little chapel on the corner of the road that leads over Llanbedr Hill in Painscastle than the ruinous church in its remote location several miles away. Temperamentally unsuited to the tasks of rebuilding both the congregation and the physical fabric of the church, and with no vicarage available in which he might live, Price rented a small house, Gate House Cottage – it's still there – in the fork between the Rhosgoch and Clyro roads and close to the Maesllwch Arms (not to be confused with the grander establishment of the same name in Glasbury, this is now the Roast Ox Inn).

Painscastle was still a quiet, isolated community when I first knew it in the early 1960s. Curtains would be drawn back to observe strangers passing though on foot. A century earlier, in the 1850s, it must have been extremely remote. Price moved from there to a location closer to his church some time in the 1860s, having bought three defunct wooden bathing machines from Aberystwyth and installed them in the small valley where he was to spend the rest of his life. Local gossip held that he was a fabulously wealthy miser (he was in fact utterly generous with all he possessed, which eventually left him destitute), in consequence of which he was burgled by one of the tramps whom he regularly assisted. The package of love letters was stolen. They were ripped up and scattered to the four winds. His bathing machines also caught fire about this time, causing him to move to the tiny, draughty, drystone, thatched shack where Kilvert and Williams met him. His pastoral care to his parishioners was always exemplary. When they invited him to share their food, he would leave a shilling for a meal or sixpence for a cup of tea. Every Sunday morning at 10.30 he held a service solely for tramps and vagrants, who were allowed to cook food on the church stove whilst he conducted the service. He paid them to attend for as long as he had funds to do so, and for those who were in relationships, he gave them five shillings to regularise their unions in his church. One writer, David Edmunds-Owen, tells the following story about Price:

> *"One day a tramp, who does not seem to have known him very well, came to beg. Mr Price took out a half-crown, showed it to the man and said: 'There, my friend, is the last coin that I have in the world. If you think that you are worse off than I am then in God's name, take it.' The tramp refused the gift, and explained in Hay the next day that 'he really could not take it from such a dear old gentleman.'"*

The final years of "The Solitary" were ones of difficulty and decline. The end came in March 1895. A friend, Adolphus Hackman, Vicar of Llyswen, took him away to Talgarth. His ragged clothes had not been taken off for years and had to be cut from him before he was bathed. From his bed he gave profuse thanks to his helpers, *"wondering what he had done in his life to merit such attention and so many blessings"*. After which mild protestation he slipped away into deep and restful sleep and never regained consciousness. His funeral service at the by-now-restored Llanbedr-Painscastle church was conducted by Thomas Williams, who'd accompanied Kilvert in his visit twenty-three years before. During the first spell that I worked at The Woodlands, in 1966, on my days off I often used to walk around this end of Llanbedr Hill, and was always met with the unfailing and characteristic indigenous Radnorshire courtesy and hospitality from the people I met in this secluded, quiet region (not quite the same these days, since it became a distant suburb of Hampstead and Highgate). The people hereabouts lived for the most part to immense ages, and remembered with pride their anchorite vicar. Mr and Mrs

Price of Llanbach Howey, near the church, recalled him as *"of small stature, a perfect gentleman, and of a very kindly disposition"*. The old man at the seventeenth-century farmhouse of Ciliau, above the confluence of Wye and Little Wye, looking down on that spot from the lower slopes of Twyn y Garth, also remembered him from his boyhood seventy years before. He told me of his generosity, his clear voice, and other stories too where folk-tale and glimpses of history intermingled in his conversation with the sound of the Bach Howey flowing below. Here were water-sprites on a rock below Craig Pwll-du, that it was better not to approach lest their enchantment lured you into inescapable green underwater mansions. Sitting with a cup of cider in his chimney-breast as the spring evening was sung to its close by chatter of water from below, he told me of cavaliers from the time of the English Revolution cantering along the lanes from Painscastle, two abreast, plumes waving, spurs jingling. The last time I visited Ciliau, twenty-five years ago, it was becoming ruinous – Radnorshire Silurian is poor building-stone. Windows were broken; courses of masonry had fallen away; chimney-stacks leaned; in the orchard fruit trees had gone un-pruned for years and were rotting from the boles. Sad to see it thus! As for The Solitary, his grave is in Llanbedr Painscastle churchyard, under a white cross with the following inscription:

In loving memory of
Rev John Price MA
Son of Thomas Price Esq
Llwynmendy Carmarthenshire
and vicar of this parish
who died March 20th 1895
aged 86 years
For to me to live is Christ
and to die is gain – Phil 1.21

I cannot help but think that the example of this saintly man, his lack of acquisitiveness, freedom from personal greed, simple holiness, are qualities of which particularly English society in these post-Thatcher, ignorant times, stands sorely in need. The country also stands in need of the landscape enclosed in this majestic easterly bend of the river. John Price is a fitting patron saint and *genius loci* for this small region of Radnorshire hill country, one of the quietly beautiful, relatively unspoiled parts of Wales. On a fine evening recently I walked up to Ireland. It's an old, now-ruined farmhouse east of the high point on Llanbedr Hill between Painscastle and Rhulen, among rounded heather hills. We all have places that are resonant in our lives. This ruined house is that for me. I first came here on a solitary walking tour of Wales when I was fourteen. Then it was sound-walled, roofed, windowed, abandoned only recently. I pushed open the door on that day in 1961, explored inside, fetched water from the cold and cress-lined spring nearby, lit a fire of ash-twigs in the hearth, swept the wooden boards with an ash-branch, spread my sleeping bag across them, sat on the doorstep to watch the shades thicken and hear the owls. I sat there again next morning, cradling my tea as the sun rose through a gap in the hills above Colva. This was sixty years ago. Almost forty years ago I wrote an environmental piece about Ireland, Radnor, in the *Guardian* newspaper[26]. All that was left then to maintain some pretence of uprightness were a few feet of cracked chimney-breast. Now there's only a mound of rubble, nettle-girt beneath the trees. For half-a-century I'd wondered who had lived here? Then, quite by chance, when I was living not many miles away at Clun (remember your Housman? *"Clunbury, Clunton, Clungunford and Clun/Are the quietest places under the sun"*? Still true to a relative degree) in the Shropshire hill country, I read a delightful book called *An Idler on the Shropshire Borders* that recounts

---

[26] *Guardian*, 5th November, 1983: "Pass the ammunition and speed the plough".

the adventures and encounters of Ida Gandy, a doctor's wife who lived in Clunbury from 1930 to 1945. Suddenly out of its pages there was a glimpse of Ireland's former life. A keeper lived here, Mrs. Gandy tells us, "a really kind and friendly man, interested in other birds beside his own game. He showed us where a ring-ouzel was nesting in the heather, and a pet raven whom he'd rescued when it had fallen from its nest." She tells further of how the keeper's wife spoiled the bird disgracefully, feeding him biscuit meal from a spoon. These memories of hers, so simple and artless, ravished me, had me glowing with old affection for the place. At Ireland again more recently, on a glowing evening with heather and gorse in bloom and the air fragrant with their honeyed and coconut scents, it seemed this couple's kindliness had long imbued the place, was what had drawn me back time and again over decades. As I left a curlew flew soundlessly through the ash grove. I felt so grateful to Ida Gandy for the good things I'd learned.

That was a long detour from the river, which we left in Boughrood. Let's re-embark there and float down the river to Glasbury (*Y Clas ar Wy*), where I spent some of the happiest years of my life at a time when its old, rural community had not yet been displaced by wealthy metropolitan incomers. It was then very much an old-fashioned rural village. George Sturt would have felt at home here and found plenty in common with the inhabitants. It became the outdoor activities hub of the region, with many local authorities from England buying up large houses and re-inventing them as outdoor pursuits centres before the whole educational outdoor pursuits project went into decline. Nowadays the river beach at Glasbury – with café and public toilets and parking and pubs close at hand, a gentle green meadow for picnicking just above the bank, an easy place to launch canoes and practice all the elementary techniques on a fairly placid stretch of river – has become a popular resort for visitors. In the holiday seasons and at weekends throughout the year it throngs with noisy paddlers, swimmers and splashers. The wildlife on the whole has taken its leave and retreated to quieter reaches. The visitors seem not to notice the liquid manure flooding in from the Afon Llynfi. I very much doubt that Glasbury beach will ever qualify for Blue Flag status. A depressing thought! And another depressing thought is that here an old friend of mine filled her pockets with stones and waded into the deep pool at the outflow of the Llynfi. I'd known her in her twenties, when she was a young teacher, only a little older than I was. She was a fine horsewoman, used to take me riding, would smile at my ineptitude, at my complaints about the discomfort for the male of the species of cantering. In her later years she became incapacitated with arthritis, lost sight of joy. I believe suicide is seldom impulsive or sudden, but rather a process contemplated perhaps even years beforehand until finally the mental habituation is complete, the person almost unreachable, the final act an inevitability that can no longer even take into account the bewilderment, hurt and self-blaming of those who are left behind. But it is their ultimate choice, and we have to move beyond our own pain and accept their right to make it. As I had to with my first-born son, in anguish but out of respect.

When I lived in Glasbury, in the village there were three shops, two garages, a post office, a dairy, a score of small family farms, and a population infused with traditions, local knowledge, country lore. Like the bridges that preceded the current one, like the old church, like the houses by the river, almost all of this has been swept away – literally in some cases, for the riverside houses in Glasbury were notoriously prone to flooding, particularly the Old Vicarage where the writer and historian William Woods lived for a time in the 1970s, and who, with his wife, entertained me most hospitably and gave me a bed one night and a great deal of erudite talk when I'd turned up in the Maesllwch Arms after hitching down from Eryri. The old faces, the old characters, the ones you might see in the bars of the Harp Inn and the Maesllwch Arms, the Radnorshire Arms in Llowes or the Boat Inn at Boughrood – the ones with open countenances and warm hearts, ever ready to spare time to give you a hand, offer advice, or simply talk about their sense of the place and perception of life here – are gone. I remember Tom Price, who looked after the centre minibuses at The Woodlands, servicing, and also serviced for nothing more than cost of materials other than the ones of which he already had a supply in his workshop, my first car – a Mini Countryman that I'd bought from a gardener in the village for £40. It was a bargain at that. I did over eighty thousand miles in it before the sub-frames finally rusted through, and even then John Thomas at Glasbury garage gave me £10 for it, for spares, after he'd most apologetically had to fail it on the MoT. Do you get such generosity of spirit in much of Britain these days? I doubt it, yet it seems to me that it characterised the people who lived along the Welsh Wye in those halcyon days. They were as frequently encountered as halcyons themselves, flashing like sky-jewels from riverside willow to riverside willow, diving and emerging with minnows crosswise in their beaks which they'd take back to hidden tunnels in the banks that they excavated before the nesting season. This was a lovely part of the country in which to have spent some of my younger years, and I've often returned to it, to sleep out on summer nights up on Llanbedr Hill or The Begwns, to converse with the spirit of old John Price, to keep myself connected with the goodness of the place and its people, and the long traditions of the land:

> "…*no higher wage, no income, will buy for [humankind] that satisfaction which of old – until machinery made drudges of them – streamed into their muscles all day long from close contact with iron,*

timber, clay, wind and wave, horse-strength. It tingled up in all the niceties of touch, sight, scent. The very ears received it, as when the plane went singing over the wood, or the exact chisel went tapping in (under the mallet) to the hard ash with gentle sound. But these intimacies are over..."

That extract is from *The Wheelwright's Shop* by George Sturt. The closest male friend I made during my Glasbury years was a woodwork teacher called John Greenland who worked at Blackbird Leys, the roughest Secondary Modern school in Oxford – it does have them! John brought groups down to the centre twice a year. These students generally excelled at all our activities and were an appreciative delight to work with. In my time of working in outdoor centres, because of my own Manchester inner-city slum kid upbringing I was always given the supposedly roughest kids to work with, and I always enjoyed and seemed to understand their attitudes. They made me laugh. The truculence was mostly on the surface. In our divided and unequal society you could scarcely blame them for it, who had been deemed low status educationally at the age of eleven and thus had so many opportunities taken away from them. To "level things up" as the politicians now have it, I'd invite many of John's students back on the specialist courses we held in school holidays. Their attitudes were exemplary. They combined famously with girls from Oxford High School who usually made up the rest of the group and twisted the poor lads round their little fingers. A few young hearts were broken as a result of this social experiment, but perhaps a greater social awareness came from it too. With John himself, I'd drive down to Pembroke in our holidays. Together we made the first ascents of some of my best new climbs on the sea-cliffs there – exciting pioneering exploits on steep limestone, particularly that of the sunset-walled, sea-caved precipice of Mowing Word, Pembroke's finest sea-cliff. After I'd left The Woodlands, John took over my job and I'm sure did it far better than I had ever done. Eventually he too left and established a cabinet-making business in Hay. I used to call in whenever I was in the area, and relished his craftsman's enthusiasm for the woods with which he worked – the visceral appreciation of the material, his tactile delight in grain and texture, the way he described it with slow, sensual gestures of his hands, his celebration and proper use of it. That quotation above from George Sturt captures exactly something most of us have lost and which John still possessed in full measure. And there was something of John Price about him too – the mildness, the generosity, the quasi-religious approach to life, the capacity to praise. He too was disappointed in love, but rather than let it destroy him, he worked at his craft and produced exquisite things. He became an exponent of the old rural traditions of working with natural materials. You could see that capacity in him as he strove to adapt to the mediums of steep rock, of rapids in a canoe. He's another of my honorary Wyesiders.

As is the ex-ghillie John Pledge, with whom I worked from time to time during university-long summer vacations at Glasbury House. He set off walking from there one lunchtime in 1976 to eat his mid-day meal at home in Llyswen just across the river, peered over Glasbury bridge, and spotted a large salmon in a pool that the dry summer had left under it. Never the man to lose an opportunity, down he went to the pool, caught the fish, which weighed in at 33lbs, and bore it off to his wife Lil, who duly cooked him a large steak from it, and served it up with trimmings. Fresh doesn't come any fresher than that. Afterwards John sat in his favourite armchair for a post-prandial snooze, from which he never woke. So much river lore vanished with him. He's in the graveyard now, looking down on the river the keepering and ghillying along which had been his life's work. The last in this brief inventory of Glasbury characters I knew is Joyce Thomas, for years a cleaner at The Woodlands, and the bane of young male instructors' lives for the apple-pie beds she made, for the raucous laughter directed at us, the outrageous flirtation, the lifting her skirt to flash her knickers at us. There was no serious sexual intent in any of this – it was merely ribald rural play, done to embarrass the poor young males she suspected of priggishness, and never was there a more good-humoured and kindly woman. I like to think of her now as one of the earthier characters in a Hardy novel, bringing things alive with her yaffingale laughter[27]. On the first occasion that I appeared at Hay Festival, to be interviewed by Mavis Nicholson about a book of mine that had just appeared, Joyce was there on the front row, running through her entire repertoire of sly winks, rolled eyes, sidelong grins and every other device a woman can use to stop a man taking himself too seriously. Which was not an option anyway with an interviewer as deft as Mavis – an acutely sharp south Walian from Briton Ferry who'd had her own interview series on Channel Four in which she'd interrogated celebrities as various as James Baldwin, Lauren Bacall, Rudolf Nureyev and Maya Angelou (she'd shared a lover who'd been the first male pin-up in *Playgirl* magazine with the latter). When Mavis had me in her Star Chamber, her first question, without any prior warning, in front of 400 people at eleven in the morning after a long session carousing with her in one of Hay's pubs the previous evening, ran like this:

"So tell me, Jim – you're on record as saying that LSD forms an essential part of any writer's education. Would you care to elaborate..?"

It was delivered in the sweetest tones, and had the audience's immediate hushed attention. The minx! So I answered her, at some length (occasionally glancing at Joyce Thomas on the front row to see how I was doing), and Mavis and I made it through the

---

[27] Radnorshire dialect word for the green woodpecker.

hour without losing our friendship[28]. They should have made her a fixture at Hay. All that apart – and Hay is not Hay-on-Wye, incidentally, its English name (in Welsh it's Y Gelli Gandryll) coming from the Norman La Haie – after my event I walked into town past the castle, which folklore associates with Moll Walbee, but then almost everything in Radnorshire of antiquarian interest has some connection with Moll Walbee. She's reputed to have built Hay castle in a day (Abergavenny castle too, if it comes to that). When a stone splinter from one of the blocks she was carrying made its way into her shoe, she picked it out and flung it across the river, where it implanted itself upright in the churchyard at Llowes. You can still see it there today, in the church now – Moll Walbey's Stone – though the more archaeologically minded claim that it's a mesolithic menhir. Moll was also celebrated for having held out against a long siege in Painscastle, in the valley of the Bach Howey (where we recently met the Reverend Price, "The Solitary"). There's not a stone of the immense castle now standing. It was all quarried to build the houses in the village, but the earthworks left behind are impressively large.

So who was this Amazonian figure of Radnorshire legend? She was the wife of William de Breos, a descendant of Philip de Breos who came over from Normandy with William the Conqueror, performing sterling knightly service at Hastings and elsewhere, and was duly rewarded with a Marcher lordship for his pains. His great-great-grandson's wife Maud was pithily described by a contemporary at the court of King John as *"malapert and stomachful"*. She was clearly a woman of considerable character to have left such reverberations rolling down through the centuries.

---

[28] The comments were made in the course of a long interview for *The Guardian* with the American writer Peter Matthiessen, in which we both praised the influence LSD had in our early writing, and concluded by agreeing that there was a law of diminishing returns here. A few trips were all that was needed to establish acid consciousness. Thereafter, the mind can take you unaided to the same places. I'll return to this theme in a later chapter.

Radnorshire seems to have been one of the great repositories of the oral tradition, and Maud's been absorbed into it. She came to a harrowing and desperate end after she persisted in angry interrogation of King John, demanding to his face what he had done with his nephew and ward Arthur, for which insolence she was reputedly walled up in a dungeon of Corfe Castle in Dorset and starved to death, the sound of her fingernails scratching frantically on stone ever after reputed to terrify those condemned to the fortress's nether regions.

The best thing about the little town of Hay, in my opinion – it has changed much in the sixty years I've known it, and not much of that change has been well attuned to the character of the town – is to sit on the wall beneath the new bridge to Clyro and watch the dippers working the rapids beneath it. They had accompanied us all the way down from Builth on our dinghy trips, of course – they're numerous in Wales, far less so in the polluted waters east of the border – but one day years later, when I was in Hay for a meeting and to tutor a morning "creative writing" session, at lunch-time I went down to the river, sat in cool shade under the concrete bridge, and watched the rapids. And first noticed the dippers![29] There were several pairs, which is highly unusual. They were scrupulously observing social distancing, and they were not only walking down stones into the water to search for the caddis-fly larvae that are their main food. They also, having surfaced with several in their bills, flew up to – again socially distanced, for dippers are highly territorial birds, rather like the robin in this respect – nests in the gaps between concrete cut-waters of the bridge and the roadway above. You might think a more atypical

---

[29] Bill Condry mentions them on this stretch of the river in his New Naturalist volume, *The Natural History of Wales*: "In the fertile region from Builth to Hay dippers are commoner than in most of Wales. For though widespread, the dipper tends to be sparse in the acid-soiled districts of the north-west and west where the invertebrate life of the streams is so restricted. In contrast the Wye gets ever richer as, just below Hay, it flows broadly off into England."

location[30] for a dipper to build a nest is hard to imagine, but to and fro they flew – dumpy little elegantly marked and hyper-active birds, singing all the time, looking in the words of W.H. Hudson like "a big black wren with a silvery white bib". Their voices were as liquid and trilling as the river itself as they carried food to their broods in the large, mossy nests with tiny openings in the new municipal structure they had very usefully adapted into a dipper tenement: right by a readily-available source of food, safe from predators or any human disturbance save for the continual low rumblings through the layer of tarmac above. I found myself lost in wonder at these admirable little water-ouzels, water-blackbirds, water-hens; at how they had figured out a way of turning to their own advantage so gross an intrusion into their native and long-established habitat as this. And with that satisfying thought, I climbed up to the road, crossed the bridge, and made my way by field paths into Clyro, where they emerged by the house where Francis Kilvert (1840-1879) once lived.

I've been a devotee of Kilvert's diaries for many years. I even have the sumptuous three-volume 1977 cloth-bound, cased and illustrated edition – not quite up to *Golden Cockerel* standards, but nonetheless a prime example of the bookbinders' craft. I saw it in the window of the junk shop that used to be opposite one of my favourite haunts, Yarborough House Café in Bishops Castle, several years ago, went in to ask the price, which left a reasonable amount of change from £100 (it would have been several times that in Hay), so I walked out with it under my arm and have been heartily glad of having done so ever since. Not that it doesn't give me anxious moments. Kilvert was at Wadham College, Oxford, with Lewis Carroll, and some of the same doubts attach to both men. In Kilvert's diaries there are frequent descriptions of young

---

[30] Not necessarily the case – in fact, dippers make frequent use of man-made structures as nesting sites.

girls in states of undress. Delight's expressed and descriptions given when they're glimpsed without their drawers. If this isn't exactly paedophilia, it's certainly an inappropriate expression of interest in the naked pre-pubescent female form. And it gets worse, as in the case of "the incorrigible Fanny Strange":

> *"Her parents have very wisely not spared her nor the rod. She has during the last few weeks been repeatedly stripped and has had her bottom flogged naked with great severity. At one time she seemed absolutely incorrigible. The severest whippings her mother could inflict upon her bare flesh seemed to have no effect upon her. She was whipped every day, and often twice or three times in the day and then when her father came home at night he got a stout switch, stripped the girl naked, laid her on her face across his knees and whipped her bare bottom and thighs again till they were covered with weals and the blood came. I asked her mother if it would shame the girl and have a good effect if I were to whip her myself or if she were to flog her in my presence. 'No,' she said, 'she is so hardened that she wouldn't care if I made her strip herself bare and then flogged her on her naked bottom before you.'*
> *"*

The vicious prurience and sadism of this leaves me reeling, however much allowance you make for what the diary's editor, William Plomer[31], called the diarist's *"special blend of honesty and appetite for life which gives the power to record everyday happenings while magically freeing them from banality or triviality."* I wouldn't want to leave you with this one-sided impression of Kilvert. His attitudes and behaviour here, rightly suspect and illegal in our time, were normative and widely applauded, socially condoned even, in his own time – which tells you much about the nature of Victorian society. Perhaps it still goes on, so ingrained is it in the

---

[31] William Plomer (1903-1973) was a South African writer, novelist, poet and librettist (he worked with Benjamin Britten on some of his operas). During the late 1930s he was employed by the publisher Jonathan Cape, who later brought out his editions of Kilvert's diaries.

Establishment's psyche, in the major public schools the products of which all too often form the Westminster governments[32]. As far as we know there were no suspicions reported against Kilvert by his acquaintances or parishioners, as there most certainly would be nowadays, when behaviour like this (there are other instances of it in the diary) would have had him placed on the sexual offenders' register immediately and seen him vilified in the tabloid press. Vicious this behaviour certainly was, and habitual at that time, but it was vicious in a society that was itself very frequently thus. In the armed forces, severe floggings were the order of the day even for minor infringements of discipline. The last public execution in Britain took place little more than two years before Kilvert took up his curacy at Clyro. He would surely not have understood our present-day objections to conduct like his, or to his "rompings" with the young girls of his friends and parishioners which he mentions with frequency in his diary. To him they seemed innocent, and perhaps they were. He was married at the age of 38 to Elizabeth Anne Rowland, whom he'd met in Paris, and he died of peritonitis three weeks after returning from their honeymoon in Scotland, leaving behind him in the area where he'd spent the greater part of his working life a fragrant reputation as a kindly, compassionate and understanding parish priest. Would that have been the case if his behaviour in front of a watchful, judgmental rural community had really been as outrageous as it appears to us now? Or is he, in order to align himself with the conventionally desirable image in a schoolmaster (for he was that as well when a curate) of disciplinarian and martinet, merely presenting himself thus? He certainly damns himself with his own pen in the passage above. Was that out of confessional need? I'm reminded here of the way the American film-maker Woody Allen,

---

[32] The film to see here is Lindsay Anderson's 1968 satirical masterpiece *If..?*, which won the Palme d'Or at Cannes in 1969. Its insights into the psychology of the "upper" echelons of English society seem to me to have sharpened with the passage of years.

in his 1979 comedy *Manhattan,* appears to confirm all the gossipy media charges directed against him for sexual behaviour towards women much younger than himself during his marriage to the actress Mia Farrow. There are surely lessons to be learned here in our judgments of human conduct, which are so often based in malice, envy, the desire to appease our own guilty consciences by projecting our own misdeeds onto others. I've learnt never to take calumny at face value, and am disinclined to do so even when, as here, it is self-inflicted. Yes, Kilvert is unwittingly revealing sad, cruel and dangerous impulses; but there is no evidence that he ever acted upon them beyond occasional instances like his bizarre and faltering request to Fanny Strange's mother.

Shortly before his death he'd been preferred to the living in Bredwardine, six miles east of Hay on the banks of the Wye. His simple grave is in the churchyard there, close to the river, surrounded by drifts of snowdrops in spring – a place of pilgrimage, and I think rightly so, for he is, beyond doubt, one of the finest English diarists, fit to rank – although very different to either of them – with Samuel Pepys and John Evelyn. The glimpses he gives us into Radnorshire society and folkloric belief in the Victorian age are endlessly fascinating, Hardyesque even. He tells of a grafted thorn that flowered on Christmas Eve, and the oxen that were witnessed kneeling before it. He recounts the processions to the "Wild Duck Pool" at Newbuilding on Easter Morning, *"to see the sun dance and play in the water and the angels who were at the Resurrection playing backwards and forwards before the sun"*, and of the fairies, for fear of whom *"boys would wear their hats the wrong way round lest they should be enticed into fairy rings and made to dance."* He tells also about Walter Brown of the Marsh, who confides how he once saw some fairies in the hedge, but before he could get down from his cart they were gone. This account started on quite a negative note, so let's make amends for that and present a more sympathetic picture of Kilvert to conclude this brief account:

> *"As I came away from the school this afternoon a man standing by the finger-post accosted me and asked if I had any work for him to do. He was he said a Shropshire man named Wilding from the town of Bridgenorth [sic]. He was by trade a hatter and was cleaning hats and coats along the road to help him down to Cardiff where there was a manufactury and where he hoped to get work. He was penniless he said. He had not been able to get a piece of work to do all day though he had tried hard. He was fasting and wet through. 'Feel my coat, Sir,' he said. I felt his coat. It was drenched, soaked with the pitiless rain. Can you help me, your reverence?' he said, and called me by my name. 'How do you know my name?' I asked. 'I learnt it in the village, Sir.' He was a fine manly-looking fellow with a black moustache and his address was manly and pleasant, respectful and self-respectful. But there was a mute appeal in his dark brown fine eyes, which I could not resist. His eyes seemed ready to fill with tears and they had the imploring piteous despairing look of an animal in distress. My heart melted within me. I could not refuse him and I took a shilling from my purse. 'For the sake of the old county,' I said. 'My family are from Shropshire too. Cheer up. Better luck tomorrow.' 'God bless you, Sir, for your kindness,' he said. And as he spoke I thought there was a tear in his eye."*

There's so much social history in this account of a brief exchange between the curate and an impoverished and workless itinerant. It's a snapshot of Victorian Britain, and Kilvert provides those on almost every page. Of the twenty-two volumes of which Plomer had been vouchsafed glimpses, he chose to select only from the first eight. After Mrs. Kilvert's death, the remaining volumes passed into the hands of a niece of Kilvert, and beyond her death to an obscure and minor novelist of the 1930s called Essex Hope.

Plomer had hoped one day to publish the diary in its entirety and had prepared and had typed a fair copy of the entire twenty-two volumes. An abridged version of the diary was published just before the outbreak of the Second World War and has remained intermittently in print to this day. A television series scripted by Jeremy Sandford was prepared from it. To his lasting regret, though, Plomer had allowed the typescript he'd had prepared of the full diary to go missing. Initially, this was not a matter of great concern. The original notebooks were presumed still to exist, and a new text might be prepared from them. However, according to his introduction to the new and corrected three-volume edition reissued with corrections and illustrations in 1977, Plomer learned from Essex Hope, to whom the originals had passed on the death of her aunt Perceval Smith, that she *"had done away with most of the Diary"*. Justifications were attempted – that Mrs. Kilvert had been embarrassed by the intimacy revealed in accounts of the courtship by her husband; that some of the passages were very questionable; that much of it was gossipy and of dubious worth. Heaven knows how Pepys or Boswell would have fared had their diaries been subject to these parameters of judgment! *"I did not scold Mrs Hope,"* Plomer confided to a friend at the time, whilst adding that he felt like strangling her with his own bare hands. The latter did preserve three of the notebooks that had passed to her. One she gave to Plomer himself, a second went to Jeremy Sandford, and the final one to a Kilvert enthusiast, Charles Harvey. These originals survive today in the National Library of Wales at Aberystwyth and in Durham University Library. They contain enough material absent from the published versions to undermine Plomer's suggestion that his selections represented the very best of Kilvert's diary writing. But I doubt that we shall ever now know, and can only be thankful that the little we have remains to us.

Let's return to the Wye. Beyond Bredwardine, where the

Kilverts spent the tragically short weeks of their married life[33], the river in its broad flood plain meanders gently along. It passes Monnington Court, which is often and wrongly thought to be the site of Owain Glyndŵr's grave. Kilvert himself makes this mistake, shedding threnodic tears over *"the strong wild heart* [that] *has rested by the ancient home and roof-tree of his kindred since he fell asleep there more than four hundred years ago."* The Monnington Court required here, with a strong tradition of being the place of Glyndŵr's burial, is not this one, though it is confusingly close. The right one was the home of one of his daughters, and is a likely candidate as his final hiding place and resting place. It is to the south of the Wye, at the south-eastern end of Vowchurch Common, overlooking the Golden Valley. But you'd expect the old sorcerer to retain a little mystery, even in the matter of his post-mortem whereabouts, particularly given the English enemy's predilection for barbarism towards the corpses of Welsh chieftains. (His other daughter, incidentally, married Sir John Scudamore and lived at Kentchurch Court seven miles away, where a powerful masterpiece of a miniature portrait dated to the early fifteenth century is held by a Scudamore family tradition to be of Glyndŵr in extreme old age. I'd like to comment that from the hill above the correct Monnington you can look north-east across the Wye to Credenhill, where the important mystic, poet and metaphysical writer Thomas Traherne was rector in the Seventeenth Century, and where he wrote his *Centuries of Meditations* – which was not published until after the discovery of it in manuscript on a London booksellers' stall in the early twentieth century. It's one of those knotty prose masterpieces in the English literature of its century, with a cosmogony that looks forward to Blake and to the Romantic Poets. So perhaps there's

---

[33] Elizabeth Kilvert never re-married. She died in 1912, thirty-three years after her husband, and is buried in Bredwardine churchyard, several yards away from his grave.

hope yet that Plomer's fair copy of Kilvert will turn up one day? They could even hold a special celebration at Hay Festival if this were to happen. But however much the Thoreau of *A Week on the Concord and Merrimack Rivers* might approve of all this meandering, it's time we hastened through the long reaches of the Wye as it twists its way through England – through Hereford and Ross, Goodrich and Monmouth before it performs the last and most dramatic fluvial trick in its superlatively lovely course, and once more marches with its native country of Wales.

Suddenly, below Ross, instead of contenting itself with ever-more-exaggerated meanders through the red soils of southern Herefordshire and entering its sibling river's estuary somewhere along the bleak shores south of Gloucester, it makes a dive west for the hills of Wales, and surges along under the impressive Seven Sisters rocks (there used, many years ago, to be very good, sound rock-climbing on the limestone towers and corners here, but not any longer, since their 1970 designation as a Site of Special Scientific Interest. When science and recreation come into conflict over landscape use, the latter generally and I think rightly loses out). Our river then pirouettes around the craggy knolls of Symond's Yat – a tourist attraction, though I've never quite understood for what reason. After which it curls its way south of Monmouth town, shies away from a further lowland prospect to the west, and contorts itself around The Kymin before, as the Welsh border now, it heads irresistibly due south into its final valley, which has, since the early nineteenth century, been one of the most famous landscapes of Britain. It's an odd place, the valley of the lower Wye, stranded between the Forest of Dean mining area and Monmouthshire pastoral. There are fascinating villages here of a character unlike any others in Wales. It abounds with literary and radical political associations. In Penallt, opposite the Redbrook (the ironworks explain the colour), Beatrice and Sidney

Webb were married, George Bernard Shaw struggled with drafts of *Mrs. Warren's Profession and Arms and the Man*, and brought wit and lyricism into a correspondence with Ellen Terry. He also met the very wealthy Irishwoman he was soon to marry, and who was to become the founding benefactress of the London School of Economics. Three miles downstream from Penallt the valley road swaps sides, crossing over to the west bank by way of the sturdy and elegant Bigsweir bridge, within a mile of which you arrive in the village of Llandogo. Here Lord Amberley (son of Lord John Russell, 1792-1878, the Whig peer who served two spells as Prime Minister) settled at a house, Ravenscroft, near the waterfalls above the village. When Lady Amberley first saw it, she effused: *"We were quite enchanted with the wildness and beauty of the place and A and I danced with delight!"* They also danced considerably upon local Tory sensibilities by campaigning for equal wages for men and women, abolition of the game laws, availability of advice on birth control, support for single-parent families, and a League of Nations, all radical matters in their day. John Stuart Mill was a frequent visitor to the house. The Amberleys were eventually buried in its garden. The son of this unusual, open, happy, liberal and progressive marriage was born here in 1872 and died in Penrhyndeudraeth in 1970, by which time he had been accepted, through his work as philosopher, mathematician and peace campaigner, as one of the intellectual giants of the twentieth century, and his autobiography as one of its most significant and accomplished texts. He was the Cambridge philosopher and tutor to Ludwig Wittgenstein, Bertrand Russell.

Below Llandogo the river has become tidal, and still indulges itself, despite the increasingly craggy valley sides where huge exposures of high limestone cliffs are everywhere apparent, in exaggerated meanders at Tintern and Lancaut. The cliffs on the east bank, in particular the ninety-metre-high Great Overhanging

Wall at Wintour's Leap, looking west across the Lancaut peninsula, are a nationally important venue for rock-climbing, where some of Britain's major lowland classic rock-climbs can be enjoyed, if you have the appropriate degree of competence and a taste for unremittingly steep rock, colonised by hordes of jackdaws and giving out onto loose and vegetated finishes. A guidebook published by the British Mountaineering Council exists to talk you through them and all their overhangs and intricacies. Now I'm too old and feeble even to think of repeating the experiences, which I remember with great pleasure from my distant youth, so I can feel safe in thoroughly recommending them to you. They are what these days are called "adventure climbs". They were always that. And they went under names like *King Kong, Kangaroo Wall,* and *The Burning Giraffe.* Delicious faraway prospects now! Trivial pursuits aside, let's consider Tintern Abbey. I used to have an enormous Victorian photographic print of this, framed, measuring four feet by three, that I bought in a Salisbury flea market for £5 and that adorned the walls of my houses for years despite various partners' protestations against the gloominess of it. Then one day a brother of one of them cast his eye upon it, declared love at first sight, offered plenty of money for it, but in view of his infatuation and since I liked him and knew that he was even poorer than I was, I gave it to him and hope it adorns the wall of his Wrexham flat still. If it does, the one sure thing is that it will take up a lot of space there. Two things I particularly remember about it. One was the enormous amount of ivy that hung from the masonry, shadowing and softening all the architectural features, their angles and outlines. The other was a tiny male figure in the dress of the time (1860s/1870s at a guess), who was sitting near the south door, looking vaguely phantasmal. I much preferred this atmospheric nineteenth-century photograph to the spick-and-span, scrubbed, turnstiled, amenitied and secure ruin that restoration made of it in recent years. Perhaps I've always had an ambivalent relationship to Tintern Abbey?

That might derive from having had Wordsworth's poem by heart since I was in my 'teens (I plead the excuse that it was an English "A" level set text – in those days you couldn't take books into examinations and had to learn your texts by rote). Instinctively I've always felt "Father William" was something of a fraud, and have shared that gently humorous genius Thomas Love Peacock's instinctive recoil from him. He was apostate from his early revolutionary zeal (he should have listened to Hazlitt's succinct plea that "These bargains are for life!"); treacherous to his erstwhile friends (his treatment of Coleridge still shocks me); and plagiaristic (his famous description of a failed attempt to ascend Snowdon in *The Prelude* is an act of poeticised theft plucked straight out of Thomas Pennant's *A Tour in Wales*). Though these days that kind of thing is apparently no longer termed plagiarism but "intertextuality", and is viewed as a valid stratagem by several celebrated contemporary writers. My view of Wordsworth and the egotistical sublime has simmered down subsequently into a general dislike of the man's character, and a limited appreciation of a few of his early lyrics like "The Two April Mornings" and "The Fountain" ("The Matthew Poems"). So I'm not going to discuss Wordsworth here any further, other than to say that the title is anyway misleading. Wordsworth did not write a poem about Tintern Abbey. He wrote it on the banks of the Wye "a few miles above" – just exactly where is unclear. And somehow, I prefer Kilvert's shocked response to this lower course of the river on July Eve, 1875, which resonates with the shock I felt when first viewing the Lancaut meander from the cliffs of Wintour's Leap:

> *"I have heard great talk of the Wye at Chepstow but no-one who has only seen the river at Chepstow and Tintern can imagine the beauty and character of the Wye as a mountain stream between Rhayader*

and Hay. I was disappointed in the famous view from the Wynd Cliff. The weather was certainly not favourable for distant views, not a gleam of sunshine, a misty horizon, and rain driving up the Channel with the rising tide. The view may be fine and wide on a clear day but any view would be spoilt by the filthy ditch which they call the Wye in the foreground, a ditch full of muddy water at the best of times, namely high water, but now a scene of ugly foreshore and wastes of hideous mud banks with a sluggish brown stream winding low in the bottom between."

Since Kilvert's time the situation, to our national aesthetic embarrassment, has considerably worsened. All down the lower Wye now, poultry farms discharge their quotas of effluent to thicken and further tint its already toxic brown sludge. Our national addiction to Chicken Tikka Masala comes at an environmental cost. Even the abbey itself receives a blast, albeit milder and ultimately moderated, of the Reverend Kilvert's opprobrium:

"Tintern Abbey at first sight seemed to me to be bare and almost too perfect to be entirely picturesque. One wants a little more ruin and ivy and the long lines of the buildings should be broken by trees, but within the precincts of the Abbey the narrow aisled vistas, the graceful lightness of the soaring arches and the exquisite and perfect tracery of the east and west windows are singularly beautiful. I climbed to the top of the walls and looked down into the vast square deep well formed by the four great lofty arches of nave, choir and transepts which upheld the great central tower of the Church. The top of the walls was adorned with a perfect wild-flower garden of scarlet poppies, white roses, yellow stonecrop and purple mallows, which formed a low hedge along each side of the otherwise undefended footpath or thickness of the walls, and which climbed with profuse luxuriance over the ruins of the summit of the walls.."

Kilvert the alpinist! The Wynd Cliff has, over the last fifty years, enjoyed a phasal popularity among the rock-climbing community. When it had newly been stripped of its ivy and purged of its loose rock, for a time, promoted by articles in the climbing press and a series of guidebooks published between 1977 and 1997, it had a degree of popularity. In the long days of summer, adventure-starved London rock-climbers could dash down the M4 and enjoy a few hours' activity before heading speedily back again. The vogue for, and proliferation of, indoor climbing walls for the most part put paid to all that (and avoided the concomitant speeding fines and endorsements), and the discreet white buttresses among the trees have faded back into their erstwhile obscurity, retreating once again behind curtains of luxuriant ivy, the colonies of jackdaws once again undisturbed. Fashion plays a large part in the activity of climbing, and its relentless onward progress has abandoned the pioneering impulse, retreated indoors, and left the towering rock walls and buttresses of the lower Wye Valley far behind in the twenty-first century. Maybe these will enjoy a renaissance in coming decades? It's perhaps more likely that they will moulder back into the obscurity from which climbers brought up in an older tradition once excavated them. I'm happy to enjoy my memories of huge rock walls, creaking instability in the climbing medium, vegetatious exits from the top of soaring cliffs into the sudden suburbias of Woodcroft or Piercefield. It was fun when we did it, and I retain the sharp memories of scents of cliff yew trees, jackdaw nests, the ubiquitous faint stench of the mud-banked river-loops drifting up from far below.

Mention of the latter impels me to mention one esoteric claim to fame for this section of the Wye. Low on its west bank, a few hundred metres north of the stables for Chepstow racecourse, is a cave entrance. This is not the one marked on the 1:25,000 O.S. map as "Giant's Cave". In fact, it's not marked on the map at all, but it has a name, which is the Otter Hole. It was first explored only slightly later in the 1970s than the limestone cliffs in the immediate area. Most people who pass by above it on the A466 or within fifty metres on the Wye Valley Walk will remain wholly unaware of its presence, even though the co-author of the *Selected Caves of Britain and Ireland*[34] – a notable authority – describes it as *"a fantastic cave, perhaps the most beautifully decorated in Britain!"* If you're hoping to see it for yourself, there are three factors that might just deter you from that ambition. The first of these is that it's given a grade of five, which is the highest standard of difficulty. When I was living in South Wales and before that in Derbyshire years ago, I used to go caving regularly, enjoyed it enormously, and had the utmost respect for the sport's participants – a quirky, tough and likeable bunch on the whole. It always struck me that caving, whilst perhaps less technically demanding than the extreme rock-climbing that was my sport of preference at the time, was far more physically exhausting and potentially much more serious than climbing. The problems inherent in rescue from deep within a difficult cave system are immense. Even from caves of more moderate difficulty, they can still be considerable. I remember being called out early in 1967 on the rescue of a student from an outdoor centre who had fallen and broken a femur in the rift passage of a Derbyshire cave called P8 – a sporting and wet little Grade Three trip. The outdoor centre I then worked at, Birchfield Lodge in Hope, received the rescue call-out on a March evening at 6pm after we'd been out in the rain and wind climbing on Stanage Edge with students all day. By 7pm three of us instructors were wet-suited and underground in P8, working with the cave rescue team to manoeuvre the stretcher and casualty through that narrow, twisting rift passage – wedging

---

[34] *Selected Caves of Britain and Ireland* (or Top of the Pots), Des Marshall and Donald Rust, (Cordée, Leicester, 1997)

ourselves across it and sliding the stretcher across our knees whilst reassuring the lad strapped to it that we'd have him out of there in no time. In fact, by the time we reached the surface and he was raced away by ambulance to a Sheffield hospital, it was 5 a.m. and approaching dawn. One moral from this experience became forcefully apparent to me. Don't have accidents underground! Exert double the awareness of risk that you would in daylight situations!

To come back to the Otter Hole, the second factor that might put you off visiting it is the fact that this is most definitely not a show cave. It's a long and difficult sporting trip, and because of the very fragile beauty of the calcitic formations, to undertake it you would need to be accompanied, the system having been "gated" (i.e. you can't get into it without a key, which is only available from the club responsible for access). Now for the third factor, which will become explicit as you read through the cave survey description. The Wye is tidal at this point, the tidal range can exceed fifteen metres, and the system's entrance is very close to river level. Spells of prolonged rain also have an effect on access to the cave, and as you've been travelling down the river or peering across it or even just reading Kilvert's account, the tidal mud will have made an impression on you too. I'll quote at random from the survey description:

> *"Access beyond the tidal sump is only passable three hours either side of low tide …extremely muddy … Sliding, grovelling and climbing in the sloppy filth* [a] *larger passage is reached with some mud-encrusted formations. As the Tidal Sump is approached the mud gets sloppier and deeper … horrendously slippery boulders are grovelled over … to a slippery, squalid climb down to the stream…"*

That should give you the picture, as well as raise the question of "Why bother?" I told you above that cavers are quirky and tough.

They're also indefatigable, occasionally obstreperous, obdurate in the face of all challenges, and resilient. Conditions like these – albeit usually not quite so extreme – are what they're habituated to worldwide in the practice of their deeply idiosyncratic sport. Enduring these brings our passionate speleologists through to the uncanny and unseen beauties to be encountered in the underworld. It satisfies at a profound level the human need to explore his or her environment. I think of other places where I've seen this kind of unmarred, unseen splendour – Column Hall in Ogof Ffynnnon Ddu, for example, shortly after its first discovery, with calcite pearls shining in clear pools across the chamber's glistening floor, and ten-metre long straw stalactites swaying and chiming musically together from the mere disturbance to the air caused by our carefully walking through. These are some of the loveliest sights of nature I've ever seen, and to set eyes upon them is an immense and precious privilege. Back to the Otter Hole (and who in their right mind would squirm into a small entrance below a cliff within the tidal range of the infinitely loathsome muddiness of the lower Wye?) Here's Des Marshall again, explaining the why of it, extolling what you'll encounter, having persevered through the ultimate Slough of Despond:

> *"Suddenly the passage enlarges at some large stalagmites and bosses, quickly followed by the stupendous Hall of Thirty. The way out of the Hall of Thirty is a downward slot in the continuing passage. The wealth and splendour of the formations in the continuing passage is unequalled in Britain. Please keep to the taped path. Eventually Camp 1 is reached, where there is a source of fresh water entering from the roof…"*

Soon thereafter, the cave ends at a pool choked with flaky calcite, and all that remains are those stored memories of esoteric natural magnificence, and then to turn round and make your way wearily back through greasy and insecure boulder chokes and the Tidal Sump to the tribulations of the entrance series, hoping all the while that you've read the tidal tables right and that the tricky old river (the Gwy – pronounced "gooey") hasn't risen to flood the first passages. And here's one last source of anxiety for you to add to the mounting tally. People have been known to develop illnesses from cuts after entering this cave – probably leptospirosis, or even its extreme form of Weil's Disease (rat fever is its common name, and rat urine one agent of its transmission. I like rats, my cat and I spend hours at home watching them peer out of a garden rockery where they live, standing on their hind legs to see if there's anything to eat before warily venturing out, snatching food and retreating to their lairs. They do me no harm, are exceedingly pretty and sleek, most companionable with their own kind, caring towards their young, have twitchy whiskers and appealing faces, and hop like kangaroos. They're an acid test as to whether you truly believe, along with William Blake, that "every thing that lives is holy". Please reconsider your attitude towards rats. After all, it's said you're never more than six feet away from one). Having reminded you of that, I have a story for you.

I remember setting off to walk back to my then-home in Dinorwig from the *Anglesey Arms* pub on the seafront in Caernarfon very late after a lock-in one night in 1973. There had been days of constant rain. I headed up onto the Maes, and was beckoned urgently into a shop doorway by a policeman on foot patrol. "Watch this!" he said, and pointed up Pool Street. The whole surface of the road seemed to be moving. A deluge of small, leaping, furry brown bodies came squeaking and rustling down, tens of thousands of them. They surged across the square and disappeared down the road that leads to the quay before you get to the castle. "Always happens when there's going to be a flood", the policemen explained. "They come up out of all the culverts and drains. Good job I called you out of the way of them, or you might be bare bones by now!" I think he was joking, but am still not entirely sure. Anyway, rats and river-banks go together, so be warned. I'm sure I'll have thoroughly dissuaded you from an attempt on the Otter Hole by now, though I'll freely admit that fifty years ago, I'd have cast all doubt and apprehension aside, prepared carefully, judiciously chosen the right companions, and joined the queues (!) to see the Hall of Thirty and all the other wonders in this late ornament to the course of the Wye.

Beyond Tintern, a few more snake-like writhings see the Wye curl under the cliffs on which Chepstow Castle's built. It twists past a sewage works, a factory and the Army Apprentices' College to merge unobtrusively with the Severn just downstream of the motorway suspension bridge. Slimeroad Sands and Whirl's End are the most notable features of the Severn estuary at this point (though fans might consider a photograph of Bob Dylan waiting at Aust for the ferry from Beachley to arrive, that adorns one of his late albums, is of unparalleled significance). As a recent article in the *Guardian*[35] states, every single river and lake in England is polluted beyond legal limits. *"There's not one that's free from toxic chemicals from industries past and present. Water companies disgorge untold volumes of raw human sewage into them, while farm fertilisers and pesticides seep insidiously into rivers, accompanied by lashings of slurry."* That's how the lower Wye ends its hitherto-glorious course. European environmental standards? Forget them! The profit motive rules! English Tories have taken back control, and sooner or later, as always, the people and the environment will pay the ghastly price. We will look more closely at this problem, and its environmental effect, in the next chapter on the Afon Teifi. Before we go there, let's see how Robert Gibbings – my favourite Wye tourist by far – has been doing in his own Coming down the Wye. We last spotted

---

[35] Rachel Salvidge, 23 September, 2020

him in one of the hostelries of Llangurig. He made it as far as Tintern, and his visit to the abbey produced some masterful, subtly atmospheric illustrations. He walked back in rain and hail to the hostelry in Chepstow where he was staying, and there met up with an acquaintance from Llangurig.

"Going back in the morning. Want a lift? … Noon tomorrow we'll start."

For a moment I hesitated. Then I agreed, and as I did so I felt my spirits rise.

PART TWO

Death of a River? Afon Teifi

"…A noble river called the Teifi" is how Giraldus Cambrensis described the Teifi: "It is better stocked with the finest salmon than any other stream in Wales." There'll be many fishermen who revere this river for its former glories who wish that were still the case. Contemporary agricultural practice, fishing in the 21st Century, even eco-technology, can make unhappy bed-fellows for erstwhile-unpolluted waters. View the Teifi as it flows through the gorge below Cilgerran and you could be forgiven for assuming it was not water flowing there, but liquid manure (or even toxic sludge). The Teifi no longer scintillates. Rather it swirls brown and uninviting as the Ganges at Varanasi, though sadly far less revered – the only floating corpses here are periodically those of poisoned fish. Teifi-side is rich land, cattle-rearing country from time immemorial, flowing through seventy miles of West Wales. You'll know about rainfall in that part of the country. Slurry pits overflow. Effluent tanks suffer disastrous leaks. Pastureland is swept clean by floods, washing more dung and agro-chemicals into the river. Most years cases are reported of mass fish-deaths. Most years crocodile tears are shed by the bodies appointed supposedly to oversee, and nothing gets done. The farming lobby's so powerful in the Senedd and in Westminster that few measures are enforced to penalise serial offenders. Don't take from this that the Teifi is now devoid of attraction, nor even that all its salmon, sewin and trout are dead (though most of them are). This river is still one of the landscape delights, and a defining presence of West Wales:

"Fair Tivy, how sweet are thy waves gently flowing,
Thy wild oaken woods and green eglantine bowers."

That couplet's inscribed on Aberteifi's old bridge. If you lean too far and pitch over the parapet you might well drown, for the water below boils dramatically when flooding tide meets flooded river. Social, industrial and natural histories of Afon Teifi are fascinating. Otters, Rebecca Rioters, the flannel industry, beavers – its interest is boundless. Most rivers running through Wales rise on individual hills: Yr Wyddfa, Pumlumon, Cilfaesty Hill. Not the Teifi! Its source is the Teifi Pools, in the wide expanse of high moorland that stretches from Bro Ddyfi's Machynlleth in the north to Llanymddyfri to the south. These days this landscape is referred to in English as the Cambrian Mountains, after a national park that never quite made it to designation (too many resources to be exploited to allow even the mild planning controls available to other national parks to be imposed here!) There's an older Welsh name for this central hill-massif. You find it in the *Pedeir Keinc y Mabinogi*[1]. There it's rendered as Elenit. If the region ever does make it to national park status, it will probably be as *Parc Cenedlaethol Elenydd*. Perhaps the mapmakers of the Ordnance Survey will take heed and introduce "Elenydd" into their cartography, instead of "Cambrian Mountains" (an anglo-colonialist atrocity), but I'm not holding my breath. I know Brian Friel's masterpiece, *Translations*, on how the Ordnance Survey rejected Irish toponymy in nineteenth-century Donegal, too well!

---

[1] Literally "The Four Branches of the Mabinogi" – and usually referred to as *The Mabinogion*, which was the title given by Charlotte Guest, wife of a Merthyr Tydfil ironmaster, to the translations to which she put her name by nineteenth century Welsh scholars of the mediaeval texts when they were published between 1838 and 1849. By far the best translation, still in print from Everyman, is the 1948 one by Gwyn Jones and Thomas Jones – a masterfully redacted and stylishly rendered version of a seminal text and major classic which came down through the oral tradition and owes its survival to the work of medieval monastic scribes.

To get to Teifi Pools, you can come over from Rhayader Gwy along "The Monk's Trod"; but I'm not sure you'd like it. The problem is that it's a designated byway, and thus open to all traffic. Which includes the off-road fraternity – Trumpian libertarians always adept at exploiting these anti-conservational loopholes – in their 4WD Land-rovers, Shoguns, Fronteras and the rest, equipped with monstrous studded tyres to rip up fragile vegetation, winches and long spools of wire to drag each other out of mire and mign of their own creating, as well as the scrambles and trials bikers on their noisy, whining two-strokes, the high-pitched cacophonies of which can be heard from miles around in this wide, quiet landscape of morass and heather. The Monks' Trod originated from the journeyings of Cistercian monks between the twelfth century abbeys of Cwm Hir, near Llandrindod Wells, Strata Marcella on the River Severn between Oswestry and Welshpool, Whitland near St. Clear's, and Ystrad Fflur above Pontrhydfendigaid. It crosses high moorland of the Claerwen SSSI (also a Special Area of Conservation). Recreational off-roaders for decades have made heavy use of this ancient line of communication. They've caused appalling damage. In 1990 a *Traffic Regulation Order* was placed on the by-way, banning four-wheeled vehicles only. This was followed in 2002 by a temporary TRO (recently expired) banning all motor traffic, including motorcycles. Involved councils are currently considering closing the trail to all users, including walkers, cyclists, horse riders, and horse-drawn carriages, to give it a chance to recover, which at this altitude will take many years. Necessary repairs to the route have been estimated at running into hundreds of thousands of pounds. Neither Ceredigion nor Powys are wealthy councils. There's also an understandable degree of resentment at spending local receipts on wanton damage caused by outsiders. The off-roaders are mostly that. When I've protested against this environmental irresponsibility in the past, responses have been vicious – death threats, poison pen letters, anonymous phone calls, all the usual run of cowardly bluster that special interest groups from off-roaders to huntsmen to shooters can muster against anyone seeking reasoned restraint on anti-social, destructive and selfish pursuits.

Beyond Elan and Claerwen watersheds, once into west Wales and *Y Fro Gymraeg*, you'll find little enticement to dawdle around Teifi Pools. Take your cue from Kyffin Williams' artistic studies of these features, particularly "Stormy weather approaching", and make for the lower ground would be my advice. The pools themselves are notably bleak, marred by hideous grey concrete dams. You can head down to Ffair Rhos, site of one of the oldest livestock fairs in Wales, or make your way more attractively from Llyn Egnant – another lake skulking behind grey concrete – by following a footpath along the Afon Egnant down to Ystrad Fflur (Strata Florida), with red kites on hooked wings straddling the western wind, forked tails spread wide, bucking on the blasts and peering for prey. (Though you'll find more these days by the feeding stations south of Rhayader or at the abattoir near Tregaron.) Egnant as it descends towards the old monastery is of haunting loveliness. As the monastic ruins used to be, before CADW gave it an habitual stylistic makeover. Where once there were green lawns under spreading yew-trees, carefully tended ruins in a quiet place, open and free of access, now there's a car-park, a plethora of signs, plastic canopies, garish interpretation boards and displays peddling elementary handfuls of facts, galvanised steel steps, an entrance kiosk, admission fees. In the days before it had become a tourist attraction, when the only publicity was T. Gwynn Jones's poem, that every Welsh person of a particular generation knew by heart (*"Mae dail y coed yn Ystrad Fflur/Yn murmur yn yr awel,/A deuddeng Abad yn y gro/Yn huno yno'n dawel.*" – and so on for four perfect stanzas), I used often to come here and sleep out unmolested by officialdom under Dafydd's yew-tree on my way between Eryri and the sea-cliffs of Castlemartin in Pembrokeshire. If I had a girl-friend with me from time to time, I'm sure Dafydd ap Gwilym (1320?-1380?) would have approved. He's accepted as among the major poets of late-medieval Europe, with a sure ear and marvellous grasp of language's capacity for music, expressed in his verse through the *cywydd* and the strict metres available to the *cynganeddwyr*. He has also, as it comes through in his poetry, an endearing, mischievous, sensual nature. On romantic love and natural beauty, the world of nature, sexual play and cosmic jokery, he writes as well as any poet has ever written. Not everyone agrees with this assessment of him. My dear old Welsh tutor in Bangor, Enid Pierce Jones[2], when I tried to initiate a conversation with her about his verse, cut me off short with a peremptory "I don't think we'll talk about

---

[2] *"The hair that capped her slender frame bristled*
Iron-grey and upright, her character
Also thus, but kindly. "We hit hard on
Our consonants in Welsh," she decreed. No
Lisping with her – words crisp as schoolma'am's tawse!
She had her favourites – Guto'r Glyn, Gweirydd
Ap Rhys – and those she demonised: R.S.,
Dafydd ab Gwilym ("A libertine", she hissed.)
"Darn o hen Gymru biwritanaidd" – that
Was Miss Enid Pierce Roberts to a tee.
Throughout her life, though, she took the Church in Wales'
Communion, walked to Bangor's Cadeirlan
From her bookish home on Farrar Road twice
Each Sunday. This staunch old scholar came of
Trefaldwyn stock, born in Llangadfan, knew
By heart the hymns of Ann Griffiths, preferred
Them to Pantycelyn's. We'd sing them to
Each other in her tutorials. "You were
Flat there, Mr. Perrin", she'd jibe, a wry smile
Teased out for me, eyes bird-sharp, searching my
Face for any trace of the mockery that
Would have ended our friendship at a stroke."

Dafydd, Mr. Perrin – he was a libertine!" Tersely accurate, of course, and hence his appeal. Had I wanted to talk about Guto'r Glyn or Gweirydd ab Rhys, she would happily have indulged me, but Dafydd with his Morfydds and Dyddgus was simply not respectable, and sometimes the semi-amused glint as she cast an essentially kind but scrupulously appraising eye upon me suggested that in her view perhaps neither was I. But then, her birthplace Llangadfan ever since the time of William Jones the Madogeion was always rather a stern place.

We rejoin Afon Teifi in one of the supreme landscapes of Wales. At the end of the last ice age it was a lake, penned in behind a moraine as the ice sheet that had covered most of Wales melted away. Teifi, being a vigorous, thrusting, youthful river, eventually forced its way through, leaving the former lake to be colonised by beds of phragmites, that grew and spread and died. In doing so they were transformed into peat. Incrementally, over millennia and with the addition of sphagnum mosses, the lake transformed into three gently profiled domes where Marsh Harriers hunted small birds and mammals and the Teifi followed a sinuous, deep and dark course in which otters hunted salmon and brown trout, and cotton grass unfurled its black-braided tight buds into white flags every summer. What do you see when you walk there along the riverside path? There's a flash of azure and translucence across the Teifi's smooth flow, then stillness. I followed the darting trajectory. Clipped to a winter-blanched last-year's stalk of water-sedge was a Keeled Skimmer – common dragonfly of our running water. Along with the intertwining starred complexity of water-crowfoot, it made an illuminated manuscript of the stream. Sun dappled a bank from which an adder slipped away. I thought of Bill Condry coming across a female adder, sleepy in the cold of a spring morning, and stooping to stroke her head softly:

"She lay in a coil with her head raised just off the ground and held rigidly immobile with no flickering of the tongue. She seemed more like a wood carving than a living snake. Gingerly I bent over her and after long hesitation, because I am no snake charmer, I dared to touch the top of her head very lightly. She did not react in any way. Then very softly I stroked her head. Still no sign that she was aware of my presence. Just as lightly I caressed her throat. She remained entirely indifferent. It was not until I stroked her back all the way from head to tail that she decided that it was time for her to go, which she did slowly as if in a dream, leaving me grateful to have experienced such a rare encounter in the wild."

Two green hairstreak butterflies, gracefully viridescent, danced past on a soft wind sifting through reeds. Tall golden flower-stems of bog asphodel waved, and silky white plumes of cotton-grass that have colonised the old peat-diggings. From pillows of sphagnum, carmine glitter of round-leaved sundew attracted my eye, slowly digesting captured insect-life. At pool-margins opening flowers of yellow water-lilies gave off their subtle wine-scent. Marsh-marigolds – index-plant to glacial retreat – adorned black flats of stinking mud. A kingfisher[3] whirred past, stickleback in its beak, and disappeared into a thicket of riparian willow. Here and there on the board-walk, otter-spraints told of another blessing presence along the trout-and-minnow-rich river. It's not one that you often see, though when we arrive at Newcastle Emlyn I'll

---

[3] If you want to see kingfishers in Wales, the Teifi used to be a good place to start, though the most reliable Welsh location I know for sighting of these spectacular small birds are the sea-caves at the western end of Morfa Bychan, where they seem to have roosted safe and out of sight for decades now. Though neither is as reliable as the River Till in Northumberland, which flows into the Tweed by the Norham Castle of Turner's painting. Another good Welsh location for sightings are the phragmites beds behind Poppit Sands on the Teifi estuary. And finally, there's a riverside pub just downstream of Welsh Bridge in Amwythig (Shrewsbury). Go there for lunch, sit in the window and keep a watch on the willows along the opposite bank. Chances are there'll be kingfishers flying between them.

introduce you more fully. This great bog of Tregaron is a natural treasure-chest, spacious and lapidary. So lovely in its extravagant detail, the wider view is uncannily beautiful too. To walk here is to attune to landscape's evolving nature. The ghost of the great glacial lake that once spread through this melodic hill-basin still thrills at my senses, as does slow process of the ages that has shaped its present form. These low rising domes of peat are still infinitesimally proving with life-yeast of the long centuries. For me, nowhere better expresses landscape's dynamic of change. Two red kite – miraculous survivor of the Welsh uplands – glide overhead. A drake teal skitters into osiers. Muted harsh discords of unseen geese flying low from pool to pool rouse in me a queer plucking sensation, compounding awareness of time, and of the harm we do to this temporal heaven. The calling of geese always makes me think of the hauntingly poetic passage from the early Chinese divinatory text, the *I Ching* (Book of Changes), that talks of the migrations of the wild geese as being like the great movements of the soul, of souls transformed to birds, of life as a flight and migratory journey made in pairs, gliding and settling at each stage of their journey, bound by the red threads of fated relationships. In landscapes like Cors Caron, your mind tends to run on change and time's slow passage. You peer into densely knotted stands of willow rising from interlinking pools and wonder what life inhabits there. The plentiful orchids demonstrate their capacity to hybridise and hence confuse our obsession with taxonomy, our tendency to fixed definitions in a world continually evolving. You may glimpse a water rail stalking its jerky way across the black margin of a pond, or precipitate the zig-zag swift flight of a snipe. There will surely be black-headed gulls drifting overhead. If you're exceptionally lucky, for their populations have tragically declined even here, there'll be the calling of curlews.

We'll make our way out of this exhilarating landscape by

returning to the car-park, itself on the old railway line that linked Aberystwyth to Carmarthen, which was constructed by Davies of Llandinam by laying the track across sacks stuffed with bales of twigs and sheeps' fleeces, so that the rails essentially floated.[4] There's been talk in recent years of reinstating the line, but the engineering problems would be so vast, the cost of purchasing back land that had been sold off prohibitive, the outcry against impingement on and disturbance to so supremely important a conservation site would be so vehement that I'm not sure this will ever happen[5].

_____

[4] In later editions of his *Tour in Wales*, when describing W.E. Madocks' construction of the embankment across Traeth Mawr, Thomas Pennant mentions how the stonework was laid on thick beds of rush matting staked down on the sand, so the idea obviously had slightly earlier provenance.

[5] This, edited from the *Cambrian News* in March 2021, presents a marginally more positive view: 'A report from Cardiff University's Wales Governance Centre finds that under a fully devolved system, Wales could have received an extra £514m investment in its rail infrastructure between 2011-12 and 2019-20 compared to what it received, with several projects called for in Ceredigion, including the return of the Aberystwyth to Carmarthen railway, closed in the 1960s under the Beeching cuts. Campaigners have called for the return of the railway for more than a decade. The scheme was included in the Welsh Government's rail strategy document 'A Railway for Wales - Meeting the needs of future generations', in which it said that it wants to 'improve connectivity on the nation's key corridors – especially the western corridor from Ynys Môn to Aberystwyth, Carmarthen and Swansea Bay'. The report finds: "These amounts can be compared to the cost of several major Welsh rail infrastructure projects that have been estimated by external sources, including the Carmarthen to Aberystwyth line (£620-£775m), electrification of the North Wales Coast mainline (£764m), and electrification of the South Wales mainline between Cardiff and Swansea (£433m)." Although operations of the railway in Wales are a Welsh Government, *railway infrastructure remains the responsibility of the UK Government*. The Welsh Government can spend its own resources to fund railway schemes, but because infrastructure is not devolved to Wales, it is not provided with extra resources to do this through the Barnett Formula. Wales Fiscal Analysis researcher Guto Ifan said: "When it comes to the Welsh railways, the evidence is clear that funding would have been substantially higher under a fully devolved system – to the tune of £500m since 2011." "That funding over the course of eight years would have enabled significant improvement projects to take place. Wales is also set to lose out on transport funding when the Treasury next sets multi-year budgets, due to technical changes.' in Barnett formula calculations." "This is a double whammy for Wales, with the historic under-funding being baked in to the system. It is now clear that only full devolution of rail infrastructure - similar to Scotland

Emerging from Cors Caron, the Teifi describes a sequence of extravagant meanders around the little town of Tregaron – once a significant centre for the drovers of Wales. Samuel Taylor Coleridge and Joseph Hucks passed through here as they headed south from Aberystwyth on their 1794 tour of Wales, which produced a book, of course, the following year – Hucks's *A Pedestrian Tour through North Wales in a Series of Letters*, which is lively enough in a scabrous fashion, and makes the following comment on Tregaron:

> *"Tregarron* [sic] *is a miserable hole, in the which however we were constrained to sleep, and to break the windows in our bedrooms to let in the fresh air. We took a guide from thence to Llanindovrey, over the lonely and trackless mountains of Cardiganshire; it rained hard the whole way, and we had not even the consolation of seeing a partner of our misfortunes: for, to speak within compass, we neither beheld a single habitation, nor even a human creature, for more than twenty miles."*

George Borrow stayed in Tregaron after searching unsuccessfully for Dafydd ap Gwilym's grave at Ystrad Fflur. On his way from Pontrhydfendigaid, in the darkness he fell in with a pipe-smoking former drover who regaled him with amusing moral tales about the rascally deeds of Twm Siôn Cati, "a wild wag of Wales". In one of the most memorable passages in the whole long length of *Wild Wales* the ex-drover conducts him four miles along the road:

> *"After descending a hill we came to what looked like a small suburb, and presently crossed a bridge over the stream, the waters of which sparkled merrily in the beams of the moon, which was now shining bright over some lofty hills to the south-east. Beyond the bridge was a small market place, on the right-hand side of which stood an ancient-*

– will address the underfunding of Welsh railways."
Interesting to compare the amounts under consideration here with those being spent by Westminster on HS2, of course.

looking church. The place upon the whole put me very much in mind of an Andalusian village overhung by its sierra. 'Where is the inn?' I said to my companion. 'Yonder it be,' said he, pointing to a large house at the farther end of the market place. 'Very good inn, that – Talbot Arms – where they are always glad to see English gentlemans.' Then touching his hat, and politely waving his hand, he turned to one side, and I saw him no more."

Not often that Borrow mocks Welsh vernacular use of English in that manner! Let's pick up again with Coleridge and Hucks, and take a jaunt on the mountain road (which was not their route) in the weather they experienced from Tregaron over to Abergwesyn. Even in our time you might well arrive at the same negative viewpoint on this terrain as theirs. It's still perhaps the wildest road in Wales, through desolate moorland marred with conifer plantations for most of the way between Tregaron and Llanerch Yrfa in the Irfon valley. Though the latter place has its compensations. It's one of the starting places – the shortest certainly, but by no means the best – for a walk up Drygarn Fawr, presiding spirit of the great wilderness, the three massive quartz-cored summit cairns of which can be seen for miles around in any direction. It may only be 2,115 feet high (641 metres), but it's a spectacular viewpoint from which you can see to Ynys Enlli on the clearest days (if you're an habitual hill-goer, you'll be all too well aware that in Wales these generally presage rain). It's certainly one of the great and lonely hills of Wales. The better route is to approach it from Llanafan Fawr, where there's an excellent pub, the *Red Lion*, by another of the "mother churches" of Wales. Climbing Drygarn Fawr by this route you can take in the neighbouring height of Gorllwyn, and the likelihood of your seeing anyone else in the course of a long and arduous day is as remote as the terrain you'll be traversing. These are the gathering grounds for Claerwen reservoir, and very wet, but with a sense about them of infinite space. From Drygarn Fawr, looking north, there's no major settlement and only a couple of roads between you and the Dyfi valley. Years ago, on a soft morning of the shortening days, I headed into this wild, watershed country. A kite ghosted past, its plumage glowing against a watery sun, as I squelched round the moorland pool of Llyn Gynon and on to the long ridge of Esgair Garthen. East of the moorland gable above Claerwen, deeply incised valleys lead down to lush country, their sides blotched with heather, patched with pink-tinged scree. North, south and west a carpet of peat, seamed, cliffed and stratified, dark chocolate against sage, tawny and purple moor-shades, spread wide. The moor appeared featureless, but when I headed south and followed vague long depressions where streams start, there were rocks with smooth green turf around them, pools of viridian and bright ochre, emerald patches of sphagnum. Across the whole scene a subtle illumination flickered constantly. Drygarn Fawr slipped constantly in and out of view. It was after mid-day when I reached it, wet of foot and aching of limb. A summit spine of seamed and quartzy conglomerate runs north-east to south-west. Bronze Age man built the two huge burial cairns on it, perhaps a quarter-mile apart. They are visible for miles around, beckoning, the northerly one magically crowned with white, glittering stone. I sat with my back to it, the moor-grasses all around taking on the colour of a reddening western sky, and was suddenly, delightedly conscious of the utter isolation here, and the long miles home, with the moor in front of me "like the continual experience of this life wherein the wise firmly admit vast Presences to stand in what is an apparent emptiness, unperceived by any sense"[6].

The last time I came here, I chose the shorter, easier route from among the three I know, the terrain being thoroughly sodden after

---

[6] Hilaire Belloc.

weeks of rain (why do you think so many reservoirs are located in Wales?). Bemired, after consuming my flask and sandwiches with my back against one of those quartz-centred cairns, I made my way down into the Irfon valley. The peregrines that nest on the slatey cliffs above Llanerch Yrfa were screaming noisily around as their eyasses left the nest for the first time and took to the wing. The air was full of their urgent sound and activity. In the field beyond the Elenydd Wilderness Trust hostel at Dolgoch, a tousled grey mountain pony with a heavy black fringe sidled up to nudge at my rucksack. He took the apple I offered him and departed munching and satisfied. Eastwardly, Drygarn Fawr was gauzed now in light mist. The Afon Tywi, here a peat-inflected moorland river, rattled over its stony bed and an observant carrion crow – sole sleek thing in this sodden hill-landscape – hopped from one turk's-head to another in optimistic emulation of the pony's quest. I sat on a boulder and tossed him a biscuit. He dipped down to collect it, glided away to perch on a ruined wall. The path heading downriver had been churned to a quagmire by trekking ponies' hooves. Like the crow, though without his bounce, I played hopscotch across the tussocks. Saturated peat of the moor above maintained the Nant Cwm Du as torrent. I found a leaping place, hurled myself across, tumbled over into the mud in fits of involuntary laughter. On each side long, dark bulwarks of alien conifers were crowding in, squeezing light from the valley.

On the map is the old sub-text to this occluded landscape: Castell Llygoden (mouse castle); Nant yr Hwch (sow stream); Nant y Fleiddast (wolf-bitch stream). Each of these names had a story. The land to which they were attached is lost. Stolen two centuries ago by those sufficiently privileged to make use of the Enclosure Acts[7], for the last seventy years, slowly, with government approval

---

[7] Read *This Land is Your Land* by Marion Shoard if you think I overstate the case. Or anything else by Marion if it comes to that. She and another dear friend of mine, the equally redoutable Kate Ashbrook of the Open Spaces Society, are the two outstanding

and lavish subsidies to descendants of the original perpetrators of the legalized acts of theft that were the Enclosure Acts, it has been erased. Here once was open mountain pasture and laughing water. Now Afon Tywi slid fast, dark and foam-streaked over shingle-beds, accelerating between shaley outcrops towards a sombre, concrete-towered weir beyond which the new reservoir awaited its tribute. The mountain pony leapt a fence and followed me, plunging and whinnying in pleasure along the free river to where it deepens. His ears went back as he looked ahead. Out he climbed, and trailed back disconsolate through the mire. I followed him, started up the car, and for all the Old Etonian Hucks's dire pronouncements on Tregaron[8], made my way back to the Talbot Hotel there, where he and Coleridge had stayed over two centuries before, booked myself in, a friend came to join me, and we spent an enjoyable evening in that friendly place, the good Welsh and the good beer flowing, and the good rural company of Wales as friendly, hospitable, communicative and interesting as ever all around me.

On the grey streets of Tregaron next morning I took note of how the old drovers' bank on the main street was plastered with ultramarine plastic signage that would have panicked the herds in previous centuries as they set off across by way of Abergwesyn to the English smithfields. I tried to imagine that way of life. These narrow streets would have echoed to the bellowing of steers, the frantic baa-ing of sheep, the hiss and cackle of geese, the whinnying of ponies and cobs, the drovers' continual high calls of "buwch, buwch", by which Welsh farmers still summon their cattle from the fields. Slowly the great caravanserais would get under way and in a controlled frenzy head for the uplands, where the small farmers, hearing the brouhaha from below, would corral

---

campaigners for countryside access throughout Britain.

[8] Never trust anything an old Etonian says – vanishingly few of them speak for the people, and particularly not for the people of Wales.

their own livestock lest they be absorbed into the herds bound for slaughter in England. Thirty thousand head of cattle a year were leaving West Wales by the late eighteenth century, heading for the abbatoirs of England, making their way over routes like this rough and narrow one to Abergwesyn before descending to fords over the Wye. Llyswen, Glasbury and Hay were the narrowest crossings of that river's floodplain, so settlements grew up around them and became important stopping places for the drovers, benefiting from all the subsidiary trade (sale of hosiery communally knitted by the women of places like Tregaron or Y Bala; delivery of money; chaperoning of young people to and from the English cities) they dealt in and the dissemination of news and information for which the drovers acted as important conduits. For the present, though, we're following in Roman footsteps downriver along the Teifi. The next significant settlement to the south is Llanddewi Brefi. But there's a catastrophe to be dealt with first that took place in December 2016. It was announced in a media which on the whole paid it little attention through an article by my good friend, seasoned cave explorer and occasional climbing partner David Rose, the best investigative journalist we have left in contemporary Fleet Street. His piece appeared in the *Mail on Sunday* for 20 May, 2017. *"This green and poisoned land: River is devastated by toxic tsunami of sludge from a 'green' energy plant receiving thousands in subsidies from YOU"* is how the banner headline read. The gist of the story was that at Pencefn Drysgol farm south of Tregaron on the flank of a hill overlooking Nant Carfan – a tributary of the Teifi – lived two brothers, Jim and William Lloyd, hill-farmers in a poor area. They were attracted by government subsidies available for installation of anaerobic digesters and sale of the electricity they produced at more than double the normal rate to the National Grid.

So they had an anaerobic digester installed. Both the contractor who installed the plant and the manufacturer who produced it ceased trading shortly thereafter, leaving the Lloyd brothers solely liable for any incidents that might take place during the period of its operation. What happened next was as predictable as it is unbearable. Without proper quality controls[9] or inspection of manufacture and installation, in a feeding frenzy of investors seeking to profit from generous grants that were likely to be available only for a strictly limited period, the substantial apparatus known as a "green guzzler" that is required to turn animal and human excrement into methane for burning off to produce electricity was sited west of the farmhouse and on a slope that falls seventy metres to the Nant Carfan. A joint in a plastic pipe underneath (hence difficult to inspect) the huge – and by now full of mixed human and animal excrement – storage tank failed in the night, through pressure from capacity content and methane production emanating from the same. Its contents streamed in a noisome runnel of black slime straight downhill into Nant Carfan, which carried it away into Afon Teifi less than a mile away. That disaster has an ongoing effect even now. At the time, the numbers of dead salmon and sea trout (sewin) that had been making their way up-river to spawn and were poisoned were ghastly to see. Magnificent fish of a size anglers would have had the experience of a lifetime in engaging with; that had returned to their home river and battled their way upstream to arrive close to their spawning beds were now drifting downstream belly up in foul and toxic water. An incident like this, wiping out as it does the imprinting of home environment on generations of a species, can mark a tipping point in its viability and return to a river. Ill-thought-through government policy; saloon bar arguments propagated by the trash press; ill-trained cowboy workmen after a quick financial killing – all these in unholy alliance had destroyed

---

[9] To avoid these was, in fact, a prime and stated aim of the tories in taking Britain out of the European Union.

what Afon Teifi had been celebrated for through a millennium. It was not the Lloyd brothers' fault. The finger of blame points ultimately at a government that has no thought of implementing proper environmental safeguards, planning controls, or quality inspection of workmanship on schemes in environmentally sensitive areas; that insists on rewarding expansion in energy production where education into reduction of demand would be more appropriate; whose regulatory overseers since the 1970s, have been either ineffectual or collusive with agencies inimical to their independent operation or both. This – one of many recorded mishaps involving "green guzzlers" – has left its long-lasting mark on one of the loveliest of all Welsh rivers. Because that river was a favourite with anglers, who have for a century and a half been important contributors to the rural Ceredigion economy through their use of local inns, employment of local fishing guides, need for transport and food and all the associated facets of sporting tourism, this event has been disastrous to an exponential degree. As we follow downriver now, the effect is palpable time and again of what was far more than a small parochial tragedy. It was an ecological catastrophe, an affront to, a destruction of, a prime asset for a whole nation. They did better than this in the 1870s, as we shall soon see. And though the Lloyd brothers were not to blame, the nature of the deal to which they had signed up means that they receive princely tariffs amounting to tens of thousands of pounds for years to come, and – not an insignificant matter in these straitened times, particularly on a farm with large wintering sheds to heat – free electricity into the bargain.

Two miles downriver we arrive in Llanddewi Brefi, with its dominant church on a large mound, which had a significant role to play in the religious history of Wales. Let's allow George Borrow to tell the story and give the atmosphere in his idiosyncratic way:

> *"Llan Ddewi Brefi is a small village situated at the entrance of a gorge leading up to some lofty hills which rise to the east and belong to the same mountain range as those near Tregaron. A brook flowing from the hills murmurs through it and at length finds its way into the Teivi – an ancient church stands on a little rising ground just below the hills, multitudes of rooks inhabit its steeple and fill throughout the day the air with their cawing."*

The church at Llanddewi does indeed have a steeple, an awkward, squat little affair characteristic of this area, nestling within the battlements of the sturdy tower. And yes, it stands on rising ground in the form of a mound that surely pre-dates the church and is most probably an example of early Christianity's propensity to take over pre-existent religious sites. Though anyone who was at the Synod of Llanddewi Brefi in AD 569 might disagree with that conclusion, for they – according to hagiographers who recorded it six centuries later – witnessed the earth rise beneath the feet of St. David as he began to preach against the heretical doctrine of Pelagianism that had taken root in the fertile soil of the Celtic Christian church. This was the same doctrine that in all probability led to the massacre of the monks at Bangor Is-Coed by Saxons at the behest of the Machiavellian power-broker Augustine of Canterbury. The church hierarchy of AD 569 deplored the way Pelagianism queried the doctrine of grace, upheld the notion of free will, presumed Adam to have been sinless, believed that unbaptized infants would not eternally roast in the flames of hell, and maintained that animals have souls. I just ran that list of central tenets in Pelagian belief past my cat, who slumbers on my knee as I type. She rolled her lovely green eyes and purred softly that it all sounded perfectly reasonable to her, and what in heaven's name were those founding fathers of the church in Wales getting so heated about? "Humans!" she yawned. Then she went back to sleep, as I imagine most people would these days, having rolled their eyes a little at the vision of a mound rising under the feet of Dewi Sant as he preached to the excitable multitude who huzzah-ed him to the stars, as they were exhorted to do by their attendant priests. If only Brother Cadfael had been among the throng to speak reason to the mob; but he came centuries later and anyway was a fictional creation, unlike the thumping dogmatisms of these Pauline creeds of the Roman church. I'm glad I didn't live in those days. Even thinking of them brings the stench of burning human flesh to my nostrils. But I mustn't be too sceptical, too ardent in my support of Mr. Morgan (for that good Welsh name, translated into holy Latin, becomes Pelagius). Borrow – as staunch an Anglican Christian as could be found in his time – goes on to comment that this place is *"just the kind of spot in which some quiet pensive man, fatigued but not soured by the turmoil of the world, might settle down, enjoy a few innocent pleasures, make his peace with God and then compose himself to his long rest."*

Dewi Sant, on the other hand, withdrew into a cell here, laboured in it for three days, and *"produced a treatise in writing in which the tenets of Morgan[10] were so triumphantly overthrown that the convocation unanimously adopted it and sent it into the world with a testimony of approbation as an antidote to the heresy, and so great was its efficacy that from that moment the doctrines of Morgan fell gradually into disrepute"*. Especially, of course, with the kind of audience who believe in miracles like advantages accruing from Brexit or the rising up of a mound beneath a preaching Saint's feet, the building of a huge church upon it, and the installation in that church as a "holy relic" of a horn of one of the great humped oxen of Hu Gadarn, which had helped drag the fearful Afanc out of the beaver pool at the

---

[10] i.e. Pelagius, of which Morgan is an approximate translation. (Morgan is, of course, popular both as forename and surname in West Wales to this day, I'm glad to say.)

confluence of Afon Conwy and Afon Lledr. But to quote the concluding line of Robert Graves' poem "Welsh Incident" – the one that begins in the great black caves near Cricieth from which I've often seen kingfishers fly – *"I was coming to that."*

Of this ox's horn formerly revered in the rather forbidding ("huge, grand and simple" in Elisabeth Beazley's and Peter Howell's view, which is a charitable one) church of Llanddewi Brefi, Principal Rhys in the second volume of his magisterial study of Celtic folklore[11], had the following to say:

> *Brefi is the name of the river from which this Llanddewi takes its distinctive name; and it is pronounced there much the same as* brefu, *'the act of lowing, bellowing, or bleating.' Now the Brefi runs down through the Foelallt Farm, which lies between two very big rocks popularly fancied to have been once united... a wild tradition* [has it] *that when the church was building there were two oxen to draw the stone required; and one of the two died in the effort to drag the load, while the other bellowed nine times and thereby split the hill."*

An obstacle thus removed, the remaining ox brought the load of stone to the site, whilst a fragment of the horn from the dead ox was preserved in the church once it had been built. From there in the nineteenth century it was removed to Aberystwyth and the eminent geologist Professor Boyd Dawkins[12] pronounced it as having belonged to *"the great urus (Bos Primigenius), and added that its condition proved it to have been derived from a peat bog or alluvium."* Principal Rhys goes on to add that *"on the whole, it seems to me probable that the wild legends about the* Ychen Bannog *in Cardiganshire have*

---

[11] *Celtic Folklore: Welsh and Manx*, Oxford, 1901 – an invaluable work of reference and scholarship.

[12] Sir William Boyd Dawkins (1837-1929) was an eminent geologist and palaeontologist, one of whose areas of expertise was the study of extinct European animals. He and Principal Rhys were both Honorary Fellows of Jesus College, Oxford, so it was natural that consultation would take place between the two very different authorities.

underlying them a substratum of tradition going back to a time when the urus was not as yet extinct in Wales. How far the urus was once treated in this country as an emblem of divinity, it is impossible to say." So there you have a richly suggestive provenance for a probably-no-longer-extant holy relic, some pregnant suggestions around the possibility of a prehistoric ox cult in Wales, and he even manages to work in a rather caustic jibe (not quoted here) against the postal service in late-nineteenth-century Ceredigion – his native county. The mind of Principal Rhys (1840-1916) is indeed something of a quality still to be treasured! Before leaving Llanddewi Brefi, it's certainly worth mentioning that this was the site of one of the most important *clasau* (Celtic Christian religious communities in which men and women lived on equal terms) of early medieval Wales. It was one that outlasted most of the others. Here was written Rhygyfarch's 1095 hagiographical life of Dewi Sant. When the *clas* came under the control of Thomas Bek – a loyal placeman of Edward Longshanks in the latter's ongoing conquest of Wales – in the closing decades of the thirteenth century, it produced one of the early religious classics of Wales – "The Book of the Anchorite" – an anonymously-written set of tracts from the mid-fourteenth century now in Oxford's Bodleian Library. *"...let the reader pray that the name of him who wrote them should be written in Heaven and never blotted out from the book of life"*, pleads its gentle author from seven-and-a-half centuries ago.

The prospect of continuing on from Llanddewi alongside Afon Teifi by way of the fine old bridge at Pont Llanio, near which are the remains of *Bremia* Roman fort and an associated Roman bath house, was tempting, as was the alternative from Llanddewi of rejoining the river at Pont Gogoyan with its even finer old bridge (the bridges of Dyffryn Teifi are worthy of a monograph all to themselves, and each seems to come with a bevy of attendant swans). Being perverse by nature, I opted for neither, and climbed into the hills, hoping to find my way to Lampeter along stretches of the ancient road through Wales called Sarn Helen, that takes you through this remote country long settled by incomers who lead their "alternative" lives on smallholdings along back lanes and are "into" veganism, naturism (when the Welsh climate allows), permaculture, Shiatsu massage, orthorexia, mung beans, the People's Market in Lampeter's Victoria Hall, and such-like associated enterprises from Tai Chi to the Tarot. I have no argument with any of this except for when it leads to gullibility when assailed by eco-ethical arguments peddled by "green" entrepreneurs like those responsible for Afon Teifi's eco-catastrophe, and prefer it on the whole to the spiteful acquisitiveness of English torydom. But this is just a personal view, and I won't push it at anyone. Instead, let's head into the hills by one of two roads leading up the valley of Afon Brefi. The other heads to the Elenydd Wilderness Trust hostel of Tŷ'n Cornel – a place of infinite delight at the head of the Doethie (pronounce it 'doy-thee-a') valley, which is one of the loveliest in Wales, though sadly the mountain bikers with their turf-ripping tyres have taken to using it, and the former green path that contoured its eastern slope, from the junction in a beautiful, deep and dangerous confluence pool with the Afon Tywi underneath the oakwood hill of Dinas[13], is now a sloshy groove of mud, ruining the former experience of this exquisite landscape.

In the grey damp of a long-gone forenoon I followed the lane that climbs to a moorland brow above Llanddewi before descending into quiet Cwm Twrch and joining Sarn Helen, which has been in use since the time of those who erected the great megaliths and cairns that resonate across this landscape. Red road signs above Llanddewi gave warning of its closure; sheets of

---

[13] An RSPB reserve, and a delightful walk, abounding with both varieties of flycatcher at the proper season.

highway notices enforced the prohibition. Beyond them, the surface was crushed and comminuted by heavy contractors' vehicles hauling timber from clear-felled conifer plantations across Bryn Glas and Bryn Du – the green hill, the black hill. The texture of the land there now is raw, ruined outrage. Mametz Wood to Insane Hill hath come! A few dead trunks still stood, stripped and blanched like bone. Investors who grasped Thatcherite opportunity were paid their dividends, earned of land compulsorily purchased decades ago for the commonweal. I wrote a short piece in *The Guardian* a decade or so ago in protest at forestry depredations across Welsh hill country, with all its destructive effect on rural community and traditional agricultural practice. A forester wrote in to respond in the most positive fashion. Here's his letter, from the paper's correspondence columns:

> *"I am a forester and erstwhile steward of some of the forests in the Welsh hills above Llanddewi Brefi. The poetry of Jim Perrin's Country Diary struck a painful chord. The spruce plantations of the 20th century originated in the very war that killed the poet Edward Thomas. I regret that we marched them in lines over the hills long after their genesis, as a timber reserve in time of submarine blockade, had become a redundant justification. The Welsh poet Gwenallt from Rhydcymerau wrote (in Welsh – I translate) of the 'trees of the third war' claiming the farms. Worse ... we still persist, uniform conifer plantations are clear-felled, in 'Somme-like' scenes (to use a poignant word, now English), and then replanted in another 'rotation' of trees much the same. It goes on quietly, with public subsidies, accompanied by sophisticated talk of 'standards' and 'sustainable forestry'. It does not have to be so. Some foresters now advocate more natural continuous-cover forestry, eschewing clear-felling, and using thinning, natural regeneration and more native species. Uniform monocultural plantations could be consigned to the dustbin of history, along with the wars of*

*the early 20th century which gave birth to such violent forestry practices
on the hills of Britain."*

I thank Alec Dauncey for that commentary, with which I
profoundly agree, and hope his truthful outspokenness did not get
him into hot water with his employers. That soured land of the
plantations is now being washed away by the hill-rain of Wales,
has become the cause of silting and flooding downriver. When
Giraldus made his "Journey Through Wales" in 1188, passing
through Llanddewi Brefi as companion to Archbishop Baldwin
in his drive to recruit for the Crusades, the Teifi was the only
Welsh river where you might find beavers, whose civil engineering
propensities are a natural safeguard against flood-ravages.
Mankind being the obtuse and brutal animal he is, he destroyed
this natural ally against natural disaster. Here's Giraldus again:

*"I thought that it would be useful to include a paragraph or two at
this point about the habits of these animals: the way in which they
convey their building materials from the woods to the water; with what
artistry they construct their dams in the middle of rivers from the
materials which they have collected; how they protect their dwellings
in Western countries and in the East against those who hunt them;
and a word about their tails, which are fish-like, so to speak, rather
than what one would expect in a land animal. Beavers build their
castle-like lodges in the middle of rivers. They have an extraordinary
method of conveying and carting timber from the woods to the water,
for they use other beavers as wagons. The beavers of one team gnaw
down the branches, and then another group has the instinct to turn over
on their backs and to hold the wood tightly against their bellies with
their four feet. Each of these last grips a branch in its teeth which sticks
out on either side. A third group holds tightly on to this cross branch
with its teeth and pulls the animal in question along backwards together
with its load. Anyone who witnesses this manoeuvre cannot fail to be
impressed..."*

That last statement is surely true! But the relevant passage to the beaver as man's unwitting helpmate comes next, and is a relevant plea in support of the beavers' reintroduction to Welsh rivers:

> *"...in some deep and tranquil bend of the river the beavers piece together with such skill the logs of wood which form their lodge that no drop of water can easily enter, and no storm however violent do harm to it or loosen it."*

So far, so sensible, and applicable to Welsh river environments. Where Giraldus strays from the helpfully sensible is when he quotes Classical authorities – Juvenal, Cicero, St. Bernard of Clairvaux – to argue that the beaver, when hunted, preserves its own life by gnawing off its testicles (he makes no mention of how the female beaver fares). From that point on his argument grows ever more fanciful and obscure. That reference to "fish-like tails" – which they're not, remarkable appendages though they be – turns out to be yet another early-medieval way round dietary prohibitions in the ecclesiastical calendar. A beaver's tail, his reasoning went, is fish-like and therefore can be eaten on Fridays along with fishy-tasting birds: Scoter, Barnacle Geese, herons:

> *"In times of fasting, the great leaders of the church eat these tails instead of fish, accepting them for their flavour and their colouring, for in this, they say, they could be taken for fish..."*

I came across a recently-shot beaver a few years ago in northern Saskatchewan. By no remote stretch of the imagination could the tail of a beaver be mistaken for a fish. But self-interest has always been a powerful force in the formulation of rules within any community. If the monks at Strata Florida were ever served beaver-tail in their refectory, discontent would have been writ large on those vigorously chewing faces. As I write, a news story has just been released about the introduction of beavers to the nature reserve of which Bill Condry was for so long a warden at Ynys Las. That news would certainly have delighted Bill, and will delight his widow, Penny! Here's a final thought on beavers and their re-introduction from the fine Scottish nature writer Jim Crumley, who concludes his passionate and coherently rational plea for their reintroduction to Britain in the following fashion:

> *"Scotland is a better place because beavers have begun to re-shape it, to reinvigorate it, to reinvent it, to cast their spell wherever they ply their architect's trade. ... Beavers make a difference. Unlike other reintroductions we have attempted – or are likely to attempt this side of the wolf – they initiate and then sustain a rolling regime of constant landscape evolution and the associated liberation of literally endless opportunities for other creatures to thrive in their shadow."* [14]

With that thought, let's leave the subject of beavers in Wales – on which Professor Dawkins might have had something historically well informed to say – and head over the hill into Cwm Twrch, which is to cross from the Teifi catchment into that of the Tywi – a river for which I have far less affection, though some of its headwaters are particularly fine (Afon Cothi in particular in its upper gorge to Pwll Uffern Cothi is a little-known, sculpturesque gem). Cwm Twrch, all the way down from Bryn Brawd to Ffarmers, is also an esoteric delight and has one of the best surviving fords in Wales – one to which I love going, to become a "watcher at the ford", a Welsh Morrigan (does that Irish word hold Morgan in itself too – Pelagius, remember, was reputedly an Irish monk?). On an early March evening I headed out to watch at the ford, knowing the brown Afon Twrch – the pig-river – would be foaming past. A raven called. I thought of Aldo

---

[14] Jim Crumley, *Nature's Architect: The beaver's return to our wild landscapes* (Saraband, 2015), p. 190. It should be noted that of late (summer 2021) the Scottish Parliament, at the behest of various Neanderthal interest bodies, has issued licences to shoot beavers on Scottish rivers.

Leopold's prophetic musings on the odyssey of an atom; thought too of how precious is Welsh hill-country, especially as it swills and surges before your eyes, suspended in this brown flood on its way to the sea. On I went by way of Esgair Crwys – the shoulder of the cross – and descended towards Cellan. The lane was slick with algae. A dark dog-fox emerged from the dusk and leapt a fence stapled between native oaks chain-sawed maliciously to the quick, so that this and all coming year's leaves would wither away. The fox entangled momentarily with barbed wire. A brief convulsion and he was free. I looked for badger-runs in this habitual ground. None were in use: "...*far more ancient and dark/The Combe looks since they killed the badger there."* (Edward Thomas, who understood typologies). Another sleek streak of russet pelted down a field, making for the hen-run of a friend I intended to visit. Instead of expected cacophony, I heard dogs bark, plodded on up-field to seven Scots pines by a ruin. The old enclosure beyond was beech-ringed. This was drover-territory, the cattle were penned here for the night. One wall had collapsed in an explosion of white quartz, the quarry for which would have been a former cairn from the bronze age on the bluff close by. Every hill-top and ridge-end visible from here has one, white-cored with spirit-stone.

Up on Craig Twrch two were prominent. I drifted off in that direction. A slant line of ascent from Ffordd Helen was scored across the slope. A stone wall from the time of the Enclosure Acts and a barbed-wire fence of modern provenance prevented the use of what had been right-of-way through millennia. Casting about, a line of long marker-stones, laid low and turf-obscured, indicated another route by which to climb the ridge. The cairns are atop its south-west gable, looking down on a hillside pecked with pits of Roman metal-working all around the enormous prone megalith of Carreg y Bwci – the hobgoblin's stone. It's distance, though, that preoccupies the eye. Even in dimity light I could see Cader

Idris and Y Berwyn northerly; Preseli in the west; long rimming southern scarps of Wales from Bannau Brycheiniog to the Black Mountains on the Herefordshire border, and floating beyond them the perkily distinctive little shapely outline of the Malvern Hills above the Severn Plain. Rough mountain pasture around this sentinel ridge was still winter-grey. Gravid ewes (they lamb late at this altitude) knelt to tug and chew at sparse fescues. Overhead a buzzard mewed; from a fence-post a solitary raven observed, waiting for her annual portion of afterbirth and eyes of sickly lambs, to bring to red throats already agape in tree-top nests by the Long Wood beyond the Teifi. Spring, she knew, was coming to the hills. Descending back towards Cellan, I overtook an old couple, arms linked, walking sticks giving an easy, patient impetus to their uphill progress. They were climbing the lane as I descended through its wild avenue of alder, oak and ash, asked if I was bound for the ford, told me how special a place it is for them, intimated that a proposal had been made and accepted there long years before. We talked about the place far to the north where Pryderi was slain. A blush of early-opening buds glowed along the overarching boughs. I heard the stream running over slabs before I reached it. Under the hazels on this near and mossy bank leaves of bluebells had speared up through a fading litter of celandines. They come late into flower among these cold hills. Only a few stems were drooping into bloom, hinting at the coming richness of colour and pervasive scent. Pale delicacy of primrose-clusters was badged luminous across deep shade, and water rippled across the penetrations of light. I caught at a muted flash of yellow, focussed on incessant flitting activity among gleaming stones. Two grey wagtails, not yet in the cadmium intensity of summer plumage, their slender long tails bobbing incessantly, shrilled at me in alarm and flitted urgently upstream, away from my intrusion. My shoes and socks came off, trousers were rolled, and

I waded across, the water shin-deep, forceful and chill.

There is something about a ford that thrills. It's not just the excitement of encounter with nature's uncertainties – the memories of times when I'd driven this lane, had my headlights pick out the fierce dark flood of a hill-stream in spate, and reversed chastened back up the twisting lane. It's that as the progress of civilisation and convenience has forced the old crossing-places higher up the tributary streams and towards the sources, their typological resonances have retreated thus too. So that in a quiet and remote place like this, your subconscious mind might still encounter the watcher at the ford, daughter of the god of war in the old tales, premonitory, washing the clothes of warriors slain or to be slain as the raven – *cigfran* in Welsh, "the meat-crow" – circles overhead, reminding of the many bloody conflicts to which humanity is prone. Down in the valley the Teifi was a wide and gleaming thread of silver. Another day on this road, in front of me I saw a black, bedraggled thing, flattening down into long grass of a shallow ditch by the road as I approached. I stooped to pick him up. Fierce, grey-irised eyes fixed on me. He hurled raucous abuse, red throat and pale-pink gape-flange working furiously, sharp bill spearing repeatedly at my thumb, infant talons raking my wrist. What to do with him, this lost little carrion crow already on the vulnerable cusp between nestling and fledgling? His parents were calling from high in a row of nearby beech. I negotiated barbed wire, climbed ten feet up the most amenable trunk, and found a safe, mossed bowl soft with mast into which to drop him. A last glimpse of him shuggling down into dry warmth, and I walked away, within minutes through my night-glass I saw the adults fetching food. I like crows, am glad to see his own kind treating him kindly – as most passers-by hereabouts would not. The rushy pastures on either side were heavy with the sweet scent of lesser butterfly orchids. Fragrance intensifying in the dusk, their ghostly pallor attracted night-moths that can reach nectar in the long spurs, and in doing so pollinate. Flower-spikes of a lovely, violet-flowered *salvia*, meadow clary – distinctly rare in the region and perhaps a garden escape – indicated base-rich rather than the apparently acid soil. I wandered on and came to Carreg y Bwci. Its five metres of greywacke sprawl across turf where suggestions of circles, alignments, ditches have been scumbled and discoded by the long centuries – signifiers, now lost in an inexplicable past that yet evokes a certain sense of uncomprehending dread. I imagined a drover on his return from the English smithfields, quickening his pace in the stone's presence, fearful of what might roost here.

To the east, the day was vaguening down into obscurity. Ridges merged into gathering grey, the prime and threatened wild of Elenydd unmarred for once in this light. Continuing down into Dyffryn Teifi I turned down a friend's track, and within the hour she and I were sitting in the *King's Head* in Lampeter, waiting for an order from the Indian take-away next door and listening to the students who throng the place discussing which was the best "session beer", which the strongest, until the time came to pick up the takeaway and head for her fireside, leaving an appraisal of Lampeter's delights until the following day. We had to wait until the evening for one of those delights, and it takes this narrative back in Shandy-esque fashion to Tregaron. The delight was a vigorously presented and engagingly constructed and costumed account written and acted by pupils at the local school of the sad history of an elephant from a travelling menagerie that visited Tregaron in 1848[15]. The elephant died, seemingly from lead

---

[15] Wombwell's travelling menageries (there were three of them in all) travelled extensively throughout Wales in the nineteenth century. The animals were transported around in strongly barred, horse-drawn, wheeled cages and were subject to much taunting and abuse. The Reverend Francis Kilvert encountered the menagerie on Dolgellau's Marian in June 1871 and left this account: *"After dinner we went out and strolled around the town. Wombwell's menagerie had just come in and the town was alive and swarming with people. The caravans were drawn*

poisoning, as a result of which tragic incident, officialdom – more than usually slow on the uptake – thirty years later, in 1878, acted on petitions and deputations to London, reasoned that what could kill an elephant was probably having a deleterious effect on the health of human populations (or even, perhaps more shockingly to the local nabobs, on the stocks of salmon and sewin in this notable "sporting" river), and so a Whitehall Inspector of Salmon Fisheries was eventually sent to inspect. The inspector in question was Spencer Walpole (1839-1907), whose father had been Home Secretary in the Peel administration. (To avoid charges of nepotism his son's salary was reduced from £900-£1,000 to £700.) Walpole's wife's mother was one of the assassinated Prime Minister Spencer Perceval's twelve children. Her marriage had been a love-match regularised in East Grinstead after the pair had eloped, and an air of genial competence survived the pall cast over the family by Spencer Perceval's assassination at Westminster by an aggrieved merchant who was subsequently hanged for his murder. Walpole, the Victorian Inspector of Salmon Fisheries and a distinguished historian, wrote a biography of Perceval. Walpole commented on his own work as a civil servant that "in its promise of many a pleasant wandering by river, lake and sea-shore [it] was most congenial." His daughter, long after her parents' happy

---

up in the 'Marian Mawr', the marshy meadow at the back of the hotel just outside the Golden Lion garden … Up at 5.30. Not a soul stirring in the house, the front door locked and the key gone. I got out by the garden door and through the wicket inti the Marian Mawr. There was the caravan. The people were all asleep, but the lions were rustling and growling about their dens hungry for breakfast. I knocked at the lions' door and at the door of the ostriches, gnus and antelopes, eliciting divers roars, groans, howls, hoots and grunts. A large black dog was chained at the entrance." The menagerie was made up of fifteen vehicles for the animals, accommodation for the showmen, and also for the accompanying brass band. In the 1840s George Wombwell (1777-1850), the then proprietor, had been consulted by Prince Albert about the deaths of several of his pet dogs, and had correctly identified the cause as lead poisoning from their drinking water. I wonder if he arrived at this conclusion after the loss of the elephant in Tregaron? George was buried in a coffin made from oak salvaged from the *Royal George* in Highgate Cemetery, under a statue of his favourite lion, Nero.

marriage had been concluded by their deaths, left an affecting vignette relating to their time spent investigating that matter crucial to the members of gentleman's clubs in St. James and Mayfair – the health of the salmon and trout stock along the upper Teifi:

"I sometimes wonder in how many wayside villages and fishing hamlets may still linger a memory of his genial courteous passing..? There was a certain simplicity about him and a ready sympathy, very different from condescension, which was so natural to him that he made it seem natural to others."

On Walpole's swiftly delivered recommendations, regulations were imposed on mining proprietors, and water issuing from the mines had to be collected into settling pools to allow the toxic residue to be filtered out instead of being discharged directly into rivers and streams. But the sense that human welfare was of less significance than that of the fish which were the gentry's object in examining the issue remained (their capture being these same gentry's sole prerogative); and it fuelled resentment in these towns along the upper Teifi, just as Nant Carfan's eco-catastrophe has done more recently.

To return to Lampeter, the Teifi appears to weave a web of channels around this charmingly plain and unpretentious little early Victorian university town. In fact, this is an illusion. The Teifi winds its way in to the Pont Steffan that gives the town its Welsh name through a wide strath from Llanfair Clydogau that encircles the town to the south, and the little river that pursues a course directly through Lampeter, flowing along the eastern boundary of St. David's University College, is actually Nant Tawelan that dawdles its way in from Silian to the north. The history of the University College is interesting. The land on which it stands belonged until the early nineteenth century to the

Peterwell estate, the ruins of which can be found (beware of unpleasant ghosts!) just west of the town, along a tree-lined avenue heading south from the Llanwnnen road to where a couple of decayed stumps of towers do little more than provide the vaguest hint of what former baroque splendour rose here to bankrupt the squire who was its profligate proprietor. When indentures on government loans he had taken out became payable, he defaulted. His estate passed to a staunch old Quaker banker and abolitionist friend of Wilberforce, John Scandrett Harford, whose name is commemorated in Harford Square in Lampeter, where one of the surviving South Walian Italian cafes is to be found. A chance meeting between Harford and Thomas Burgess[16] in Gloucester in 1820 had led to the former offering Burgess the site of Lampeter Castle for the scheme for which Burgess, who had been Bishop of St. David's since 1803, had long been collecting. This was for a college in Wales devoted to preparing men through a seven-year course for holy orders. Its foundation stone, on the site gifted by Harford, was laid in 1822.

Before that Harford, Burgess and a young architect, C.R. Cockerell, had met in Lampeter to look over the site and discuss the venture. Cockerell (1788-1863) was another fascinating character, best known for his work on the very sympathetic and harmonious extensions to the Ashmolean Museum in Oxford. He had spent seven years on the Grand Tour (five of them during the period of the Napoleonic Wars, which argues a certain steeliness of character). He excavated temple sites in Greece, shamelessly

---

[16] Thomas Burgess (1756-1837) was a remarkable character for his time. He was an *eisteddfodwr* who took a great interest in Welsh life and gave his patronage to the group of Welsh literary clergy who were active during the early part of the 19th century, and to the Carmarthen eisteddfod of 1819. As Bishop of Ty Ddewi from 1803, he refused to induct clergy unable to preach in Welsh to Welsh-speaking parishes – a remarkable and enlightened stance given what came later, when the *Brad y Llyfrau Gleision* ("Treachery of the Blue Books") had led to the "Welsh Not" and other such educational atrocities against the Welsh language and cultural community.

"collected" Classical artefacts in the manner of the day, visited Egypt, Troy and Mesopotamia, was a founder member of *The Travellers' Club*, and was first recipient of the *Royal Gold Medal* for Architecture. The Royal Academy's summary view of his approach runs thus:

> *At the heart of Cockerell's emotional experience of the power of the antique to fire the imagination lay an extraordinary visual sensitivity to the mass and volume of the components of architecture, which for him were never mere abstract, weightless forms or quotations borrowed from the past, but acted together as a constantly renewable expression of man's innate need to create beauty on earth.*

An enthusiastic Hellene, he nonetheless put that aside in the commission he received from Harford and Burgess, and came up with a design more like his Tudor-style brick buildings of 1818-1820 for Harrow School. His designs for St. David's College, Lampeter, focused on a quadrangle, with staircases running off it to give access to student rooms made cosy by corner fireplaces and box beds. Water came from pumps in the quadrangle, grey pebbledash rendered the external walls, the windows were iron-framed. Harford stumped up a further £1000 towards the building costs, and the library – a wonderful institution – benefited from the bequest of Bishop Burgess's 7,000 volume annotated collection, as well as further gifts particularly from Sir Thomas Phillipps (1792-1872), the so-called "Vello-maniac", who bankrupted himself in the collection of rare early manuscripts. At one time he had thought to house all of these in Wales, but family and financial pressures diverted him from that aim. Nonetheless, what the new college at Lampeter received was generous and fascinating, forming the basis to a first-rate collection. As to the college itself, it still pleases and charms in an Oxford manner with its air of quiet and remote scholarship

among the green and peaceful Teifi-side hills. At times I've wished
I'd come here to read for my first degree, as several of my friends
in the outdoor world did. I made a film in County Mayo for the
BBC as part of a Cameron McNeish series with two of them,
Richard and Meg Else. My fellow columnist these last more-years-
than-either-of-us-cares-to-remember on *The Great Outdoors*
magazine, Chris Townsend, was also a student there before
heading north into the Scottish hills to make his name as
formidable long-distance walker and outdoor gear guru. But then,
at a Welsh Union of Writers conference in Llanberis, to which I'd
been invited as guest reader for the Saturday evening session by
the late Robin Reeves, long-time editor of the *New Welsh Review*
before it became a dull mouthpiece for adherents to the latest
critical *isms*, I spent a long time in conversation with the John
Cowper Powys scholar, Belinda Humfrey, and not just because she
had brought with her two delectable little terriers (once you've
shared your life with a terrier, any other breed of dog seems dull
by comparison). Belinda was for many years Head of the
Department of English at St. David's, and her blood-curdling tales
of misogyny, blocks on career advancement, internecine warfare,
Senior Common Room conflict and all the other downsides to
what ought to be a quiet discipline of study made me very grateful
I'd gone north instead, though I recognised all the traits Belinda
described among the academics I met in the college I did attend.
In what sphere of life does cut-throat competition not hold sway?
It seems at times that the elbow is the most evolved human organ.
In academia, where the mutual pursuit of knowledge is surely the
beau idéal, that's a very saddening thought.

Before we leave Lampeter, in order to expiate the memory of
those conifer plantations above Llanddewi Brefi we should pay a
visit to the Long Wood, along the crest of the ridge north of
Dyffryn Teifi, between it and Betws Bledrws, and when we've

done that, perhaps we'll call round at Denmark Farm? *"Whose woods these are I think I know"*, wrote Robert Frost in his most famous poem; but I'm proven wrong as I slip between river and trees into this Teifi-side Long Wood at end of a day in the dark time of the year. No longer is the Forestry Commission proprietor here. A trust administers now, and slowly transforms. Rectangular blocks of spruce give place to native and haphazard trees. Quirkily carved benches line the track-verge, as though for spectators at nature's return. Stones chipped to heart-shape rest against trunks, signifying the something-heartening that's afoot in this place. I sat and registered green buds of sycamore, black tips of ash, a subtle carmine in the cherry. Midwinter spring. Slow clouds were dove-grey, last leaves luminescent in a bloom of late sunlight. The warblers and flycatchers were away south, vespers now a magpie cacophony. Winter stilling was yet on the land. One solitary chaffinch flitted away. In the silence it left behind, rattle of a dry leaf's descent startled A blackbird busy around my feet cocked his head, stabbed down, drew forth an elastic worm. His volleying triumphant song told briefly how poets are born not made, before he scudded away to shadow's safety. Had you attended close as a bird, you might have heard spores swelling through the loam; the seeds uncurl; or faraway Swordy Well of the finest English eco-poem gurgling under the landfill that covers it now. I fancy, in this renascent wood, that we should listen more to land and how it might feel; consider more its silence and its absences; come to know its nature and its need. Though what chance empathy when we no longer know what land is? Around me ferns are brilliant green among brown needle-litter: fish-spine of hard fern; soft shield fern; male fern the root of which was carved to hand-shape and baked before Midsummer's Day to be worn as amulet. Ravens chattered from their roost in beech-trees at the wood's margin. From a sweep of easy wind, wary of us, they communicated. Meanwhile, mushroom collectors who had been active beneath the trees since morning, stooping, inspecting, scuttling excitedly selecting from among the daily crop of chanterelles and fairy-clubs, russulas, lactarias and clitocybes, were finally emerging from the trees into afternoon light, bags crammed with jew's-ear and wood-blewit, parasol and penny-bun, to confer over identifications, chatter recipes, trade specimens. I passed them on the lane as I headed for Denmark Farm.

Three miles away from the smallest British university town, across the old railway line and on the next ridge north from that along which the Long Wood was planted, is the former agri-industrial site (or working farm if you prefer that term) now owned by the Shared Earth Trust. It has seceded from the suspect world of progress that has done so much damage along Afon Teifi, and its forty acres are reverting to a state of nature. Hedgerows un-battered by over-dense livestock-containment are burgeoning. They seethe with flitting and quarrelsome bird-life. Field-drains have been blocked. Economic desiccation of the land is thus subverted. Pasture becomes sodden and waterlogged again, provides habitat for dragonflies, damsel-flies, even otters. Small numbers of Highland Cattle and ponies graze the fields, and no hay is cut until after seeding. What grows here arrives naturally. Along the walks that now thread the area, beech-mast crackles underfoot as you tread softly on moss. Everywhere you look, a gentle helping hand is being offered to bio-diversity. The contrast with the surrounding landscapes is becoming ever more harsh. Metallic hues of ubiquitous Euro-grass have given place to natural greens; to the flower-rich and various; to textures of delight. No artificial administration of chemicals pollutes this ground, or promotes the growth of algal blooms in its ponds, or runs off to poison the river-fish. Butterflies and moths dance and feed here as if in thankfulness. Twilight bats feast on the land's enabled density of insect-life. All the native Welsh *mustelidae* shuffle and lope along their trails unconfined and unmolested. This natural abundance is the physical manifestation of a holistic organizing principle where nothing is forced or killed. Visitors may camp and assist. Rather than desolation-by-progress, here is a work-in-progress, to be observed in hopeful pleasure through decades to come. It's the most heartening spectacle I've seen along the Teifi.

I drove back into Lampeter and out again by way of Cwmann, where the rather dark inn overlooking the river used to host invigorating music sessions to which all the aforementioned alternative community of the hills used to cram in, and perhaps still do, especially when the local mage Andrew Hawkey and his effortlessly competent "Blues Occasionals" are playing. The last time I was there I had a late-morning rendez-vous with Andrew. Knowing I was friendly with the Welsh singer Meic Stevens[17], and being a rare records dealer (look up his home page on Wikipedia), Andrew had asked if I had any of Meic's early records. I told him I had a mint copy of *Gwymon* (seaweed), from the 1960s, that I hardly ever played because it wasn't Meic at his rousing or his

---

[17] My closest near-death experience – and there have been several - came as a result of a drinking bout with Meic. When I was living at Brithdir in Cwm Pennant he phoned at ten o'clock one February morning many years ago to tell me he was in the Bryncir Arms, that it was market day at the mart opposite, he was drinking with the *ffermwyr*, there was an all-day licence, and I should get myself down as soon as possible. So being weak-willed I did, to join in a very entertaining session of boozing and Welsh conversation, very little of which was on the prices of sheep and cattle. In the early evening we all had some food. In the late evening Meic asked me for a lift to Bangor. I thought I'd better test the air before making a decision, so I went out into the car-park and walked over to the fence at the back of it; which was the last thing I remember until, hours later, I opened my eyes to see the stars shining brightly above in a clear sky, and to find that I couldn't move. Eventually I managed, with a great splintering sound, to wrest an arm free, put it to my face, which was encrusted with frozen vomit, and realised that I'd tippled over the fence and landed , fortunately face up, in the ditch beyond, into which I'd been frozen. I crawled out, realised Meic was long gone, found my keys, drove back to Brithdir and spent two days in bed thawing out and recovering from a monumental hangover. When I next saw Meic, he told me he'd had a lift with one of the farmers to a pub in Caernarfon, where Gwenllian, his girlfriend at the time, had eventually found him. Good, dangerous company, that man!

lyrically plaintive best. Andrew offered £500 for it. I was astonished. That was a lot of money at the time. I think he gave me only slightly less for a copy of Endaf Emlyn's *Hiraeth*. He explained that early Welsh acid rock at the time was very collectible in Japan, so I combined clinching that sale in the Cwmann Tavern with negotiating a book contract at the now sadly defunct as a publishing house, but once seminal Gwasg Gomer in Llandysul[18]. After I'd parted with the record, I made my way along a dull road with the river snaking like an infuriated whip-snake down to my right. I was thinking of the previous occasion when I'd caught a bus this way and had sat on the back seat next to a parka-wearing, henna-plaited hitch-hiker who smelt vaguely of patchouli and goats, and had every variety of face-piercing I'd ever seen. She told me her name was Sheba, shared a continual succession of small herbal cigarettes with me (you could smoke at the back of buses in those days), and said that she was bound for Llandysul. In those days the Gomerian Press had its offices in the town of Llandysul itself, rather than by the roundabout on the way to Synod Inn, so we hopped off the bus together, spent a pleasant hour in the pub, and when the time came for my meeting we bade each other farewell. She planted an alarmingly frank and garlic-hued kiss on my lips to thank me for lunch which I remember to this day (the kiss, not the lunch, which was not at all memorable), and sashayed on to a bus that was to take her back to Llanllwni with a quick and mischievous glance back at me to make sure I was paying sufficient attention to her performance, and a big smile when she saw that I was.

("Ah, but I was so much older then, I'm younger than that now...")

---

[18] I remember how proud I'd been when my first book came out from the firm that had published all the major poets of the twentieth-century Welsh literary renaissance. Waldo Williams, Robert Williams Parry, Sir T.H. Parry-Williams – all their collections had been printed in that Dickensian building on Llandysul High Street looking down on the Teifi.

There's a substantial tributary to Afon Teifi. Afon Tyweli races down a deep, glaciated valley from Pencader and joins the main river by Pont Tyweli at the bottom end of town. The water at this location, especially when the river's high, looks ferocious. The kayak fraternity – "paddlers" as they prefer to be known (an obsessive bunch of neoprene fetishists) – call it "The Cauldron". A little farther downriver another tricky section with overhanging trees saw the death of a popular South Walian canoeist, who was trapped in flood conditions by a branch and drowned whilst his companions looked on helplessly. At Pantycroi, a mile upstream from Llandysul on Afon Tyweli, Caradog Evans (1878-1945) was born. His father, an auctioneer, had recently died, leaving a widow and five young children. At fifteen, Caradog – "the great Caradog" in Dylan Thomas's phrase – was apprenticed to a draper in Carmarthen, and thereafter worked in drapers' shops at Barry, Cardiff and London. The publication of his first book of short stories, *My People*, brought him immediate and lasting notoriety, and he compounded the effect in subsequent publications like *Capel Sion* (1916); *My Neighbours* (1919 – about the London Welsh); *Taffy* (1923 – a play about Welsh village life); and in the 1930s a sequence of novels that were variously labelled "libellous" and "dangerous and pornographic". Dylan Thomas was a disciple, and paid him a pilgrim's visit when he was living in Aberystwyth in the 1930s. He was the malignant icon to the emergent modernism of Anglo-Welsh literature between the wars, and the vehemence of his assault on his own country's religious hypocrisy, greed and sadism still has power to leave you reeling with shock. There is a vein of profound misanthropy running through his stories. These are horror stories of a claustrophobic and sadistic bent, peopled by grotesque and malevolent characters, never redeemed by even a glimmer of fellow humanity. They would serve well as a critique of the underlying values of

Boris Johnson's twenty-first century Tory England, where everything has a price and nothing has a heart. The style in which they're related is perhaps their most remarkable achievement – a sneering, lisping, excoriating, Bible-parodic patois. The plot of the first story in *My People*, "A Father in Sion", gives the flavour for the whole body of his work, and it was wormwood and gall to the respectable Wales of his time, which viewed him ever thereafter as the country's sworn enemy. The "Father in Sion" was Sadrach Danyrefail:

> *"He was a man whose thoughts were continually employed on sacred subjects. He began the day and ended the day with the words of a chapter from the Book and a prayer on his lips."*

He marries an older woman, Achsah, for her good farm, and he sires eight children on her. She appears to lose her sanity and he locks her in the saddle loft:

> *"Once a week when the household was asleep he … threw a cow's halter over her shoulders, and drove her out into the fields for an airing."*

He moves another woman into Achsah's house, is elected to the Seiat Fawr of Capel Sion. Six of Achsah's children die:

> *"Rachel developed fits; while hoeing turnips in the twilight of an afternoon she shivered and fell, her head resting in the water-ditch that is alongside the hedge. In the morning Sadrach came that way with a load of manure. Rachel was silent. Death had come before the milking of the cows. Sadrach went to the end of the field and emptied his cart of manure. Then he came back and cast Rachel's body into the cart, and covered it with a sack, and drove home singing the hymn which begins 'Safely, safely gathered in…'"*

On the wedding day of Sadrach and Achsah's first-born, the wife escapes her loft, watches the marriage procession go by, wonders at the absence of six of her children, finds their graves in the chapelyard. When the first-born son returns with his new wife to Danyrefail, the wife is embraced by a lunatic. So much for Caradog Evans' "Tales of the Peasantry of West Wales". It wouldn't be the last assault upon Welsh religious hypocrisy. Patrick O'Brian's 1952 *Testimonies* (under its original title of *Three Bear Witness)* was the first published novel of a writer who became in a particular genre – that of maritime fiction – a cult figure of worldwide popularity, first recipient of the Heywood Hill Prize for a lifetime's contribution to literature, his admirers including Charlton Heston and John Bayley. O'Brian's fame rests on the Aubrey/Maturin naval cycle set at the time of the Napoleonic Wars – a fluently-written though notably uneven series for which devotees make substantial claims. Jan Morris, writing in *The Observer,* came close to the heart of the matter when she commented that "aficionados scarcely feel them to be novels at all. They are a world of their own, full of excitement, mystery, charm and good manners of which, over three decades, we have ourselves become citizens". The Aubrey/Maturin novels, as Jan acutely implies, are essentially escapist literature, a high-class maritime soap-opera, breathtakingly erudite, flattering their readers' pretensions, and drawing forth some extravagant plaudits. One reviewer in *The Times* – best afforded protection of anonymity – proclaimed O'Brian "the greatest historical novelist of all time". Lovers of Scott and Tolstoy, Stendhal and Balzac will flinch from such crassness and mutter under their breaths the useful couplet from Young's *Night Thoughts*:

> *"Unlearned men of books retain the care*
> *As Eunuchs are the guardians of the fair."*

For all his engaging wit and vivid characters, as an historical novelist O'Brian is a throwback to what György Lukács, in his seminal work *The Historical Novel* (1955), calls the "ideological mediocrity of Legitimist pseudo-historicism", with its "extraordinarily powerful influence... distorted and mendacious". The Saunders Lewis of the suspect pre-war writings would have identified with many threads here. This may prove an interesting line of enquiry to some other commentator, but it leaves me grateful for the one Welsh novel O'Brian did write before the rigging of his imagination became entirely salt-encrusted. *Testimonies* is a fascinating piece of work, a kind of Welsh *Antigone* from an external though far from dispassionate viewpoint. It convincingly bodies forth the landscape in which the story is set (not on Teifi-side, unfortunately, but in Croesor, near Porthmadog), and uses it as emotional sounding-board in the traditional manner of English fiction:

> *"It was September when I first came into the valley: the top of it was hidden in fine rain, and the enclosing ridges on either side merged into a grey, formless cloud. There was no hint of the two peaks that were shown on the map, high and steep on each side of the valley's head. This I saw from the windows of the station cab as it brought me up the mountainous road from the plains, a road so narrow that in places the car could barely run between the stone walls."*

The subtle typologies here – the ascent from the plains, the road so narrow, the clouded peaks – are noteworthy in a novel that engages with the theme of religious hypocrisy and its effect on the lives of the unquestioning devout. They chime too with the introduction of a delicately-suggested folkloric theme of ill-omen. I'm reminded of a comment by Empson on *Ulysses*, that leads me into autobiographical and psychological speculation about O'Brian:

> *"Most readers of* Ulysses *do not believe in omens, but Joyce eagerly did; in this he is genuinely like Homer. Four of the characters receive*

omens, and Joyce would regard these as an assurance that some great event would occur."

The note is apposite, particularly in adducing Classical example, to the complex allusiveness of O'Brian's novel. On his first night in the rented cottage of Hafod, the chief protagonist, John Aubrey Pugh – a character who might have narrated an M.R. James story – looks out of his window and sees this:

> *"The last grey light and a parting in the mist showed a huddle of buildings down there; I supposed them to be the farm and while I stared a light appeared, travelled steadily along to a door and vanished; a faint ghostliness filled the windows of the building and then the mist blotted it out."*

Principal Rhys glosses this in the first volume of his *Celtic Folklore*, where he tells of the *"canwyll gorff*, or corpse-candle... as a means of warning each to get ready in time for his death; that is to say, to prevent death finding him unprepared." It's a preoccupation also that crops up throughout George Borrow's *Wild Wales* of 1862. O'Brian's understated use of the motif to evoke eschatological atmosphere – hovering, sinister and deadly – demonstrates his early literary skill. The structure of *Testimonies*, too, is interesting, pointed up in both alternative titles. An obvious affinity is to Ron Berry's *So Long, Hector Bebb* (also, of course, to Faulkner's *As I Lay Dying*), in the device of the multiple narrator. O'Brian further complicates this by the use of a Grand Inquisitor-figure, anonymous and unexplained throughout, dragging tales out of a group of Jamesian flawed "reflectors", even extracting explanatory testimony *post mortem* from the main female character after the novel's dramatic climax – a fictive device that intensifies the "faint ghostliness" of the anticipatory early passage into very eerie illumination (which is further intensified by a powerfully resonant running fox-motif). These peculiar dimensions of the novel aside, the acuity in observations of a rural community under the spell of late-Calvinism at its most hypocritically malevolent is bracing. We are in *Tartuffe*-territory here, though differing in plot-drivers that are not only to do with sexual desire[19].

The villainous minister Pritchard Ellis shamelessly practises on the Orgon-figure of Emyr Vaughan whilst lusting after his wife Bronwen; but he's also characterized by a naked lust for power and an appalling (and, for the object of his lust, ultimately tragic) manipulation of the unbridled, easily-aroused and community-wide indulgence in calumny. I know of no other work of English literature (America can throw up some good examples, *The Scarlet Letter* and *The Crucible* prominent among them) in which the regrettable and ubiquitous human tendency to calumniate is more precisely and excruciatingly portrayed. What O'Brian gets precisely right in psychological terms is the nature of calumny as projected guilt – what Thomas Merton calls the "fanatical projections of all one's own evil upon 'the enemy' (whoever that may be)"[20]. The unremitting malignity of Pritchard Ellis derives from the chasm between depraved personal morality and assumed position in society. As a Calvinist minister, his physical advances to Bronwen Vaughan, his pathetic attempts at voyeurism (through an enlarged rat-hole), his possession of "dirty things in his bedroom" (O'Brian excels in the use of the unspecified to add imaginative force – the sexual behaviour of Emyr Vaughan which arouses such anguished disgust in his wife is left similarly vague and gains potency thereby), make his situation so potentially parlous that his necessary defence is a calculated and merciless discrediting, regardless of consequence for them, of all those by whose knowledge he is threatened, and an inculpation of the whole chapel-community within his designs.

---

[19] The issues raised by Iago's practising upon Othello are quite different to those at play in *Testimonies*.

[20] Thomas Merton, *The Wisdom of the Desert* (New York, 1960) pp. 21-22.

There is acute psychological insight in O'Brian's recounting of this from several perspectives (so vehemently imagined it might suggest an origin in the author's having personally suffered through the same dynamic)[21]. The ending of *Testimonies* is an everyday horror-story of an intensity scarcely surpassed even by Caradog Evans. As it draws to its conclusion, foolish wickedness masquerading as the good is entirely triumphant. To quote Auerbach on Molière's great play, *"Everywhere the ass looks out from under the lion's skin"*[22]. The moral realism of Kate Roberts is supercharged here, the vision that of a demon-ruled Calvinist hell, Pritchard Ellis a Welsh version of Hogg's *Justified Sinner.* It would be interesting to know how this fascinating and accomplished novel was received in the community on which it was based. "Cwm Bugail" is clearly identifiable as Cwm Croesor, above Traeth Mawr in Gwynedd. Description of the cottage where Pugh lives, Hafod, is an exact match for the real cottage of Fron Wen near the head of the cwm, "square on a little dug-in plateau that almost undermined the road…the smallest habitation I had ever seen; a white front with a green door between two windows, and a grey roof the size of a sheet." Having known Cwm Croesor over many decades, I recognize flesh-and-blood characters behind O'Brian's fictional ones. They would not have been best pleased at their portrayal. Where the co-incidence of autobiography and novel does have a happy influence is in exact, atmospheric description of scenes such as the "otter-boarding" at Llyn yr Adar in the wild country between Croesor and Nant Gwynant – a scene worthy of the evocative, knowledgeable, neglected writings on Welsh landscape by Ian Niall – or of sheep-shearing at the

---

[21] Some support for this intuition comes from Nikolai Tolstoy's compassionate and worthy biography of his step-father, *Patrick O'Brian: The Making of a Novelist* (Century 2004). The same book's account of O'Brian's time in Croesor gives excellent background to *Testimonies.*
[22] Erich Auerbach, *Mimesis: The Representation of Reality in Western Literature* (Princeton 1953) p. 361.

Vaughans' farm. The temptation is to quote at length from this latter, and compare its accuracy and energy with flimsier direct counterparts in other recent novels with Welsh settings. This would be cruel. Kinder, perhaps, simply to note that here the description derives from personal experience lucidly recollected and described, whilst the others, in time-honoured tradition of metropolitan and "Program Era" writers, are gestural, synthetic, source-derived from a very limited range of reference. The novels I have in mind are, in Edward Thomas's terse phrase, "books made out of books founded on other books" – not terribly well-chosen ones here, either.

O'Brian occasionally lapses into a mockery of Welsh-speakers' use of English that can claim direct line of descent from Shakespeare's Fluellen – *"Sit down, Mr. Pugh, sit down: I have putting your tea to Bronwen's table, isn't it."* – but his general response to the Welsh language is sympathetic and informed, approving even, as here, talking of John, the gwas at the Vaughan's farm:

> *"There was that strange flash of poetry in him too, something that is not paralleled (I think) in any other country... he told me... stories that must have come to him straight from the Mabinogion, or from the verbal tradition before that."*

Close to an Arnoldian museumising of Welsh culture[23] perhaps, but at least there is cultural knowledge and awareness of tradition here? A very interesting explanatory point is made about the appeal of this primal, mountain landscape of "Cwm Bugail" to Pugh, the effete and deracinated Oxford scholar (and by extension to the author, whose naval novels constitute an interesting enquiry into aspects of the masculine):

---

[23] For a brilliant brief exposition of this pitfall and its historical background, see M. Wynn Thomas, *Corresponding Cultures: the two literatures of Wales* (U.W.P. 1999), and particularly chapter four, "The Good Thieves? Translating Welsh literature into English"

*"...the vast country opened and strengthened my being in ways that I
had never imagined... I began to feel more of a man – more complete
and masculine – and less like a neutral creature in an unsatisfactory
body... The strength of the country; that was a new concept for me...
a man's natural reaction would be to become more virile.*

That was a digression almost worthy of *A Week on the Concord and
Merrimack Rivers*. And it's left us high and dry in the country – to
continue the religious theme – of *Y Smotyn Du*. In the late
eighteenth century radical intellectualism in Wales (as in England)
had begun to move away from the life-denying ordinances of
Calvinism. Independent congregations here and there were
rejecting it, and Dyffryn Teifi was particularly strong in its drift to
other shades of belief. There were half-a-dozen Calvinism-
occluding Chapels such as those at Llwynrhydowen near
Llandysul and Alltyblaca close by Llanybydder, led by serious,
thoughtful and eloquent educated ministers like David Williams
and John Jenkins, who had turned initially to Arminianism[24].

From Llandysul to Henllan the Teifi wanders from side to side
of its wide and gentle valley until it reaches Llyn y Badell, which

---

[24] Jacobus Arminius (1560-1609) believed and preached that Christ had died for all
mankind, and that God had woven into his offer of salvation the human response and
freedom. So free will was restored, and each individual can either accept the Gospel
through faith, or reject it through unbelief. The Calvinists were understandably nervous
about this new liberty, considering it a dangerous threat tantamount to heresy against
Christian orthodoxy, and perhaps their suspicions were well founded, given that these
Teifi-side rebels rapidly progressed from Arminianism to Arianism, Socinianism and
beyond that to the ultimate heresy of Unitarianism, where the central tenet was that Christ
was human and human reason the key to salvation. This revolt of the Age of Reason
against dogmatic religiosity reached its peak in the late-eighteenth century and early
nineteenth centuries when its followers included figures like Joseph Priestley, Samuel Taylor
Coleridge, and William Hazlitt. Unitarianism's rejection of predestination, Biblical
infallibity, and Original Sin carries echoes of a long tradition in Christianity that stretches
back to the Irish monk Pelagius, who we met before in this narrative at Bangor Is-coed
and Llanddewi Brefi. I'll leave you to speculate on what it is in Welsh river-water that has
this effect of freeing the riparian believers from the straitening hold of dogma. Something
jettisoned into it during the Operation Julie investigations, perhaps?

does become a lake (hence the name, which translates as "lake of the bowl") when the water's high, but at other times remains a waterlogged field across which flocks of Canada geese graze. The gorge below the bridge at Henllan bears all the hallmarks of a glacial overflow channel, and certainly water from the shrinking ice-sheets that had covered much of West Wales during the early Holocene period had careered down here in awesome quantity and with landscape-sculpting power. Geomorphologists and glaciologists have suggested figures of 2000 square miles of ice-sheet producing 60,000 cubic feet per second of meltwater tearing and grinding its way down this slim and nowadays picturesque channel guarded by an Iron Age promontory fort. The water rushed out into the wide strath below, where it takes one of its periodic rests and dawdles between the present-day settlements of Pentrecagal and Llandyfriog. At the head of this tranquil reach it's joined from the south by an anything-but-restful tributary, the Afon Bargoed, which spills down a long sequence of oakwood valleys to join with the Nant Esgair at the former centre of the Welsh flannel industry in the twinned villages of Drefach and Felindre.

Weaving and farming have a long and in the main sensible association in West Wales. This was sheep country, it had ample water-power to hand, and the mills that still stand on many of the river banks testify to flannel production's former importance in the local economy. *Amgueddfa Genedlaethol Cymru* (the National Museum of Wales) has taken over and restored the former Cambrian Mill in Drefach, which village was known locally as "the Welsh Huddersfield", and its admirably curated displays are now a major tourist attraction here, as well as selling high quality Welsh naturally-dyed woollen yarn. A late girlfriend not long before her death[25] knitted me a long, soft, rainbow scarf in

---

[25] Of a brain haemorrhage – she had talked often before this of the "red threads" that she

delightful shades of sea-green, salmon pink, muted red, purple and electric blue from wool she'd bought here. I still treasure it and occasionally return to Drefach to buy more when it's in need of a stitch in time. The former woollen and flannel industry of Wales of which we're now at the heart was extant as a cottage industry at least from medieval times. We've already seen during our visit to Tregaron how the drovers of West Wales on their forays into England acted as ambassadors and salesmen in selling stockings and the like made by their womenfolk. The frequency of occurrence of the word *pandy* throughout Wales also argues long provenance, albeit at a cottage level, for the industry from an early date. Fulling mills were in operation at Pentrecwrt on the Teifi in 1574, at Rhuddlan Teifi in 1539, Cilgerran below the imposing castle in 1326, and earliest of all at St. Dogmael's on the Teifi estuary where it borders with Pembrokeshire in 1291. When the Industrial Revolution's impact was felt in these West Wales valleys, early in the nineteenth century, hand-weaving by rural labourers working on looms in sheds attached to farms whose proprietors had provided the relatively modest capital investment was already severely in decline. New entrepreneurs, aware of the demand for quality flannel in the South Walian mining, steel and tinplate industries, moved in, threw up new industrial mill premises throughout the region, and the nature of the industry and the communities changed radically.

There was a house-building boom too throughout the region in the last two decades of the nineteenth century. Drive round Drefach, Drefelin, Waungilwen, Pentrecwrt, Cwmhiraeth, Cwmpengraig and you'll see the neat terraces from that time clustering round the social and cultural focus that was and hereabouts in a dwindling way still is the chapel –

---

saw continually. I'm sure there was a connection between these and the tragic event which so suddenly carried her off.

disproportionately large in proportion to the size of the settlement, securely at the interface between agriculture and industry, the networks of paths neatly paved in Cilgerran slate winding their way through jay-screamed woods to which the flycatchers and the redstarts return each spring. These sessile oakwoods along the West Wales river valleys are glorious environments, insect-rich from April onwards, hence the abundant birdlife. I used to love walking the network of paths that threaded through them when I stayed in Cwmpengraig. They thronged with jays – the most colourful and one of the most interesting of the *corvidae*. Is there any more startling British bird-call than that of the jay? Its name in Welsh sums it up: *sgrech y coed* (screech of the woods), though there's far more to this most beautiful of our native crows than its raucous voice of protest, which used to rouse my little terrier Phoebe to paroxysms of indignation and fruitless pursuit. The colour-scheme of jays' plumage – cinnamon and celestial azure – is exquisite, set off to perfection by velvet-black and pure white secondaries, a speckled crest, and the bright blue iris of the eye. This is a gorgeous bird. Its character too is distinctive: "Tireless energy, and a liveliness of disposition and alertness almost without parallel among British birds" is how W.H. Hudson, best of our avian writers, described it. You more often hear it than see it, though. Centuries of persecution by agents of the shooting interest have left this vital, intelligent creature intensely wary of so-called mankind (interestingly, the British birds seem more intensely wary and shy than those in the French Pyrenees where, for health reasons, I've spent a great deal of time over the last fifteen years. I'm inclined to see this as a reflection on particularly English brutality towards our native wildlife, though that's something a true-born English "sportsman", pendulous of belly and broad of backside from over-indulgence in roast beef and Yorkshire pudding, his mind larded with jingoistic sentimentality, would always be at pains to deny). The jay's tireless energy in collecting and hiding acorns in well-hidden caches that the birds themselves at times have difficulty in finding is surely responsible for great tracts of oakwood throughout Britain. It is truly, to adapt the title of Jean Giono's beautiful and redemptive 1953 eco-fable, *"l'oiseau qui plantait des arbres"*. Adaptation has a Darwinian relevance here too. The jay's gullet relative to that of other corvids is enlarged, and copiously supplied with saliva to make regurgitation into the cache easier. In the spring acorns (they can carry up to nine at a time) are off the menu. At that time you'll catch the visionary flash of their dipping flight across the low sun-rays, heading downriver to estuarine fields for worms before returning lapidary in the last westering light to their oak-tree roosts.

Of the human community in these oakwood valleys, workers whose families had been employed for generations in the old hand-loom industry were snapped up by the new factory proprietors, re-equipped and re-skilled, and set to work in a way that was exponentially more productive. This little area of West Wales is quite unique in my experience, possessed of a remarkable community coherence and gentle individuality, located in as damply lovely a location as you'll find anywhere in Britain, dedicated to its music, its eisteddfodau, its long traditions, its communitarianism. I remember an evening some years ago spent watching on the large screen a World Cup semi-final in Felindre's *Tafarn John y Gwas*, when the whole population of the two villages seemed to be crammed into the pub. Naturally they were cheering on any side that wasn't England, whilst the landlord and landlady kept every table supplied with endless free brechdanau sglodion (chip butties) to be washed down with copious draughts of the Reverend James that flowed hoppily and good-humouredly throughout the long and sociable evening. It was the best night I'd spent in a pub in years, and inclined me to think very well of the former community of the Teifi-side flannel industry, the decline of which was set in train by West Yorkshire's canny re-investment after the Great War compared to traditional Cardi tight-fistedness and reluctance around spending money, which meant that it was left languishing as trade to the mining areas ceased in the strike-crippled 1920s, and fashions changed thereafter to ensure it never recovered. But the shells of the great mills still stand as testament to former prosperity and enterprise. Take a look at the huge, dank, desolately overpowering one on the Teifi's south bank at Pont Alltcafan, currently being divided up into echoing apartments for holiday visitors. It's no doubt a better use for it than allowing the former neglect to slide into dereliction, but it sits ill with the industry and imagination that not so very many decades ago held sway alongside our river as it journeys through history.

History is what's on tap in the next important settlement downriver from Henllan – Newcastle Emlyn, which is one of my favourite small Welsh towns. It was the site of the first Welsh printing press in 1718 (the first book printed in Wales followed in 1719), as a slate tablet fastened to the wall by a shop at the Adpar end of the Teifi bridge, placed there by the "Committee of the Happy Winter Evening Entertainments", proudly informs you. Castell Newydd Emlyn even has a castle, the new one of the town's name, which is not one of the usual Longshanks abominations that sustain the Wales Tourist Board, blight and oppress so many Welsh towns with their overpowering colonial presence, and draw American and Japanese tourists annually by the tens of thousands to enrich the – mostly English – investors in the tourist trade. This one in Emlyn is ruinous and small, enclosed within a grand loop of the Teifi (in high flood the river takes a direct line across to the weir, cutting out the meander – you have been warned!) When I lived close by, I used to come here most days to walk my little Parson Russell Terrier Phoebe – a delightful little creature, very timid because she came from a "D'ye ken John Peel"-like breeder, red-faced with long side-whiskers, in Aspatria, who had kept her locked in a cage in a barn until she was three years old because she "wasn't up to show standard" in his view. This despite her grandfather having won "Best of Breed" at Cruft's! Needless to say, in my eyes she was incomparably beautiful as well as sweet of temper, and I doted on her right to the end, when she breathed her last on my knee by the stove at the age of sixteen. Her grandfather had been bred by a dear friend of mine, the great Cumbrian rock-climber Paul Ross, who'd put him to stud now and again. He phoned me up from Colorado one night, asked me if I had another dog yet (my previous Russell, "The Flea", had died six years before at the age of seventeen)? If not, he told me, I should "get my ass up to Cumbria", where there was one waiting for me. It would stop me moping after the deaths within nine months of my two dearest-beloved, he added. He told me to give the breeder £50 for the injections, and to smack him in the teeth for keeping her in those conditions (in the event I did the former but not the latter – not out of fear, but simply because I wanted to get little Phoebe out of there as quickly as possible).

Next day I was on my way. "The more I see of humanity, the more I love my dog." She was my dear and closest companion for thirteen years thereafter and soon became a confident, secure and playful little dog. When she died I was heartbroken, and buried her beneath my bedroom window in a small grave across which sweet-smelling dog violets now grow in profusion. Our walks around the castle at Emlyn in the time we lived in Dyffryn Teifi became a daily habit, the air there seeming less sodden than the valley in which we lived, more healthy. Also, in the course of them Phoebe would meet many of her friends and her social circle. She was still very wary of humans, but loved the company of other dogs. Which is how we came to meet Chelsea Pete. Pete arrived at the castle most afternoons at much the same time as Phoebe and myself. He had two dogs – a Shar Pei (Chinese wrinkly dog), and a Jack Russell. They and Phoebe became immediate friends, and would tear around the bailey in great circles of mutual pursuit until they flopped down panting together for a rest before the next bout of frantic pursuits. Meanwhile Pete and I would chat away inconsequentially as chaps of a certain age will. I learnt that he was a Londoner: that he was called Chelsea Pete because that was the football team he supported ("Never missed a match in twenty-five years!"); that he came from Acton, which I vaguely knew through a dear woman friend of mine, a painter living in Chiswick, whom I visited from time to time despite a lifetime's aversion to London. Pete had moved to West Wales, married a woman, unmarried her on his account because of certain indiscretions on her part, suffered a stroke in his fifties from which he had recovered well, and now lived with his dogs on the outskirts of Emlyn, occasionally venturing out for a pint in the *Pelican*[26], where the beer was well kept. I can vouch for that, and it sold draught Bass which is a delectable rarity over which George Borrow, an aficionado of *cwrw da*, would certainly have enthused at length.

---

[26] The last duel fought in Wales reputedly came about as the result of a pub dispute in either the *Pelican* or the *Salutation* between two Teifi-side "gentlemen" – a unique, numerous and idiosyncratic social order on whose activities an entire literature has been written – on the question of a barmaid's honour. Mr. Heslop defended it, the dastardly Mr. Beynon questioned it, and in the subsequent ritual combat with pistols on 10 September 1811, seeking to steal a march on his opponent Beynon turned early and shot Heslop fatally in the back. He now lies in Llandyfriog churchyard in a simple box tomb inscribed with the epitaph "Alas; Poor Heslop." Alas indeed, but as our present British Prime Minister's behaviour confirms, the English (or Anglo-Welsh, which amounts to the same thing) upper classes have never been ones to play scrupulously by the rules. Another duel claimed as the last in Wales, also over a young lady's honour, was reputedly fought on the riverbank walk of Fortune's Frolic alongside the Cleddau outside Haverfordwest, but this time there was no fatal outcome. However, this took place in 1779, so it proves nothing except perhaps that the inhabitants of the Landsker were more Eirenic than those of Teifi-side with its disputatious squirearchy throughout the period in question.

One afternoon Phoebe and I were walking our usual riparian circuit, Chelsea Pete and his dogs not yet having arrived, when I happened to glance down at a point where the river bank was palisaded with fine alders hung with purple cones and catkins. It was a golden autumn afternoon. I mused on the alder's remarkable qualities: its capacity to fix nitrogen and fertilise the ground through *Frankia* bacteria in its root-nodules; its red sap, once used as dye for those referred to in *Trioedd Ynys Prydein* as "sacred kings and warriors of the alder cult"; its wood, that served a variety of purposes from clog manufacture to the making of whistles. As I looked up into slender branches of the tree's crown that were used for these, a piercing note, more squeak than whistle, came from the bank right by my feet. It was followed by muted huffings and splashings. I looked down, and there, sprawled across roots that stretched into the water, was a bitch otter and her this-year's cub, unaware of my presence, no more than ten feet away so that even in the fading light I could pick out every detail of them: the thick, spiked guard-hair of their coats; the small rounded ears; the luxuriant vibrissae (whiskers) of the broad muzzle by which they sense prey underwater; the streamlined shape and wide rudders; their wonderful strangeness. The bitch extricated herself from the playful grasp of her cub, kicked away from the bank, and with a powerful arch of her back plunged into the deep flow of the river, less polluted here than it was a few agrarian miles up- or down-stream. Hissing strings of bubbles released from her coat rose to mark her progress. Within a minute she was back, a plump roach in her mouth, her cub whickering at her, tearing at it before she'd deposited it on the moss-covered root. The gifts that come, when you move softly within a landscape! I looked round and down the path to see if anyone was coming. In the distance was Chelsea Pete with his dogs. I put my fingers to my lips to warn him to be quiet. Phoebe, however, had pelted off to greet her friends and soon the dogs were chasing round, panting and barking at each other, and the otter and her cub had slipped silently away into deep water. But it still felt to have been a blessed encounter. Afterwards I walked across the bridge, hoping the Riverside Café would be open for afternoon tea and cake on the terrace by the water. It wasn't, so Phoebe and I huddled into the Pelican and shared a pint of Bass (she licked the froth off my finger as I held it out to her). In the twilight we went to watch surging currents from salmon ladders and the mill-race rejoin the river above a rippling reach upstream of the town bridge. What struck me forcefully was the lack of life, for which I didn't know the reason at the time. No birds, no fish leaping.[27]

---

[27] A newspaper report from February 2021 told of the catastrophic decline in freshwater fish numbers. Nearly a third of the estimated world total have gone, and of the remaining population nearly a third are now threatened with extinction. Conservation charities know of 80 species that are now extinct,. Sixteen of those extinctions have come within the last twelve months. Worldwide there are human populations running into millions who are dependent on freshwater fish, not only for food but also as a source of income. Numbers have plummeted through factors that include river and lake pollution, catches that are too large and cannot be sustained, the damming and draining of rivers and wetlands. Of fish that migrate seasonally in shoals, 75% have disappeared in the last half-century, and in that time populations of larger species have fallen by 94%. Entitled "The World's Forgotten Fishes", the report was commissioned by 16 conservation groups, including WWF, the London Zoological Society (ZSL), Global Wildlife Conservation and The Nature Conservancy. Within waters around the United Kingdom, sturgeon and burbot have vanished, salmon are disappearing and the European eel remains critically endangered. According to the WWF, much of the decline is driven by the poor state of rivers, mostly as a result of pollution, dams and sewage. It has called on the government to restore freshwater habitats to good health through proper enforcement of existing laws, strengthening protections in the Environment Bill and championing a strong set of global targets for the recovery of nature.

Dave Tickner, from WWF, said freshwater habitats are some of the most vibrant on earth, but - as this report shows - they are in catastrophic decline around the world. "Nature is in freefall and the UK is no exception: wildlife struggles to survive, let alone thrive, in our polluted waters," said the organisation's chief adviser on freshwater. "If we are to take this government's environmental promises seriously, it must get its act together, clean up our rivers and restore our freshwater habitats to good health."

Carmen Revenga of The Nature Conservancy Council said freshwater fish are a diverse and unique group of species that are not only essential for the healthy functioning of our

Next day I drove to Cenarth and walked upstream to see how those observations were borne out there. Chelsea Pete had told me a horror story from when he'd worked here as a water bailiff in 2004. A young grey seal had swum up from the estuary and arrived in the pool beneath Cenarth's famous bridge. It made itself at home, became a fixture, was popular with visitors who heard of its presence there and inevitably gave it a name, as though it were a pet. "Sammy" fed heartily on the salmon and sea trout then making their way up-river to the spawning grounds beyond Tregaron, and thus adversely affected the anglers and coracle men who are licensed killers of fish on this exclusive stretch of the Teifi, where the fish rest before battling their way up the falls, perhaps using the tail-in-the mouth catapult tactics described by Giraldus in the twelfth century:

> "...the Teifi ... is better stocked with the finest salmon than any other stream in Wales. Near Cilgerran, at a spot called Cenarth Mawr, on the topmost point of a rock which Saint Llawddog hollowed out with his own hands, there is a flourishing fishing station. The waters of the Teifi run ceaselessly over this rock, falling with a mighty roar into the abyss below. Now it is from these depths that the salmon ascend into the concave rock above, which is a remarkable leap, about as far as the height of the tallest spear."

Giraldus goes on to describe how this feat is managed, displaying as he does so something of the imaginative power when it comes to natural history of Pliny the Elder, or even Gilbert White in his "conglobulating swallows" mode by which account Dr. Johnson

---

rivers, lakes and wetlands, but millions of people, particularly the poor, also depend on them for their food and income. "It's now more urgent than ever that we find the collective political will and effective collaboration with private sector, governments, NGOs and communities, to implement nature-based solutions that protect freshwater species, while also ensuring human needs are met," she said. Dr Jeremy Biggs of the Freshwater Habitats Trust, commenting on the report, said that "to protect freshwater biodiversity, we need to consider both large and small waters, and to protect all our freshwaters: ponds, lakes, streams and rivers."

was so taken.

> *"This is how the salmon contrives to leap. When fish of this species swimming, as is natural, against the course of the water – for fish swim upstream, just as birds fly into the wind – come to some apparently insurmountable obstacle, they twist their tails round towards their mouths. Sometimes, in order to give more power to their leap, they go so far as to put their tails right into their mouths. Then, with a great snap, like the sudden straightening of a bough which has long been held bent, they jerk themselves out of this circular position and so leap from the lower pool to the one above, to the great astonishment of anyone who happens to be watching."*

I would certainly be greatly astonished to see that happen, and I've watched Atlantic salmon leaping their way up cataracts in Wales, Ireland, Scotland, Quebec, Gaspé; I've seen Pacific salmon – a marginally different fish that has undergone a longer evolution than the Atlantic species – doing the same in the mountain streams of British Columbia and Vancouver Island. But Giraldus was a man of his time, and Michael Drayton (1563-1631) reinforced his account in the vast and meandering topographical poem *Poly-Olbion* of 1612:

> *"Here, when the laboring fish doth at the foot arrive,*
> *And finds that by his strength but vainly he doth strive,*
> *His tail takes in his teeth: and bending like a bow,*
> *That's to the compass drawn, aloft himself doth throw;*
> *Then springing at his height, as doth a little wand,*
> *That bended end to end", and flerted from the hand,*
> *Far off itself doth cast ...*

To return to our time and the errant seal, a firing squad was assembled locally, and one morning whilst the young grey seal was swimming round the gathering-pool below Cenarth bridge, volleys of shots rang out and the long pool was stained red with the seal's blood (seals have a lot of blood!). I was reminded of one morning at Resolute Bay in the High Arctic when a pod of beluga whales entered the bay after a shoal of fish. The Inuit community, rifles at the ready, took to their boats, rounded them up in the middle of the bay and massacred them, the water once again turning red with the blood of senseless slaughter. Beluga are small white whales described by those Europeans who first recorded them as having gentle, hare-like expressions. By contrast, in my view, as Estragon says in Beckett's *Waiting for Godot*, "People are bloody ignorant apes".

A slippery path heads upstream along the north bank from Cenarth Falls. I took it one June afternoon. Many months before the first frost, even in late spring, perhaps from some reason connected with their roots being in tainted water, the overarching riverbank ash-trees were taking on pale autumn tints that are a prelude to their fall. Even though it was way out of season, the other signs being so misleading I thought to look for ash-keys, that vary so much from year to year. I thought back to my childhood when lime-green bright bunches clustered heavy on each branch, spinning down with the equinoctial gales or hanging as grim, dry, umber swags throughout the winter until late black buds of spring opened into leaf to hide them from view. I like ash-trees: Yggdrasil, the world-tree of Norse mythology; the maypole-tree; the husbandry-tree of folk-craft, its timber springy and strong-jointing; the best clean-cleaving wood wet or dry for scented fires of winter, "fit for a queen to warm herself by", flaking away to fine grey ash. In D.H. Lawrence's novella *St. Mawr*, the Welsh groom Morgan Lewis tells the American Mrs. Witt of how he ate ash-seeds as a child; how they gave the former people of the land ability to hear how the trees felt and lived; and how, in our ill-mannered times when we cut them down without propitiatory ceremony, ash-trees have come to dislike people[28].

Of course I found no ash-keys here; but later, a little way down-stream, I was astonished to encounter one on the river-bank with green clumps of keys weighing down the branches. It glowed in the low sunlight. I plucked a few keys, peeled back the winged seed-case, picked out the slender nuts within. They were gritty and bitter as I'd remembered from childhood, the after-taste long lingering. I thought I would plant them where I often stay in Ariège, in hope that squirrels in future years might play there, owls nest, and blackcaps sing (theirs the purest notes you'll find in all birdsong, finer by far than those of the nightingale). Slithering my way up-river along the slippery slate path, the silence of this part of the river was oppressive. I saw not a single bird to where the path reached a junction with the little road coming down from Cwm Cou, and only one solitary dipper when I turned back from that point to return to the car-park in Cenarth. But what I did see were glaring white tide-lines blanched by agrichemical pollutants along each bank. All was preternaturally quiet. I sang quietly to myself Schubert's setting for Goethe's haunting lyric:

"Über allen Gipfeln
Ist Ruh,
In allen Wipfeln
Spürest Du
Kaum einen Hauch;
Die Vögelein schweigen im Walde.
Warte nur! Balde
Ruhest du auch."

---

[28] Felling trees plays an interesting role in English rural fiction, and one replete with atavistic resonance. As examples, I'm reminded of the Scots pine the felling of which kills Banford in another novella by Lawrence, "The Fox". And in Hardy's richly textured and beautiful novel *The Woodlanders* the fall of the tree growing by the door of old John South's cottage precipitates the novel's tragic dénouement.

('Over all the hill-tops/ is calmness,/On all the tops/You hear scarcely a whisper;/The little birds are silent in the woods./Only wait! Soon/You too will be at peace.")

The wagtails were gone, no birds sang in the woods. A solitary dipper worked the farther bank beneath the chemical tide-mark. The life of the place had departed. When I arrived back at the long pool below the falls, the salmon, *sewin*, and brown trout that once drew anglers and coracle-fishers here raised scarcely a ripple on the river's smooth and dying flow. I thought back to my frail and wizened history teacher in his black gown in my Manchester grammar school sixty years ago, spinning out a sardonic-jocular riff on the names of Manchester's rivers. The Inkwell, the Mudlark, and the Murk was how he referred to the Irwell, the Medlock and the Irk. I knew each of those rivers in my childhood, and the filthy state of them from industrial Lancashire's heavy industry. I thought of Friedrich Engels' description, from his 1845 classic text on *The Condition of the Working Class in England*, of the immigrant Irish communities who lived on the noisome banks of these rivers in conditions of unimaginable degradation and squalor. It would be vastly to overstate the point if I were to attempt to argue an exact equivalence between 1840s Manchester and twenty-first century Ceredigion. Nonetheless, the Teifi is a river that was once bounteous and thriving, and which is now showing the early signs of moribundity, of serious ill-effects on the wildlife it once so abundantly sustained. Who's to blame? Agri-industry, agrochemicals, a vile government that refuses to enforce European community environmental measures and has deliberately taken Britain away from their close scrutiny? The apathy of the electorate, that believes false news, lies, deceitful promises? The clock is being turned stealthily back, by people who will personally profit from that retrograde direction. From the top deck of the bus home from school every day, I peered down over a bridge parapet into a scene Engels, a hundred and fifteen years earlier, had described thus:

> *"The view from this bridge, mercifully concealed from mortals of small stature by a parapet as high as a man, is characteristic for the whole district. At the bottom flows, or rather stagnates, the Irk, a narrow, coal-black, foul-smelling stream, full of debris and refuse which it deposits on the shallower right bank. In dry weather a long string of the most disgusting, blackish-green slime pools are left standing on this bank, from the depths of which bubbles of miasmatic gas constantly arise and give forth a stench unendurable even on the bridge forty or fifty feet above the surface of the stream. But besides this, the stream itself is checked every few paces by high weirs, behind which slime and refuse accumulate and rot in thick masses. Above the bridge are tanneries, bone-mills and gas-works, from which drains and refuse find their way into the Irk, which receives further the contents of all the neighbouring sewers and privies. It may easily be imagined, therefore, what sort of residue the stream deposits..."*

Of course this is not comparable to the present day along the Teifi (apart from the 2016 incident below Tregaron): but – "freed" from EEC constraints, having "got Brexit done" – we are inching back in that direction instead of towards a cleaner, less polluted, more wildlife-friendly future. Once a negative trend has been set in motion, it is very difficult to reverse. Take a look around the farm drain outlets, or those from the abattoirs at Tregaron or Llanybydder. These are the reverse coinage of natural beauty and the picturesque. Count the number of sewage processing plants between Pontrhydfendigaid and Aberteifi (the huge one in the latter town is just up-river from the otter sanctuary, so-called). Not long ago I stood at the head of the Teifi gorge a little way west of Cilgerran castle. The scene in front of me, if you neglected to look too closely, seemed as beautiful as when I'd first seen it many years before. I'd even heard of it years before that, when I'd accompanied a Welsh girlfriend from Cilgerran who was resident in London at the time, reluctantly and on her request, to a production of *Under Milk Wood* (at the name of which I always involuntarily flinch, and remember David Holbrook's terse summary of it as "the apotheosis of every suburban vice") at the gorgeously ornate Lyric Theatre in Hammersmith. In the pub afterwards she'd talked rhapsodically of the beauty of the Cilgerran gorge, which I'd never seen at the time other than in Turner's dramatic 1798 sketch of Cilgerran Castle during an exhibition at the Tate. She'd described its swift deep water that was so clear you could peer down to infinite depth, the tree-lined sides, the clean flooding rush of it. I envisaged pristine splendour and purity. My contemporary experience is that the river here flows darkly down past a long succession of abandoned quarries, the spoil from which was dumped in the river, raising the level of its bed, making it much more shallow and narrow, and causing water to back up and create regular flooding across all the fields above Llechryd bridge. Standing in the small riverside car park just downstream of the confluence with the Afon Plysgog , and watching the Teifi flood down into Cilgerran gorge, its depths brown and turbid with slurry run-off on its last inland reach before the saltings around Cardigan, I'm oddly reminded of the prelude to the famous diner scene in Bob Rafelson's disturbing 1970 masterpiece, *Five Easy Pieces*, where the hitch-hiker Palm Apodaca, to whom the Jack Nicholson character Bobby Dupea has just given a lift, launches from the back seat into an intensely scatological attack on all aspects of American culture. Chance observers of the Teifi, formerly one of the great and celebrated salmon rivers of Wales, might be tempted to the same vehemence.

To lift my thoughts, I can tell you of two much more positive experiences. In the first I was below the mouth of the gorge among woods already dappled with autumn's palette, but before the fire-tones had set in. Squirrels dipped and scurried for nuts among hazel foliage. A solitary leaf drifted downwards, presage of pattering quiet tumult through coming weeks. From the riverside path, suddenly I glimpsed a flash of brilliant white, focused my glass in time to see a drake goosander arrowing upriver, low above the surface, its chuckling call carrying through still air, its large wing-patches startlingly white against cloud-reflecting water: *"So arrogantly pure, a child might think/It can be murdered with a spot of ink"* (Yeats). Though, to revert to the negative mood, this gorgeous, visionary bird's demise is more likely to come about by government decree, the Welsh Senedd having granted a limited number of licenses to shoot them on Welsh rivers because of insufficiently researched concerns among the fishing interest regarding their possible predation on salmon and trout. These government culls on behalf of interest groups have always made me uneasy. Forty years ago Bill Condry wrote in *The Guardian* on the shooting of thousands of oystercatchers in Burry Inlet by Llanelli to protect the cockle industry, declining at the time through over-fishing and effluent discharge from nearby tinplate factories. But the oystercatchers took the blame, so out came the guns as they always will at the least pretext under a Tory government. Consider the more recent Tory onslaughts on badgers. The Burry cull proved useless because oystercatchers from surrounding areas quickly moved in to make good the losses. On goosanders, they used to be a rarity on Welsh rivers. Thirty years ago sightings were notable. In the early 1980s that fine naturalist Hilda Murrell – herself an honest, doomed irritant to government, abducted, assaulted, and left half-naked in a wintry field outside Shrewsbury to die, probably on a nod and a wink from some lowly government official because of her educated and incisive opposition to the construction of Sizewell B nuclear power station – recorded one with delight on the wooded lower reaches of Afon Tanat before its confluence with Afon Efyrnwy by Llanymynech. My glimpses of these spectacular, shy, tree-hole-nesting ducks have grown more frequent in recent years. One flew directly over Mark Cocker and myself on the Dwyryd estuary within the last five years. May that hopeful trend continue, and authority pay heed to Aldo Leopold's heartfelt plea: "Let wildlife manage wildlife." And not the wealthy angling interest (the demotic element among anglers will know who they are). Perhaps the goosander is safer in the last place where I saw one, and that at very close quarters? I'd taken a walk from Llanfairfechan's sea-front along the path heading west and looking out onto Traeth Lafan's wide expanse of sand. It's a landscape that draws you in, like the Elenydd moors of mid-Wales, or like the high Arctic, through its abstraction. Nothing's solid here; all's sketched and coloured in shifting tones of water and light. Even history has become ambiguous, uncertain. These are drowned lands, their legends tide-steeped, wind-honed. I come here frequently for the birds, to which the fluid landscape accords a peculiar gift of subtle concealment. Its bas-relief undulations, its distances, absorb and hide. What on first glance appears empty, on closer scrutiny teems with life. Though on the grey and turbulent day and a flooding tide when this sighting took place, little stirred. A couple of oystercatchers, disproportionately heavy-billed, sped past. A little egret lifted out of a filling channel and braved the buffets as it headed back towards the heronry in the trees above the old salt-water swimming pool at Penrhyn Point that it shares with its cousins the grey herons.

In the stand of Scots pine at the westernmost end of Llanfairfechan promenade, ravens discoursed, sheared down to the water's edge, soared aloft with shellfish in their bills to drop them from a height on the concrete sea-wall before folding their wings and swooping down to pick out the morsel of flesh. I returned, rain at my back, to the boating lake by the car-park where the boys of summer circled their battery-powered, radio-controlled craft. The usual cackling gaggle of mallard chased after white and mouldering crusts dispensed to them from strollers' bags. A glorious presence suddenly surfaced – a drake goosander, low in the water, bobbing on small waves. This element in nature of surprise, of the unusual, so enchants. He was 20 feet away. I circled round and caught in a glimmer of wan sunlight the subtle pink infusion of brilliantly white plumage, amused myself with making up *Farrow & Ball* tags for it, and for the slicked-back, bottle-green, teddy-boy mane, before suddenly, with an arch of his long neck, in a quick spasm he dived again into that shallow water and was gone.

The second positive experience took place a little farther down-river from Cilgerran Gorge, and alongside the well-appointed hide on the river-bank just up-river from Cardigan. For three or four weeks one spring I'd been watching the gullery upstream of Cardigan as it changed from being virtually deserted to thronging with life. It's on a long sandbank where the Teifi curves west before twisting and roiling past old wharves to make its last seaward dash. Settled into the grass of Rosehill Marsh with telescope and tripod, my particular focus had been on the Lesser black-backed gull (*Larus fuscus*) and its slightly larger near-relative the Silvermew. (*Larus argentatus* is usually referred to as the Herring gull. I much prefer the older, more poetic name, which is a direct translation of the Linnaean.) I've spent hours watching the ritualized courtship, the aggressive tussles, the beak-wrestlings and displays of the males, the incessant territorial disputes here at this season for years. I call my area of study a sandbank. Of late, however, it's seen a steady greening, a binding web of vegetation, increased alluvial deposit. It's received flotsam from the tidal seethe of the river and its propensity for periodic flooding. Here crates, cartons, plastic containers – desirable bird-shelters! – have come to rest. Together with spreading vegetation and access to open sea two miles downstream, they've made this fluvial feature a thriving breeding site for the Laridae (gulls, as well as terns and skimmers) – one of my favourite bird families.

"Yr wylan deg ar lanw, dioer,/Unlliw ag eiry neu wenlloer" (The fine gull on a warm tide-flow,/One colour with snow and white moon), wrote Dafydd ap Gwilym – Chaucer's early contemporary, peerless among medieval Welsh lyricists. Gulls are majestic birds. Dafydd's description best applies to Ivory gulls, occasional visitors from the High Arctic to Wales. Identification not only of species but also of generations between these large, white-headed gulls, particularly since recent taxonomic revisions, is a notorious area of ornithological difficulty. As with train-spotters in a different era, appearance of a rarity causes great excitement among watchers at harbours or refuse-tips. My favourite gull probably is *Larus fuscus*: for the male's skirlingly resonant calls, his buoyant flight, meticulous courtship rituals; and the female's soft croonings as they beg for food. On their longevity, W.H. Hudson, most observant of our great bird-writers, thought they may live for a century, though that was surely surmise on his part. Perhaps they do, but I can find no research that establishes the accuracy of his observation[29]. On another morning, on the riverside path and bound again for the hide in the Teifi Marshes reserve, I leant

against a fence and a Cormorant arrowed into view, threw up its broad, webbed feet to brake, and touched down on the water. Seeing it reminded me of a spring morning twenty-five years ago in the wheelhouse of a fishing boat as she careened into Roonagh

---

[29] Through ringing, Ronald Lockley, one-time warden of the nature reserve island of Skokholm off the Pembrokeshire coast, did establish a likely life-span for the storm petrel that parallels the human.

Quay, County Mayo, on green combers that were the aftermath of an Easter storm. A cormorant had kept us close, wave-skimming company. I asked the skipper, Jack Heanüe, what the folk of Inishturk – an English-speaking island – called these weirdly beautiful and atmospheric birds?

"We do call her the old hag of the sea. They say she brings bad luck, but I don't think so. She shows us where the fish are, and only takes the little ones for herself. I like to see them…"

Here on the Teifi I thought of Jack – his watchful blue eyes, his powerful hands on the wheel, his measured, generous talk – as I focused my glass on the cormorant. I'd trust his testimony over any *Natural Resources Wales* wielder of rubber stamps or caster of blind eye over agricultural polluting iniquities. Lovely bronze scalings of its plumage were prominent against an overall black, that sunlight shimmered into green and purple iridescence. The whole rich palette was set off by a startling yellow mandible-patch. Sinister they may be to some, particularly when standing on rocks with wings held out to dry – a pose that always brings to mind Milton's description of Satan from Paradise Lost: *"…up he flew; and on the Tree of Life … Sat like a cormorant … devising death"*. But they fascinate me.

These days it's humanity again that devises death for cormorants. The Welsh government in its wisdom also issues licenses to shoot these birds as well as goosanders on the country's rivers. As I watched, the cormorant drew back its long neck and with a serpentine spasm slipped under the surface. *Bilidowcar* he's called in Welsh – Billy the Ducker, which is so descriptively apt. After thirty seconds he re-surfaced holding a dab perhaps eight inches across, which after some effort he bolted down. "Not exactly little, Jack!" I thought with a smile. Though perhaps it was by west-of-Ireland standards.

Like the river, I'll skirt round Cardigan Town. I spent a few months here in a light apartment with large windows looking on to the river and close to the paddle-board centre where in 2018 a little girl, two-year-old daughter of the proprietors, tragically drowned in a car parked on the slipway which rolled down into the river. No-one noticed it was in the river at first because of the murky water. It was reported stolen. As the tide ebbed what had happened became apparent, and the body of the little girl was recovered – agonizing for all concerned. How does a parent ever recover from a moment like that?

> *"I do not know much about gods; but I think that the river*
> *Is a strong, brown god – sullen, untamed and intractable,*
> *Patient to some degree, at first recognized as a frontier;*
> *Useful, untrustworthy, as a conveyor of commerce;*
> *Then only as a problem confronting the builder of bridges.*
> *The problem once solved, the brown god is almost forgotten*
> *By the dwellers in cities – ever, however, implacable,*
> *Keeping his seasons and rages, destroyer, reminder*
> *Of what men choose to forget. Unhonoured, unpropitiated*
> *By worshippers of the machine, but waiting, watching and waiting.*
> *His rhythm was present in the nursery bedroom...*"[30]

His rhythm seized upon a chance moment of insufficient attentiveness. To chime with Eliot, the river plucked this child from her life centred around a safe nursery at Cylch Meithrin Drefach Felindre, and left her parents to endless grief and loss. A strong brown god indeed, hiding his sacrifice within turbid water. Primitive people knew and respected the power of rivers. Others, less wary, are taken by surprise and left desolate. Take this harsh lesson to heart and be forever on guard. As the mute swans were, who arrived on the river across from my apartment with a bell-

---

[30] T.S. Eliot, "The Dry Salvages", from *Four Quartets* (1943), T.S. Eliot's profound meditations on the relationship between time, eternity and the divine.

beat of wings in a grey dawn in early March, 2017. The pair touched down in Afon Teifi's tidal reaches just upstream of Cardigan town bridge, right across from the slipway where young Kiara Moore was to drown a year later. On wind-ruffled waters they kept proximity with each other, gliding around in search of food, accompanied at a respectful distance by small flocks of teal and unruly gangs of mallard drakes. I could lie in my bed dawdling over breakfast and watching through a glass the swans' courtship. The old shipwright from the small boatyard on the opposite bank, last of his kind on the Teifi where once there were many like him, ventured out of his workshop most days to sit on the slipway and talk to the swans. He fed them by hand, so calm was his presence. They responded with sonorous high grunts that belied their name. Occasionally the huge cob, neck outstretched, tore off downriver, wings flailing, to warn off some presumptuous intruder. This was his territory, and no other's. By April, closeness between cob and more delicate pen became pronounced. Long mutual grooming sessions took place on the slipway. Their necks intertwined as they drifted on flooding tides. Around the middle of the month the pen disappeared. The cob held to his stretch of the water, looking muddier and more dishevelled as weeks passed. I kept watch, noted the inaccessible region of nearby Rosehill marsh to which he gravitated each day, presumed the nest-site would be there among the reeds, hoped the otters that also visit this reach of the river from time to time would stay well clear, and the rats too, which are ubiquitous, endearing to watch, but always on the look-out for food.

In the first week of June, scanning upriver at dawn, I saw cob and pen paddling in golden light. Between the two of them was a single, black-billed ball of grey down. Over the next weeks, constantly looking for the cygnet's presence, I was fretful as a parent. One cold day they coasted along shallows at the farther bank, the cygnet nowhere to be seen. I focused the glass. There, between the pen's folded wings, a tiny dark head peered out. Normally there are four or more to a brood. Did otters take the others? Did rats have the eggs? Have the frequent agro-chemical poisonings of this once pure river, have agri-industry's "accidental" slurry discharges into it, or the toxic black sludge from Tregaron, taken a toll on swan fertility? I don't know. I suspect they have. Research needs to be done. As Arturo Gramsci[31] wrote in his *Prison Notebooks*, *"We need to turn violently and face things as they really are."* One crucial and unbearable aspect of "things as they really are" is the extent to which a river like the Teifi has been polluted by the practices of profit-and-growth incentivised agricultural and agro-chemical industries over many decades now – a process of which we are only beginning to see the effects and realize the harm that has been done to nature by our heedlessness and greed.

For the moment, how precious is this little, single scrap of avian life that I watched over every day for months with the utmost attention, every day with my heart in my mouth! For me, it stood as a symbol, occupying a place somewhere between hope and despair, forever resonating with the grief I felt for my own son and the cosmic despair to which I had been insufficiently attuned when he returned from working in India, where capitalism's grandiose growth projects were destroying nature and paying scant heed to the needs of those employed in their construction. And I was too immersed at the time in writing a difficult book, took my eye off the ball, neglected to pay the sufficient attention that would have discerned how far his spirits had sunk. Don't take your mind's or your physical eye off your children for a moment when they are

---

[31] Antonio Gramsci (1891-1937) was one of the most lucid and influential twentieth century Italian political thinkers. His critique of the malignant effect of bourgeois cultural hegemony seems to me more than ever necessary and apposite in an era of politicians as narcissistic, tawdry and devoid of conscience as Trump and Johnson.

vulnerable (they are always vulnerable!) is the lesson to be taken from all this. Don't let those who are destroying the formerly proliferating wildlife of the Afon Teifi, or condoning and enabling that destruction, get away with it. What kind of a world do we want to leave to our children if they survive into it? A desolate, chemically-tidelined, turbid one, or a cleaner, safer, thriving and thronging one? *Silent Spring*[32] is still a real threat hanging over us. One cygnet where there ought to have been four or five? Nervous parents ever attentive? We have so much to learn.

I'll not linger long in Cardigan, though I'm fond of the place. In its old quarter, behind Finch Square, along the streets leading to St. Mary's church and the site of the priory, or the back lanes by the river, it still retains something of the atmosphere of a tight-knit, brawling little port where barges carrying stone from the Cilgerran gorge quarries moored along the quays and transferred their cargoes to the brigs and sloops plying their trade across to Ireland, up to Liverpool and Chester, or around the dangerous coasts of Pembrokeshire to Swansea, Barnstaple, Bristol. Walk down Quay Street or along the Mwldan late on a winter's night with a spring tide running against a river in spate and flooding the car-park at its foot, with banks of mist lacing the void where the river lies, and you can feel the presences, hear the drunken shouts of the seamen, the slap of wave against hull, the sharp cat-calls of the prostitutes. Walk across the town bridge by the castle with its sentinel bronze statue of an otter in upright stance when the tide's flooding or ebbing, and the turmoil and eddying swirl of the water beneath is a truly frightening thing. Then turn right

---

[32] Rachel Carson's 1962 environmental classic of this title is as relevant and radically important today as it was on its publication 59 years ago, when it drew attention to the dangers of pesticides and their myriad deleterious effects on wildlife. The current debate on neonicotinoids and the continuing licensing of them despite their link to momentous decline in bee populations seems to indicate that corporate capitalism still holds the whip hand in controlling environmental legislation in Europe and America.

by the Eagle – another pub painted in that overpowering local tone of orange-yellow that has me wondering if there's a code at work here or simply an available cheap job-lot of otherwise unsaleable paint – and take the road for St. Dogmael's. Within a mile and with the river down to your right, its bank difficult of access and given over to well-kept allotments, you arrive in the last of the Teifi-side settlements. It's a thoroughly charming place, the start of the Pembrokeshire Long Distance Coastal Footpath. It's laned and alleywayed and architecturally of a characterful homogeneity – the sort of place to which old sea-captains might retire to sit outside friendly pubs over their pipes and pints and look out across a final widening of the river called The Netpool to study the antics of the coracle men who used to fish for salmon here in considerable numbers, and now do so hardly at all. It has an attractive ruined abbey rich in detail and history, and two or three decent pubs (*The Netpool Inn*, by a green near the river, is my favourite among them and has the best beer).

If you turn sharp right at the end of the high street, another mile takes you to Poppit Sands, which has a youth hostel and a café of sorts, a huge car park at the official start of the coastal path, an impressive expanse of sand dunes, and is dog-walkers' capital of Ceredigion, for the freedom to pelt around at great speed and plunge in and out of the water in total safety that those sands confer. It's a place of which I'm very fond. Along the dune-path, sloes and haws at their proper seasons hang from thorn thickets. Late flowers grow in profusion: bladder campion, herb Robert, guelder rose, colonies of evening primrose, michaelmas daisies, clotted blooms of faded meadowsweet, rustling dry spikes of ladies' tresses. By stepping stones marking the change of spring-fed stream to saltwater rhine, a kingfisher might burst from the phragmites to whirr low above the water, its flash of orange and azure in brilliant contrast to mud banks between which a little egret, infinitely graceful of form, stalks on yellow feet and stabs down with dark dagger beak. Skeins of geese, calling plangently, wheel high overhead before gliding down to pools upriver of perilous Cardigan Bar: Barnacle geese, Canada geese; Greenland white-fronts down from the cold north to over-winter here. They have to run the gauntlet of "sportsmen", their blued barrels loaded with deadly ejaculate, against whom the Welsh government – its environmental record a perpetual disgrace to this small and beautiful country – affords these declining and lovely water-fowl scant protection. Small fishing boats that had spent the day pulling pots in the lee of Cardigan Island bob through the surf and run for home on the flood, keeping close to the northern shore before heeling round to shelter behind the mole. *"Such a tide as moving seems asleep"* whispers across the sands. The whole wide estuary, sunset and evening star-reflecting, shimmers like creased satin. Sweet rattle of a curlew rises from the shoreline, pitched up to descant against the distant roar of bay-rimming white waves. Dowdily adolescent cygnets congregate in little groups, whistle strangely to each other, dawdle far in the wake of their pristine parents. More geese take flight. Brutal echo of a single shot rings out upstream. Some father, maybe, initiating a son into murderous mysteries of his wildfowling craft (I doubt many mothers pass this on to their daughters)? Why, I wonder, must the brutish kill creatures that others love? Is Franciscan mercy no more than *"the lost traveller's dream under the hill"* of Blake's last poem? When the halcyon mood is lost, in a brown study that often comes upon me in this place, I generally turn for home. Though at other times, on ebbing or flowing tides, the muddy rhine that curves behind the dunes can grip me with its fascinating allure. That's at those seasons when the estuary throngs with geese. Plangent calls tug at your emotions as they pass in vee-formations overhead.

Occasionally – all too seldom nowadays – as accompaniment a curlew's bubbling call pitches to crescendo then cascades down, the massed choirs of thousands a thing of the past. What memory might the few survivors hold of legions so drastically dwindled away? I harbour a strong belief in the intelligent connection between living creatures, have seen it manifest time and again in the natural world. It gives rise to some odd liaisons and intriguing behaviour. This draining rhine, for example, often as not is fishing place for a solitary little egret – a bird that, if collective avian memory does exist, would know something about declining populations. It might be a better symbol for the RSPB than the avocet[33], for it was awareness of the little egret's fate in Britain, driven to extinction on the altar of female fashion at the end of the nineteenth century, which brought that organization into being. Now they have made a heartening British comeback, often to be seen sharing heronries with their larger relative, the grey heron, but the elegant sentinel of this muddy tidal creek is usually solitary. Or at least, unaccompanied by his own kind. Often I've encountered him fishing here with an oystercatcher or redshank for company, the pair of them mincing through the shallow stream, watching acutely, spearing for small fish and crustaceans. On another day of cold, louring drizzle when only the mud gleamed, suddenly out of the bed of phragmites upstream darted a whirring swift vision in lapis lazuli and Indian orange. It dipped

---

[33] I have only seen an avocet once. I was sitting on the bank of the gravelly stream that winds its way through Tapovan, the sublime alp high above where the Ganga roars out of ice-caves in the snout of the Gangotri glacier at Gaumukh – a place of great power and significance in Hindu cosmogony – lazing my way through a rest day after attempts to climb Shivling, perhaps the world's most beautiful mountain, when an avocet stalked past along the sand flats of the stream on coppery-blue legs, upturned bill probing, pied plumage gleaming in the fierce clarity of sunlight at altitude. It felt to be a visionary moment. I recited R.D. Laing's acid illumination as prayer to her: *"I have seen the bird of paradise. She has spread her wings before me and I shall never be the same again. There is nothing to be afraid of. Nothing. The life that I am trying to grasp is the me that is trying to grasp it."* The implicit lesson here is perhaps to stop grasping and accept the gifts as they come to you?

between egret and redshank, came up with a small fish in its beak, sped back whence it came. The first-comers glanced significantly at each other and stalked over to the pool from which the kingfisher snatched its prey. A reed bunting clung to an adjacent reed stem and watched as the halcyon bird gulped its stickleback or minnow down. Another gift, but only for those who move quietly, watch patiently…

Afterwards, the tide ebbing, I walked far out on the sands and along the slender sand-spit that's Cardigan bar, to where the narrow navigable channel scours the eastern bank below Gwbert. Through its fast flow the salmon — formerly in huge numbers but these are now sadly declined — swim this way at spawning time into the river where they had hatched out from eggs laid and fertilized in the redds – the gravel beds at the river's head – perhaps as much as four or five years beforehand. They're returning from their North Sea feeding grounds at the interface between cold arctic and warm Gulf Stream waters, where krill and the fish that feed on them are plentiful. In that environment the salmon and sea-trout post-smolts quickly increase their size and weight, the colour of their skin and of their flesh changing, until their developing brains tune in to the recall that will take them back to their childhood land. How do they locate it? How do they retrace the stages, the sequences, the smells they first encountered just post smolt-hood?

"Now sometimes a fish fails to find its way to its parent river because it has lost the guiding currents of familiar fresh water, spreading root-like into the sea. When Salar came in from the Atlantic feeding banks the rivers of that coast were low, for little rain had fallen since the New Year. Owing to raids of seals he had left prematurely the meeting place of currents in the Island Race, and now he was travelling in a bay where the freshwater layers gave no memory-pressures to his brain. He swam on without direction, followed by the school of young salmon

*which was making for the coast. The grilse were in familiar water, for
here as smolts they had travelled during the year before.*[34]

Williamson was working from intuition and close observation in
1935. Since that date, detailed research unavailable during his
lifetime has made some very significant and fascinating discoveries
in the areas not just of how fish, but also birds navigate across
immense and often featureless distances of ocean and desert.
Much of the work in this area has been done by marine biologists
at the Atlantic Salmon Trust's research station at Redgorton near
Perth, Scotland, in conjunction with research establishments in
other countries. It has been fascinating and persuasive, radically
changing our perceptions about the levels of sophistication
attained by some of our fellow inhabitants of this planet.

These scientists have made important discoveries about the
physiology that enables fish to navigate accurately back to their
native rivers. In the lateral line (a skin-covered groove along each
side of salmon, sea trout and some other fish), they have identified
within nerve cells minute particles of magnetite, the function of

---

[34] From *Salar the Salmon* (1935) by Henry Williamson – a book I prefer for its scrupulous
quality of close observation and marvellously evocative writing to his earlier, remarkable
Tarka the Otter (1927), which established Williamson's reputation but in its harsh tenor was
as much war book by proxy as portrait drawn from nature - a book in which he worked
through affect of his Great War experience (he enlisted in 1914 and was a soldier right
through to the war's end). I have an immense regard for this uniquely gifted and prolific
writer, endlessly calumniated for his misguided friendship with the English fascist leader
Oswald Mosley and his attendance at Hitler's 1936 Nuremburg Rally. The key to
Williamson's naivety here is his presence at the 1914 Christmas Day Truce, and the
camaraderie when British and German soldiers fraternised freely between the trenches,
exchanged gifts, sang carols, until being ordered back at gunpoint behind their own lines
by an officer class whose interests the war served far more clearly than those of the ordinary
soldier. We're back with Gramsci here, and the perils of bourgeois hegemony. Williamson
was without question one of the finest exponents in the great tradition of nature writing
in English, and Salar, whose author did not have access to the most modern research into
the life-cycle of the Atlantic salmon, is certainly one of our great nature-classics, and easier
to take somehow, less brutal, than Tarka. (A grilse is a salmon returned to its native river
after a year at sea.)

which seems to be similar to that of a built-in compass to guide the fish home. They have also suggested a process called "sequential olfactory imprinting" that directs returning young fish to their home rivers, and enables adult fish to locate for their own spawning purposes the exact locations in which they hatched from eggs. The surmise of scientists at the research base is that a central nervous system stimulated in infancy, through imprinting at that time, can – probably hormonally – be re-triggered to re-play in reverse the scenes and scents of that first dangerous trip downriver to the sea, and those instinctive snapshots are what bring the sexually mature adults back to the redding grounds. I find this an astonishing piece of research, highly persuasive as explanation for a mystery that has puzzled naturalists for many years. And it brings with it a further specific and contemporary concern. If this was the stage of natural evolution during environmental conditions of far greater purity than obtain contemporaneously, then does the present degree of pollution in, for example, the Teifi – at one time one of the great salmon rivers of Britain – have a savagely deleterious effect on these sophisticated sense-mechanisms of the returning adults? Do they, to put it crudely, take one sniff at the disemboguement (that Borrovian word again!) of the Teifi as it floods out of its narrow channel through Cardigan Bar and think "This doesn't smell right – it's all chemicals and cow-poo here. Let's try another one." Is this a partial explanation for the fact that British wild salmon are in crisis, with a decline of 70% in just 25 years? I'm no scientist, and I wish I knew. But it certainly makes sense to me that on a river so palpably polluted as the Teifi is now, with mass deaths of fish a regular phenomenon because of deteriorated water condition consequent on poor agricultural practice, the maintenance of natural fish stock is going to be a matter of the gravest concern.

Now, let me take you to the island, and a more innocent time for nature-study in Wales. It's a scrap of land set across a narrow, deep channel from the north-eastern cape of the Teifi estuary and it's called, aptly enough, Cardigan Island. It's uninhabited by humans. There was thought to be no fresh water on it. The salmon streaming down from sub-Arctic waters have to pick up on the scent of the Teifi in the narrow tide-race between it and the mainland, where the local fishermen know of their teeming presence. Bill Condry persuaded the skipper of a local fishing boat to land him here on a sun-filled afternoon in July 1961, so that he might spend a night alone on the island. Here's his account of the experience, which captures not only the place itself in precisely evoked detail, but also the benign character and presence of one of the finest-ever writers on nature and landscape in Wales – a Cymric Desert Father of great wisdom and equanimity:

"I landed on Cardigan Island amid a clangour of anxious, aggressive herring gulls that swooped at me to protect their young ones crouching in the scurvy-grass along the cliff-top. The sea was calm. The boat had swayed in the tide-race, but it slid smoothly in between the rocks of the island's landing creek and let me jump out with my tent and my rucksack. Then it backed out gently, turned its bows towards the mainland, and in a minute was gone round the point, leaving me alone to explore the island."

Bill goes exploring, and he finds, significantly, not only traces of former human habitation, which he had suspected there would be, but also, with gratitude, a spring of fresh water. Then, after these two gifts, comes an unpleasant shock. His observant eye picks up on the fact that he will have to share his night on a desert island with company most people might think undesirable.

...there were rat-holes, dozens of them, round the cliff-tops wherever there was soft earth for burrowing, enough to chill any hope of finding puffins or shearwaters breeding there, for it is particularly those birds

that nest in holes that are preyed on by rats. How, I wonder, did the dreadful brown rats get on to this otherwise delectable island? Could they have swum across from the mainland, attracted by the smell of the island's bird cliffs? For at the lowest tides the channel narrows from 200 yards to less than half that distance. If you doubt that rats are so enterprising you may prefer the shipwreck theory, in support of which I can offer you the 6,500-ton liner Herefordshire, *which was being towed from the Dart to the breakers' yard in the Clyde. She tore adrift from her tugs in heavy seas on 15th March, 1934, and was deposited by a north-west gale on to the north-west corner of the island … where she lies to this day in no great depth of water.*

Always some flaw in the paradise place! Rats on Cardigan Island (how they must have appreciated Bill's sandwiches! As no doubt the silvermews appreciated the rat-nibbled pieces he would have torn off and thrown to them!) Bill's masterful account of the natural life of Cardigan Island is enticing enough to make me seek a commemorative bivouac there and compare notes. I had a very moving experience, not long after his death, in County Mayo. I was descending from the western gable of the Sheeffry Hills down a steep gully with fascinating flora to the shores of the Doo Lough. During the whole of a tricky and complex descent through shaley cliffs I strongly felt his presence there, drawing my attention to and commenting on particularly the ferns. It was as though he were whispering in my ear, the soft Brummagem tones, unchanged even after a lifetime living in Wales, directing my attention to, for example, a vigorous growth of hay-scented buckler fern. These psychogenic episodes, so convincingly real as you experience them, are surely convincing evidence at one level of life *post mortem*? Back to Cardigan Island:

Besides gulls there were shags and a few cormorants and oystercatchers nesting; a fulmar flew close round the island; six kittiwakes stood on the north cliffs, five adults and a young one. I saw gannets, razorbills and guillemots off-shore. Three kinds of birds sang: skylark, rock pipit and meadow pipit. The crow tribe was well represented: dozens of jackdaws and a pair each of ravens, carrion crows and choughs. Earlier this century puffins used to nest on the island, but as from some other Welsh islands they have now gone. (Enter rats, exit puffins?) I lay awake till after midnight and woke several times before dawn hoping to hear night birds such as owls or shearwaters, but there were none. The other living creatures were a mixed bag. There were a few grasshoppers, woodlice and ladybirds. I saw three kinds of butterfly: meadow brown, small copper and grayling; and there were six-spot burnet moths …. Finally there were the sheep: 21 small, nearly black, horned sheep called Soays, a primitive breed said to date back to the Vikings. The flock on Cardigan Island was put there a few years ago by the West Wales Field Society. Soays may be the nearest we have to true wild sheep in north Europe and wild their behaviour remains.

Soay sheep are certainly delightful little animals. Two places in Wales where you find them are Ynys Llanddwyn on the west coast of Sir Fôn, where the colony has also been established by a naturalists' trust, and in Llanymynech quarry south of Oswestry, where I once saw, at sunset, a huge and broken cliff face lit up at sunset as their topaz eyes caught the rays of the declining sun.

So there was one animal of distinction – this fine-horned, ibex-like primitive sheep grazing on what are perhaps the fields of primitive man. For birds of distinction I would choose the choughs whose cheerful voices woke me soon after dawn. A plant of distinction? Yes, I think two: first the vernal squills[35] that must have been a sheet of blue in May and which had now gone to seed. For my second plant I

---

[35] All the offshore islands of West Wales and most of that coast's headlands are good places to experience the ethereal drifts of blue produced by spring squills – an important plant to herbalists. Lovers of Dr. Johnson will remember his use of vinegar of squills as a treatment for dropsy in his declining years.

would choose the tree mallow, a splendid species that belongs so much to the islands, even the isolated stacks, of our rocky western coasts and is often, as on Cardigan Island, the only plant that gets anywhere near to being a tree, growing tall and rather woody and producing large leaves and big pink flowers in defiance of all the salt sea-winds that blow.

The topic of favourite bivouacs often came up in conversations between Bill and myself. In his delectable Gregynog Press anthology, *The Mountains of Wales*, Ioan Bowen Rees includes the account over which he and I often enthused together from Bill's *New Naturalist* volume on the Snowdonia National Park of bivouacking on Moel Hebog that's certainly one of my favourite pieces of writing on Welsh hills. It locates not far above the farm of Cwrt Isaf with which you'll make an acquaintance in the *Envoi*. Meanwhile, here's the bivouac on Cardigan Island:

That night I unrolled my sleeping bag on a soft bed of grass in a hollow circled by a low bank that I like to think was a hut-circle. But even if it was no such thing, someone had made it and I am sure a very long time ago. For a while I sat in the still warm dusk watching the four bright flashes of Strumble light 18 miles to the south-west. But Bardsey's light, which I had hoped would shine nearly 50 miles to the north, was either lost in cloud or too low on the horizon to be visible. Then I lay awake under the stars watching the play of grasses very close to my face and hearing the very softest wind swish through grass, the very slightest rustle of water against rock: sounds you miss in the daytime. Waking in the night I heard oystercatchers piping to one another, the calls of passing redshanks and the occasional unaccountable alarms of the gulls rising up in sudden shouting bursts into the dark sky, then slowly subsiding. I also heard a gnawing close to my ear and discovered that a rat had got into my rucksack and was helping itself to a packet of sandwiches.

You might think that this hint of a scenario for a horror film within the account of a night spent on a Welsh desert island adds in its own quota of apprehensiveness to an anxiety that will be familiar to many who have fretted about changing weather as they wait for the boat to take them off Enlli, Skomer or Skokholm. He captures the feeling of anxiety particularly well as he concludes his testimony:

When I woke in the morning as the choughs called and bounced through the air over me I was conscious first of grasses shaking wildly against racing grey clouds. There was an autumnal touch in the light twitter of passing finches. I felt the wind stronger over the island and heard a heavier sea than that of the previous night. I stood up to see white water breaking all round the rocks and spray flying far. I looked at the creek, the one possible landing place in this island of rocks, and saw the waves surging heavily into it. If it was like this on what was merely a breezy summer day, what, I asked myself, was it like in winter? By the afternoon, when the tide had ebbed, the waves fell a little and when the boat came I was able to fling my pack and then myself into it. Quickly on the south-flowing tide we slipped through the narrow sound. We looked up at the south cliffs gasping with summer; at three young cormorants on a nest, their mouths agape and their throats vibrating to get air; at the sea-beet hanging great seeding heads from the ledges. Then the island was behind us and soon we were entering the Teifi river and our boat was dancing through the wavelets of the bar.

Man's continuing destructiveness along its course has reduced Afon Teifi from what Bill described as "a totally beautiful river" to something lesser and more disturbing. But surely, ultimately, it can be returned to the good, even though for a time much of the life in it has been destroyed, if only the political will were there to do so, the system made just and representative, and the electorate not continually duped by amoral and uncaring profiteers and despoilers who so seldom represent their best interests? If not, our natural world will not long survive as we now know it, and we might even begin to notice its decline. It might for once register with us as something disastrous taking place that it's our human responsibility to do something about. I wait in hope on that epiphanic day.

PART THREE:

The Folklore Rivers:
Cynfal, Dwyryd, Glaslyn

Here's the ending of a poem, "An Tobar" ("The Well"), by my good friend Cathal Ó Searcaigh, the Donegal poet who lives in the townland of Gort á Choirce, in the Donegal Gaeltacht under the shadow of Errigal, one of Ireland's most dramatic hills. Cathal's a remarkable personality, one of the outstanding contemporary Irish language poets. What he writes in the lines below is widely relevant to the situation in which we find ourselves in the contemporary world, as well as to how we treat our rivers:

Aimsigh do thobar féin, a chroí,
óir tá am an anáis romhainn amach:
Caithfear pilleadh arís ar na foinsí.

(Seek out your own well, my dear,/for the age of want is near:/There will have to be a going back to sources.)

Cathal's a brave man, open about his sexuality in still-conservative, rural Ireland. I've read with him at festivals and tutored with him on writing courses. He's always challenging, entertaining, breathtakingly frank, lyrically articulate. His poem remembers how all the cottages in his townland[1] used to have their own wells; how they used to be kept clear and free from rushes; how they were cleaned out with lime every year; how this annual ritual even in deeply rural Donegal has fallen into desuetude, as it has long since in rural Wales. To fix on that idea of returning to sources, I

---

[1] There's little that's urban in the Irish term "townland".

often used to take up the topic with Bill Condry. His too-early death in 1998 meant that I missed the chance to talk to him about the source of the Afon Dyfrdwy, over which I found a remarkable primitive chapel, which I once heard referred to by an old shepherd in the pub at Llanuwchllyn as Capel Aerfen. Bill and I would, I think, have found ourselves even more bemused in the case of Afon Dwyryd, around which I've lived for much of my life. Some rivers have obvious sources. Afon Rheidol, for example, certainly flows out of Llyn Llygad Rheidol, down to the east of the summit of Pumlumon. I've made the acquaintance of Afon Tawe far underground before it ever sees the light of day, in an impressive cave passage several miles long of dark rock lightning-streaked with white calcite, "perhaps the best streamway in Britain" according to the cavers' guidebook[2], with deep potholes into which you suddenly plunge over your head into cold and rushing water in one of the linked sequence of caves that's Ogof Ffynnon Ddu. It's a passage that's both tricky to find, tricky to leave, and is the grandest caving trip I've ever been on, with the extravagant, glistening beauty of Column Hall, the finest sight I've seen anywhere underground, to be encountered along the way. Fixed forever in my mind, though it's fifty years since I was in the cave, are the crystalline pools, cave pearls bordering their margins, in that same exquisitely decorated chamber, and the sound of twenty-foot-long straw stalactites gently chiming together as the mere breath of our bodies in passing through set them softly swaying. Similarly, Afon Llwchwr gushes out of Llygad Llwchwr, within which are deep lakes with a forbidding atmosphere all their own.

For Afon Glaslyn, which we'll be coming to shortly, I'm hard pressed to trace it on the ground any further than to Glaslyn itself,

---

[2] *Selected Caves of Britain and Ireland, or "Top of the Pots"*, Des Marshall and Donald Rust, 1997.

189

right underneath Yr Wyddfa (though there is a tributary stream called Pant y Lluwchwfa marked on large-scale O.S. maps as flowing down from below Bwlch Glas). For Afon Dwyryd, however, no such certainty: is it Afon Gam, Afon Goch, Nant y Groes, or all of these or none of them? Where does it first take on its name? That's a more simple question. It doesn't appear on the O.S. 1:25,000 map until the river reaches its tidal limit just below Rhyd y Sarn at the confluence with Afon Teigl, which drains the land below Manod Mawr. Beyond the next bridge downstream, Pont Dôl y Moch, it joins with two important tributaries in quick succession: Afon Cynfal, and then Afon Goedol. Cynfal is the more important of these, and one of the great folklore rivers of Eryri. The confluence with Cynfal allows us to claim justifiably that, as with several other notable streams (Conwy, Serw, Lliw), the huge area of morass between Llan Ffestiniog and Ysbyty Ifan known as Migneint – the name translates as "place of quagmires" – is origin for all of these and many more. Let's proclaim Cynfal as most significant of Dwyryd's headwaters. We can follow Dwyryd down from the confluence at which the already rather stately stream ('the mature stage of a river' is how geographers describe it) receives a name and becomes one of the most beautiful and least sullied – with one significant exception, as we'll see when we consider Ceunant Llenyrch – of Welsh rivers. For the moment, an immense amount of interest awaits along the short course of Afon Cynfal. So let's follow that tumultuous mountain stream. To do so, we make our way to Pont yr Afon Gam, where the crooked stream that curves round the back of Foel Gron quarry and flows through a waste of slate below Cerrig yr Ieirch ("Roebuck Stones" – there are many outcrops with this name in the Welsh hills) before joining forces with Afon Goch is the best candidate for Afon Cynfal's source. It also rises, interestingly, within a couple of hundred yards of Nant yr Wyn, which is quickly appropriated by Afon Serw, and that in its turn heads away to the north-east along a wild and remote valley that will eventually merge with that of the infant Afon Conwy. From more or less the same birthplace – and remember that these moorland streams seldom have precisely delineated risings – major sources of Dwyryd and Conwy end up in bays on different sides of Wales. I don't write about Afon Conwy in this present volume, but we're very close – a mere raven's mile or two away – at Ffynnon Eidda. Given that I'm wholly committed to the deconstructed narrative principle of Thoreau's Concord and Merrimack rivers book, we should at least pay a visit to the Serw valley, and perhaps the most remote and lonely house in Wales, the shepherds' cottage of Cefn Garw (recently restored as a kind of bothy). There are places among the Welsh hills where you may "grow rich/With looking." In my copy of R.S. Thomas's *Collected Poems*, the verse from which that's taken is marked with a curlew's feather picked up by Cefn Garw. I've often followed the four-mile, climbing track to the old steading alongside Afon Serw. Rough ridge, place of quagmires, silken stream – such perfect simplicity in the way Welsh toponymy describes landscape's essence!

Decades ago old Mr. Roberts, who shepherded on horseback, departed his remote *tyddyn* for the last time, leaving it to be used by shearers who gather the moorland flock each year, or by occasional hill-wanderers, or fishermen who cast a fly to lure the small brown trout in Serw's pools. The old shepherd gone, the moor was left to fox, raven, pipit-hunting merlin, mewing buzzard. Nature set to work reclaiming her house. Frost jagged cracks into the gables. Wind rattled slates free from rusting nails. At some stravaigers' bacchanal the beam supporting the chimney-breast charred through. For years barn owls nested here – they too now gone. I walked here recently on a glorious early summer's day. Breezes riffled the tawny moor-grasses; curlew and cuckoo called distantly; merlin and kestrel dropped silently among tussocks to rise again with vole or shrew. It is so lovely, so expansive, this moor with its "clean colours/That brought a moistening of the eye". Sphagnum; bog-cotton; heather's umber soon to bloom purple. Inside the old *tyddyn* the mural of a ram that dominates one wall is faded, though still distinct. The roof's been repaired, burnt inglenook beam replaced by concrete. Graffiti's scrawled on flaking plaster: "Jac Fedw, Dewi Garmon, yn hela llwynog 10/2/80". Do Jac and Dewi still hunt the fox hereabouts? Is what brings them here the *"depth of silence, its being outside time and the chiming of a clock, the awesome quality of such a vast landscape with nobody in it"*? That's Ian Niall, the Galloway-born writer[3], who came here often. Ian first told me about it in Betws-y-coed's Waterloo Hotel bar one night in the 1970s. On this recent spring day, a gibbous moon illuminated me down-valley. By the footbridge over Afon Conwy a white owl hushed down, as I crossed the gorge to quit his pristine territory. For Afon Cynfal, we might start at the road junction of Pont yr Afon Gam, or better still a short distance away from it at the old drovers' well I just mentioned, of Ffynnon Eidda. A lane that climbs steeply through Sitka spruce plantations out of Cwm Penmachno relaxes finally on reaching the moor above, and dawdles for a narrow mile through peat hags to arrive at this road junction in the lonely heart of Migneint. Eastwards from here, the B4407 broaches the moor to descend alongside an infant Afon Conwy from Ysbyty Ifan. The experimental novelist B.S. Johnson (1933-1973) wrote a remarkable "phantom hitchhiker" story about encountering a sheela-na-gig whilst driving westwards across here on his way from Kilpeck in Herefordshire to the Llŷn peninsula one wild evening. Whenever I visit Cefn Garw, just

---

[3] For a shrewd and representative selection from this knowledgable, wide-ranging and unshowy modern master of country writing, see the volume of his writings edited by his niece, Sheila Pehrson: *If the Corncrake Calls* (The Inn Pinn, Glasgow, 2016).

across the moor (don't try walking that way!) by Afon Serw, it returns to haunt me, as though the story had invoked a tutelary spirit of this wild and watery place, more suited to wild magnificence of avian life that ghosts across than to human habitation. When I lived in Cwm Pennant in the 1970s, in a remote cottage without road access on the western flank of Moel Hebog, a bulky figure came shambling down the path alongside my house one afternoon. I was outside chain-sawing an ash tree brought down in a recent gale. He stopped to talk, introduced himself as Bryan, seemed in a fragile state so I invited him for a cup of tea. He stayed to share the rabbit stew I had on the stove (my notion of living off the land in those days was rabbit from night-time fields, salmon from the river, potatoes, onions and cabbage from my garden). He slept in the spare bedroom that night (we'd talked most of it away – he was a phenomenal talker), next morning was quietly on his way before I'd surfaced. But he left on the table a copy of his recently published Constable poetry collection, in syllabic verse for the most part, a few unpublished drafts in typescript tucked inside and a generous inscription. I have it still. This was in the summer before he killed himself. It was our only meeting. I liked him. For a long time, until I heard the news of his death, I half-expected him to turn up again. But he never did, not even in spirit form:

> *"...I began to think*
> *I knew why people left this pure valley:*
> *such peace is useful only when related*
> *to a larger world; and life is never short."[4]*

To come back to Ffynnon Eidda, you'll find this sturdily reconstructed well from 1846 at the first lane junction after

---

[4] From "Cwm Pennant" – the closing sequence to the book of poems Bryan left on my table as he left in 1975.

crossing Afon Conwy's watershed on the little road that climbs out of Cwm Penmachno. It bears the carved exhortation *"Yf a bydd ddiolchgar"* ("Drink and be thankful"). It's alongside one of the old drovers' routes from Wales to the English smithfields. There's a mystery about this well. It was not built for cattle, nor for pigs, though traces of the retaining compound for swine still abut its structure. Access to the stone basin is staggered, leading through interlocking baffles that fattened animals could not have negotiated. The name is a further mystery. It may be related to local names for understated features on these moors. Children from Llan Ffestiniog pedal noisily up here in summer to roll their sleeves and retrieve coins passing motorists fling into its chill, clear water. Fancifully, I think of the Elder Edda's tale of Odin trading an eye for a drink from the well of wisdom. If sheela-na-gigs can appear on these moors, cannot Odin also, to balance the sexual equation? West and south of Ffynnon Eidda, the B4407 passes the fine little rock outcrop of Carreg y Foel Gron above Llyn Du Bach before coming to Pont yr Afon Gam, where the road from Bala heads down right to Llan Ffestiniog. This is bracing country. The last time I was here, where the bleak and lonely road across Migneint from Y Bala joins in, a large 4WD with an aggressive grille like bared teeth was close on my tail through the bends. My filmic imagination was replaying the terrifying opening sequences from *Mississippi Burning*. Light was fading, the situation felt edgy. To make it worse, the 4WD followed me into the scenic layby where you can peer into the impressive upper gorge of Afon Cynfal. I climbed out of the car to do just that. The driver of the 4WD watched as I walked over to the fence and tried to make out detail in the dark ravine, within which thundered the rain-swollen waterfall of Rhaeadr y Cwm. He climbed down out of his truck cab. A young man dressed in light-coloured clothes, he came over to talk. "Impressive!" I commented. "Oh yes!" he responded, "I work at the outdoor centre in Rhosygwaliau. We take our kids down it sometimes. But not in these conditions. We've put bolts in for abseiling. It's very atmospheric in there!" I tell him in response about working fifty years ago at The Woodlands outdoor centre in Glasbury-on-Wye, accompanying groups of students through spectacular gorges of the Ystwyth and Rheidol rivers around Devil's Bridge. We talked of committing situations encountered in these locations: of the sculpted rock; of green diffused light reflected off moving water and mossed walls; of surprising depth both of clefts and swirling cauldron-pools within them, and a dangerous thrill in moving through these environments. After a few minutes he lifted the tailgate of his truck, took out a fly-rod, and told me he was heading for Llyn y Morwynion a quarter-mile up the hillside above. I related to him the *Mabinogion* story of how the handmaidens of Blodeuwedd drowned there, and how Gwydion the enchanter turned Blodeuedd into an owl, thereafter called Blodeuwedd ("flower-face"). Another folk-tale has women of Dyffryn Clwyd, abducted by men from Ardudwy in search of wives, becoming romantically attached to their abductors (an early example of Stockholm Syndrome?). They drowned themselves here in despair after male relatives overtook them and slaughtered their captors. The young man set off for the lake. I watched his pale form flickering moth-like, mysterious, across the hillside in crepuscular light, *"Climbing up to a place/Where stone is dark under froth"* (Yeats). An owl hooted down-valley. I glanced across to where Rhaeadr y Cwm roared in the shadow, lamented my bodily decrepitude, thought of silver bolt-heads like Blodeuwedd's eyes that pierced the shadowed gloom of its walls, and climbed back into my car to carry on down-valley. Roman Polanski filmed some of the crucial sequences in his moody, nihilistic 1971 version of *Macbeth* in this area, in small abandoned quarry workings on these moors, and the battle scenes and some of the "three weird sisters" sequences at the western end of Black Rock Sands. It's not a perfect film, and I know – all the stuff about Polanski! But if I'd had a pregnant wife brutally murdered by the Manson Family, I would have been deeply and adversely affected. The absence of compassion around this for me is the most striking thing about the controversy Polanski arouses. How people love to put the boot into those who are already down is one of the least attractive traits of human nature. On Macbeth, as well as innumerable stage productions I've seen four film versions: Kurosawa's *Throne of Blood*, which is powerful but alien; Orson Welles with RKO scenery and props you recognise from a dozen Hollywood B movies; Michael Fassbender's lamentable recent effort, where Shakespearean blank verse is reduced to incomprehensible gibberish mouthed out to a landscape much of which is pasteboard-effect CGI; and Polanski's 1971 version, which I first saw in a cinema by London's Victoria Station on its first release in autumn 1971.

Every new viewing convinces me that the latter is the best of the four. The filming, around Llan Ffestiniog, Morfa Bychan and Lindisfarne, has an intense, charged atmosphere. Landscape plays a powerful role. Jon Finch and Francesca Annis have grown on me over the years. Half a century ago I thought them weak. Now that weakness – the vitiating weakness and brutality of ambition that so much contemporary media as well as Tory aspirationalism seeks to school us into endorsing – seems of the essence in the era of ex-president Trump and the unspeakably mendacious Alexander de Pfeffel Johnson (this is a political play through and through, so the citing of modern monsters in this context is entirely appropriate). Also, I know it's odd to talk in terms of a scriptwriter when we're considering a film of a Shakespearean drama, but the one thing in this film that has gone round and round in my mind for fifty years is its closing sequence, not present in Shakespeare's text, when Donalbain – Duncan's younger son, and one of many ambiguous characters[5] in Kenneth Tynan's screenplay – rides back in the rain after MacDuff has killed Macbeth and Malcolm has been crowned to the witches' cave. Where these scenes were filmed is by the track leading up to Llyn y Morwynion from the B4391, west of Pont yr Afon Gam and on the margins of the Migneint. Wild country indeed! For my money Polanski's *Macbeth* is one of the most powerful and successful attempts at filming a Shakespearean tragedy I know[6]. It's one that's grown in stature and relevance over the years. What Tynan's nihilistic ending intimates – that evil has an eternal circularity – is far more convincing for me than the optimistic platitudes about order re-established on which the *Great Chain of Being* convention of the day insisted that Shakespeare end his play. It's also – to bring in that useful Arnoldian concept – more adequate to our own time, in which we see the truth of it being re-enacted here and in America time and again. For Donalbain in Polanski's film, read the vicious moral nonentity who at the time of writing is denizen of Number Ten.

To come back to Welsh rivers and Rhaeadr y Cwm, it spills out into the much gentler, more pastoral surroundings of Cwm Cynfal. I drove into this valley along the slant road that descends into it past a simple chapel recently, on a bright spring evening in search of a stone I'd first seen 40 years ago. At that time I'd asked directions to it of a woman cutting wood outside the interestingly-named house of Bryn Saeth. *"Fan acw, yn y gornel ym mhen pella'r maes,"* she'd told me ('Over there in the far corner of the field'). I crossed to the wood's edge. A stream cascaded over mossy slabs

---

[5] Another is the chilling Earl of Ross, suavely played by John Stride – talking calmly with Lady Macduff, then with the flicker of a smile opening the castle gate to let in the men who will murder her children and rape her and her servants. A truly horrifying moment!
[6] Polanski's 1979 version of Thomas Hardy's Tess of the D'Urbervilles is also to my mind the best film version of a Hardy novel.

confettied with wood anemones. Prone among drifted oak leaves was an inches-thick slate, four feet high, a shaped round hole in it. Perhaps this was Llech Ronw (the slate of Gronw)? A scatter of quartz rocks all around suggested a ritual site. I lifted up its heavy weight, as Gronw Pebyr had done in *Math fab Mathonwy* (the fourth branch of *The Mabinogion*, and a complex story that's one of the masterpieces of medieval European literature), to protect himself from the returned blow he owed to Lleu Llaw Gyffes. Gronw had conspired with Blodeuedd, the wife of Lleu Llaw Gyffes, to kill him. He had thrown a spear that pierced Lleu's side as he bathed with one foot on the side of a stone trough, the other on the back of a goat, the secret of how he might be killed having been wheedled from the trusting Lleu by his wife Blodeuedd before being passed on to her lover Gronw. When the spear hit him, Lleu shrieked and flew away transformed into an eagle. Gronw and Blodeuedd then lived adulterously together at Tomen y Mur (to the south of here and east of Trawsfynydd). She was a woman created for Lleu's pleasure – no feminist fable, this![7] – by his uncle, Gwydion the enchanter, from the flowers of oak, meadowsweet and broom, in order to evade the triple curse placed on him as an infant by his mother, Arianrhod, who had been thought a virgin but was disgraced by Lleu's birth. Though Lleu was mortally wounded by the spear Gronw had cast – hewn every Sunday for a year whilst the people were at Mass – he was not dead. Gwydion searched throughout Eryri for the eagle into which Lleu had been transformed, and was led to the wounded bird where it roosted in an oak tree in Dyffryn Nantlle. The putrid flesh and the maggots falling from it were being devoured by swine. It was following these swine after the swineherd released them each

---

[7] Or is it? It does place a woman's right to choose, and be more than merely an instrument for men's pleasure, centrally in the story, whilst also stressing the outcast status she acquires by so doing.

morning that had led Gwydion here. He called Lleu down from the tree, restored him to health and human form, and together he and Lleu came searching for Gronw Pebyr and Blodeuedd to wreak vengeance upon them.

When Lleu cast his spear, it pierced the shield-stone Gronw held up, killing him. (See, there's the hole!) Blodeuedd heard of their coming, and fled with her handmaidens into the desolate hills, continually looking behind them. Walking backwards, all were drowned in Llyn y Morwynion – the maidens' lake – except for their mistress, who was promptly transformed by Gwydion into an owl and mocked by being re-named Blodeuwedd ("flower-face"). These explanations for the naming of places conveyed by means of story are known by scholars of medieval Welsh literature as the onomastic element. It thrives on the precise local specificity of these centuries-old tales. Llech Ronw – if indeed it is that, and not just an arbitrary slate slab with a hole drilled in it for a gatepost[8] – has now been set upright, concreted into a plinth,

---

[8] I have my doubts about this stone. It's too light and slight, somehow, to bear the weight of story placed upon it, though that does tend to support its use in the story as a shield. There also seems to be an element of auto-suggestion here. Holed stones are numerous throughout what Myles Dillon and Nora K. Chadwick in a monumental study under the same title published in 1967 in Weidenfeld's *History of Civilisation* series called *The Celtic Realms*. The most famous example is perhaps Men-an-Toll, on the moor above Bosigran in Cornwall's West Penwith, which is large enough for babies to have been passed through it. Robert Gibbings summarises the significance of holed stones thus in a delightful book of Irish travels called Sweet Cork of Thee (Dent 1951): "*With most of them there is a tradition either of healing powers or of the ratification of compacts. Where the hole is large enough, the postulant crawls through, leaving behind him his sins or his affliction. Ailing children are passed through as a remedy for their weakness. Where the holes are smaller, clothes and cloths are treated in a similar manner, that they may relieve suffering; or hands are clasped from either side at the exchange of marriage vows. The symbolism of a wedding ring may well have a direct connection with that of these stones.*"

The notion of a ratification of compact clearly has relevance to Llech Ronw. It's much the same motif, of a blow returned, as we find marvellously played out in the middle English alliterative masterpiece of *Sir Gawain and the Green Knight*, and if you're going to read that glorious text, please do yourself a favour and choose the original, which is not all that difficult to understand, rather than in the plethora of clumsily showy and unnecessary translations by certain modern poets.

surrounded by wire, presented as a minor tourist attraction, its resonance stilled. I'd not seen it thus, thought better of finding it again, its place anyway having changed, *a loathsomeness of conifers*[9] around it now. Instead I went to Llyn y Morwynion, the maidens' wild lake, the outflow from which drains down into the Afon Cynfal. I reached it by the path from Llyn Du Bach. The sun was setting along the Llŷn peninsula when I arrived at the shore, a single teal duck gliding through silvered water as so often on the mountain lakes of Wales. Skylarks soared, distance editing out their dry shrillings until only clear, bell-like notes remained. As the dusk fell, the angry shriek of an owl drifted up from by Sarn Helen. This is not only wild country, it is powerful too.

A few days later, I parked in Llan Ffestiniog. A path descends from opposite the churchyard gate in this hilltop village, its route following cloddiau (turf and stone field dykes) bright with mats of trailing tormentil. It arrives at a wood, water loud in the ravine below, and a viewing spot for Rhaeadr Cynfal – an exquisitely lacey fall of rolling symmetry on the Afon Cynfal. The connections to the fourth branch of *The Mabinogion* are not the only literary associations in which the Afon Cynfal rejoices. There's plenty of other culturally important literary matter here. A little further along the now-vertiginous path I was following is a belvedere, below which a slender rock stack rises from the river. It's known as Huw Llwyd's Pulpit. From this, Huw (1568-1630) sermonized, scolded or even threatened, on magic and morality to congregations gathered on the bank above. He must have

---

Finally, before we leave Llech Ronw, note its appearance in *Trioedd Ynys Prydein*, in connection with the "Three Faithless/Disloyal War-Bands of the Island of Britain": "*The War-Band of Gronw the Radiant of Penllyn, who refused to receive the poisoned spear from Lleu Llaw yffes on behalf of their lord at the Stone of Goronwy at the head of the Afon Cynfal*". Frank Ward in 1934 reported on a stone discovered in the Afon Cynfal which was surely the one now railed in and embedded in concrete. The traditional burial site of Gronw Pebyr was close by, and marked by a standing stone. For more on this see Bromwich p. 67 (footnote).

[9] A favourite phrase of Bill Condry's, this; and one with which I'm entirely in agreement.

possessed a mighty voice to be heard above the noise of the river. His home was Cynfal Fawr high on the opposite bank. You encounter him in that Regency genius and amiably satirical friend of the major Romantics, Thomas Love Peacock, in whose first novella, *Headlong Hall* (1816) he appears thus:

> "...put to pe sure, Owen Thomas of Morfa-Bach will have it that one summer evening – when he went over to Cwm Cynfael in Meirionnydd, apout some cattle he wanted to puy – he saw a strange figure – pless us! With five horns – Cot save us! Sitting on Huw Llwyd's pulpit, which, your honour fery well knows, is a pig rock in the middle of the river – "

> "Of course he was mistaken," said Mr. Escot.

> "To be sure he was," said the sexton. For there is no toubt but the tevil, when Owen Thomas saw him, must have peen sitting on a piece of rock in a straight line from him on the other side of the river, where he used to sit, look you, for a whole summer's tay, while Huw Llwyd was on his pulpit, and there they used to talk across the water! For Huw Llwyd, please your honour, never raised the tevil except when he was safe in the middle of the river, which proves that Owen Thomas, in his fright, didn't pay proper attention to the exact spot where the tevil was."

Huw was a soldier, sorcerer, poet and huntsman. He was also friend and correspondent with John Dee, the Elizabethan Mage of Radnorshire stock (his family was from Pilleth, by the site of Glyndŵr's victory at Bryn Glas), who was suspected by Queen Elizabeth of casting an enchantment on her, as he may well have done, for he does that to most who study him. In Victorian times, with all its cultural and magical resonance the Cynfal gorge was a favourite on the romantic Wales itinerary, one of the highlights for tourists trekking to the extravagantly beautiful Vale of

Ffestiniog. Postcards in becoming sepia of the striking and mysterious "Pulpit" were sold in Betws-y-Coed. Less popular now, its atmospherics still thrum. Huw Llwyd's relative Morgan Llwyd (1619-1659) also came here as a child. One of the major seventeenth-century Welsh writers, among many other works he wrote the Welsh religious prose classic, *Llyfr y Tri Aderyn* ("Book of the Three Birds") of 1653 – a religious tract influenced by the mystical writer Jakob Böhme (1575-1624)[10]. The third character to be added to this significant trinity of Welsh inspiration is Edmwnd Prys (1543-1623), who was appointed Vicar of Ffestiniog in 1573, and whose appendix of Salmau Cân ("metrical psalms") to the Welsh Book of Common Prayer was an early ripple in the great late-sixteenth-century flood of religious literary achievement in Welsh that had as culmination the 1588 translation of The Bible – *"a necessary, excellent, choice and learned work, for which Wales can never repay or thank him as much as he deserves"* (Morris Kyffin, 1594) – by a humble parish priest, William Morgan (1545-1604), the incumbent at the time of his translation at the mother church Llanrhaeadr ym Mochnant, in Dyffryn Tanat. Tearing ourselves away from this nest of singing birds, the path above the plunging gorge continues to a footbridge, from which an easier route returns to Llan Ffestiniog's *Pengwern Arms* – a community pub that now offers accommodation for walkers. George Borrow stayed here on his 1854 walking tour of Wales. He'd come looking for a poet's chair – an obsession of his, this one dedicated to the fifteenth-century bard Rhys Goch Eryri. It's not here. He'd passed it unawares earlier in the day before arriving at Ffestiniog, to which he'd walked from Beddgelert – a short day for him of barely twenty miles. Cadair Rhys Goch had already

---

[10] There is no evidence that Morgan Llwyd knew of the Sufi poet Farid ud din Attar's masterpiece The Conference of Birds, nor even of Geoffrey Chaucer's *The Parliament of Fowles*, though all three texts share generic similarities.

been destroyed by copper-mining when Borrow passed by. It was above the road near Pont Aberglaslyn. It may be that Borrow's brains had been scrambled by over-proof poitín he'd sampled in Tan Lan at the foot of Cwm Croesor. Tan Lan still had a café, and a good and welcoming one too, until relatively recent times brought in stringent Health and Safety Executive regulations, and hence it was shut down, the dining room having been the terraced house's front parlour and the kitchen the proprietor's own. Poitín by then had long been off the drinks list. I often used to come here regularly after climbs on the rocks at Tremadog, have a pot of tea with poached eggs and chunky chips, and then take in one of the fiercer, steeper climbs of Joe Brown's on the impendent cliff of Carreg Hyll Drem – the crag of the frightful appearance – just a short walk along the road. Borrow would have loved Morgan Llwyd's writing. *Llyfr y Tri Aderyn* has recently been published in a fine and sensitive new translation[11] by the prolific and gifted Anglo-Welsh short-story writer Rob Mimpriss, with a powerful introduction which points up distressing parallels between English Civil War period values and those currently brought into play around the major political issue of our day, of secession from the European Union. I hope that afterwards you'll read the still-relevant debate in *Llyfr y Tri Aderyn* between Raven, Eagle and Dove. Here's a passage from near the conclusion to Rob's introduction.

> *"Like the Raven, I belong on the defeated side of a civil war. For on 23rd June 2016 I expressed the wishes of perhaps more than half the population of Wales and the U.K. in voting to maintain my European citizenship in the E.U. referendum, acting on the advice of the British Prime Minister, the Chancellor of the Exchequer, the former Deputy Prime Minister, the leader of the opposition, the First Minister*

---

[11] *A Book of Three Birds*: A New Translation of the Welsh Classic, Cockatrice Books, Bangor, 2017.

of Scotland, The Chief Minister of Gibraltar, the First Minister of Wales, the Deputy First Minister of Northern Ireland, the leader of the Ulster Unionist Party, the leader of the opposition in Wales, the President of the U.S.A. [Barack Obama at the time], and the overwhelming majority of disinterested economists in the U.K. For this act, supporters of Brexit, and of things more loathsome that hid beneath Brexit, branded me and those like me as libtards, as libturds, as snowflakes, as remoaners, as remoaniacs, as bedwetters, as saboteurs, as appeasers, as citizens of nowhere and as enemies of the people, demanding that we be silenced, be crushed, be tried for treason, kill ourselves, be killed, be hanged, be shot as Jo Cox was shot, be burnt to death, be murdered by hit men or be sent to the gas chambers; events in which it is hard not to see the seeds of dictatorship."

Rob carries on to analyse the emotional tenor of Brexiteer abuse in a passage which to my mind is required reading for an understanding of the current plight of our nations in the Disuniting Kingdom, and especially that of a small one like Wales:

"Language groups were among those to warn against the consequences of Brexit. Cymdeithas yr Iaith joined Conradh na Gaeilge, the Gaelic Language Society, the Cornish Academy, and the Cornish Language Board in a joint statement warning of 'an insecure future for our communities' under a British government which 'has shown no desire to protect and promote the rights of speakers of our nations' languages, and have throughout much of our shared history conducted aggressive language policies designed to eradicate our languages' – a phrase which in Wales recalls the request in parliament for the deliberate extermination of the Welsh language, the imposition of English as the language of schools, and the violence perpetrated upon Welsh-speaking children under the Welsh Not."

From this brief reference to the brutality of *The Blue Books* Rob brings us up to date with an excoriating critique of English exceptionalism, Tory inanity, and the whining inadequacy and endless complaining that underpinned the whole attempt by English nationalist brexiteers to justify their asinine project and promote their slippery, undeclared self-interest in pursuing it to long-term detriment of all nations that make up the historical entity so risibly referred to as the United Kingdom:

> *"To observers in Cymdeithas yr Iaith and its fellows, to speak of threats to a nation which has driven its neighbours to the point of cultural extinction, while stamping its language and culture on vast tracts of the globe, is both intellectually vapid and morally reprehensible, the self-pity of a society which complains of foreign oppression because it has never experienced any, which has never examined its past. But neither is that division felt on one side alone. For support for Brexit in England predicts a sense that England has somehow been cheated by its weaker Celtic partners, weakened by the devolution which the British government undermines, and which Brexit potentially undermines, along with a growing English separatism."*

Rob ends this introduction, written five years ago, with a prophecy that has in the intervening years essentially been fulfilled:

> *"In a time of economic hardship, English secession will seem less attractive, and a brutishly Anglo-British nationalism, a hatred of the Welsh language, and a hatred of the Welsh and Scots, will take its place."*

The vicious factionalism that's English nationalism has much to answer for in our time, just as it did in the time of Oliver Cromwell. But it's aside from the main purpose of this book, even though it glances off the thought of these two eminent former residents of Bro Cynfal, so let's leave this topic with a line from Huw Llwyd's enchanting *"Cyngor y Llwynog"* ("The Fox's Counsel"), of which Thomas Parry thought sufficiently highly to include it in *The Oxford Book of Welsh Verse*:

> *"Ffarwél, rhaid im ffoi i'r allt."*

Unlike the fox, having extricated myself from the comforts of the Pengwern Arms and all the delights of its mostly female early-evening habituées' conversation, I slipped away along the Allt Goch footpath, through delectable oakwoods full of pied flycatchers feeding on the insect life these woods so plentifully provide in early summer, to the awkward road junction just beyond which a lane leads down to the medieval Pont Dôl y Moch. From this bridge's parapet you can watch Afon Cynfal add its considerable force into what, within a quarter of a mile at the next confluence, with Ceunant Llechryd, will become unquestionably Afon Dwyryd. Ceunant Llennyrch, the confluence with which is two-and-a-half miles downriver near Maentwrog power station, is one of the most attractive gorges in Eryri, but there is a problem with it. It's the outflow from the concrete dam at the north-eastern end of Llyn Trawsfynydd. So if you're intent on heading up there – and it's popular with outdoor centres for the activity called, a little inaccurately, "gorge walking" – I need to give you some historical context, which is very instructive about the manner in which governments operate. Llyn Trawsfynydd acted as cooling reservoir for what long held the reputation of being, after Sellafield, the leakiest nuclear power station in Britain. Remember *The China Syndrome* (the 1979 film starring Jane Fonda, Jack Lemmon and Michael Douglas), that went on general release, in a piece of impeccably adventitious timing, just twelve days before the nuclear accident at Three Mile Island? If you do, then you might consider a 1988 story I wrote for that excellent small political journal, *Planet*.

> *'In the Cambrian News there is a weekly column entitled "Weird Wonders of Wales". It reflects a tradition, a taste for the marvellous,*

a credulous appetite ever craving satisfaction, and there is no body more concerned to fulfil that basic human need than our dear old Central Electricity Generating Board, the activities of which in Wales and elsewhere all too frequently beggar belief. The great strength of the CEGB is, of course, its public relations expertise. It has become so adept at this intriguing necessity of late twentieth century life that it can now happily twist conventions, manipulate argument and opinion, and even apparently convince itself – the monster of delusion having outgrown its masters – at will. Its frenetic activity has frequently been evident in Snowdonia this spring. There was the proposed experiment at Trawsfynydd Nuclear Power Station – the only inland nuclear power station in Britain – which was to have taken place in February [1988]. The cooling fans of one of the reactors were to be shut down to test if natural circulation of the gases could supply the deficiency.

Just let that sink in as an index to the mindset of the people who promote these deadly establishments!

"All perfectly safe," the public was assured, and the *Cambrian News*, perhaps to reinforce that assurance or perhaps not, printed a front-page picture of CEGB chairman Lord Marshall shaking hands with Snowdonia National Park Officer Alan Jones – though to the eagle-eyed the handshake had all the appearance of being of the masonic variety. The public, however, was not assured. There was talk of a mass evacuation of the area, of the closure of schools. There were mass meetings and special sessions of the County Council. Lord Marshall promised to fly in to Trawsfynydd on the day of the promised test by helicopter. "And fly out again if it goes wrong," muttered the public, and still was not assured. The "test" was called off. Three months later, when the reactor on which it was to have been conducted was closed down for routine maintenance, irradiation was found to have caused severe damage to welds and other components. It was not, on the whole, a public relations success for the CEGB.

There was much else to this story. Those interested in how the CEGB operated on the credulity of the populace during Mrs. Thatcher's heyday; in epidemiological statistics on childhood leukaemias and other cancers from that time; in honest accounts of nuclear accidents or operating difficulties; in local people's ambitions for materially comfortable lifestyles; in the bizarre meteorological anomaly that caused radio-active contamination from Chernobyl to be dumped 3,000 miles upwind, thus bringing about restrictions in the first instances precisely six miles downwind from the nuclear power stations at Sellafield and Trawsfynydd[12], might wish to do their own research into how crucial factors were concealed, distorted, or manipulated at will. I remember attending a symposium organised by the Council for the Protection of Rural Wales (as it then was), held at Coleg Harlech in 1988 and chaired by Eirene White, Baroness Rhymney, who had been a minister in Harold Wilson's administrations in the 1960s. A spokesman from the United Kingdom Atomic Energy Authority addressed us. He assured us that it was no part of that authority's remit to produce plutonium, and no, it was never supplied to this or any other country's military. He was pressed on his answer, and he continued categorically to deny a link that has subsequently been clearly established. The genteel members of the CPRW, being polite bourgeois ladies and gentlemen, took him at his word. He was lying. Mendacity from

---

[12] The CEGB and UKAEA at the time explained away the anomaly by saying that Caesium has a fingerprint and thus they knew that the radioactive contamination downwind of Trawsfynydd was from Chernobyl. Friends of the Earth and Edinburgh University later prepared a report, of which I was 'leaked' a copy in my then-capacity as editor of *Rural Wales/Cymru Wledig*. The report stated that radioactive contamination on the moors downwind of Trawsfynydd did in fact come from Trawsfynydd. No Fleet Street newspaper would touch this story, the surmise being that "D" notices (now "DA" notices) had been issued. This was some years before governmental lying became an established fact of British political life – though not to the extent it has now become under the Tory premiership of Alexander de Peffel Johnson.

representatives of official bodies no longer shocks us. It shocked me back then. The story of Ceunant Llennyrch and Trawsfynydd raises so many historical questions about what should be permitted in Eryri, and how the population should be safeguarded.

To take up that theme, perhaps we might head back down-gorge and follow the Dwyryd to Pont Briwet (an interesting name the origin of which may be ur- or proto-Goidelic[13]). The bridge here crosses a narrowing between rock strata at the upper end of Traeth Bach. At flood or ebb tides the force of water through here, the swirls and whirlpools, are powerfully impressive. On the Penrhyndeudraeth shore is the former site of Cooke's explosive works. It's now the nature reserve of Gwaith Powdwr – "powder works" being black powder in this context. Cooke's was a subsidiary of Nobel's, and one of the World's most advanced in manufacturing explosives. On 14th June 1988, there was a huge explosion in one of the nitro-glycerine mixing sheds which killed two workers – their bodies were never found – and injured eight others. I was living less than a mile downriver on the Aber Iâ peninsula at the time. On a beautiful sunny day I sat at the picnic table on my front lawn drinking coffee, contemplating the day's work, and the blast occurred. It shook the ground, sent a mushroom cloud of smoke and debris (including, no doubt, body parts of the two deceased employees) two thousand feet into the air. In the light of then-recent press disclosures about safety issues there, my first thought, and that of many others to whom I spoke later, was that one of the reactors at Trawsfynydd had exploded. With demand for explosives in the local quarrying industry

---

[13] Ur-goidelic is the putative precursor to the two main Celtic language branches of P- and Q-goidelic. P-goidelic includes Welsh, Breton, and Cornish, whilst the Q-goidelic languages are Erse (Irish Gaelic), Scottish Gaelic, and Manx. The meaning of Pont Briwet appears to be tautological ("bridge bridge"). However, the modern definition is for a division into Goidelic and Brittonic.

declining, after 130 years of manufacturing Cooke's was closed in 1995, the site given to the North Wales Naturalists' Trust. Grant funding to restore it came from the EU LIFE initiative's 3.1bn Euro budget for environmental and climate protection. With careful work by researchers from Bangor University, it was detoxified, cleared and planted. In its enviable location above the Dwyryd estuary, with views to Yr Wyddfa and Y Rhinogydd, it's now flourishing native woodland and heath, with birch, ash, alder, willow, oak, rowan, covering the rubble, paths threading through, hides well positioned to view abundant birdlife on the river below, in the heather, and among the young trees. When I was last there, to escape a flurry of rain I ducked into the pendulum hut where the massive cannon once used to measure the explosives' power remains. Outside Red Admiral butterflies clung to sodden blooms of Buddleia in the underbrush. A wren scolded from a drystone wall. Heather and gorse were still in flower. Rain had beaten down the year's dying bracken. No lure of sunshine brought out the adders which are plentiful here to bask in its warmth. Nightjars that have colonised the site had departed south weeks ago. I wished them safe passage, safe return, and am so glad, for once, to have a success story to impart from the natural world.

Beyond Pont Briwet on the eastern bank are the saltings of Glastraeth. When I lived nearby in Talsarnau I often walked along the embankment – one of the many early land reclamation schemes around the Dwyryd and Glaslyn estuaries. The distinctive sound from Glastraeth was the calls from high above – a yapping and yelping like a litter of young Pekingese dogs, a sound that was an identifying feature of this lovely estuary. I remember my first encounter with Barnacle Geese (*Branta leucopsis*) years ago. Curious as to what made the Pekingese yapping, I took out my glass and focused on a flight of seven birds gliding down towards Glastraeth. Their faces were white-masked. Their barred wings flickered stroboscopic silver; pale bellies and rumps glowed. They were down from breeding grounds in the Arctic, their winter population at one time running into hundreds. Thirty years ago, when I used to walk here daily, I'd encounter on a regular basis large flocks of barnacle geese, curlew and pintail. Whether through climate change, or disturbance by the very active local wildfowling fraternity I don't know; but none of these species is now present in anything like former numbers. I do know the flood of pleasure a glimpse of a small remnant of the place's former glories gives me, and when I watch ragged little remnant bands flight down to sandy rhines and samphire pastures on the farther shore to feed it is joy indeed. These beautiful, medium-sized geese have a singular presence in medieval bestiaries. Folklore had it they were the adult form of goose barnacles. Gerald the Welshman wrote of them that "Bishops and religious men in some parts of Ireland do not scruple to dine off these birds at the time of fasting, because they are not flesh nor born of flesh." Pope Innocent III whipped the recusants into line early in the thirteenth century, noting with sound good sense that since in all particulars they behaved like geese, geese they must be, and therefore were not to be eaten during Lent. May all geese be protected from unkind fates and the *"slaught'rin guns"* of Burns's great anti-bloodsports song, *"Now Westlin' Winds"*!

I often sit on rocks by the end of the track that leads down to the estuary from Talsarnau station, and hold conversations with the tawny owls in the woods on the farther shore. They remind me of an episode of great significance in my life from 1987, when I lived at Stentir above Abergafren. I found a tawny owlet in the road as I was walking up Croesor one morning. Its parents weren't around. It looked bedraggled and cold. So I picked it up, took it home, put it in a straw-filled box in my study, fed it on cat food, which it gulped down vigorously, and that evening drove back to

Croesor, hooted to call the parents, and after an hour or so, not having received any response, I took it back home and accepted responsibility for what I'd done (which was illegal, incidentally – but had I not done so, the near-certainty is that it would have died). So I had this wild creature in my workroom. I asked around for guidance, was given a few pointers, fed it regularly on cat food wrapped in fur[14] from grooming my cats, and watched it grow. Which it did very rapidly. I made a perch for it on top of a filing cabinet, from which it kept a constant eye on me. It soon began flexing its flight-power, flapped its wings, clacked its beak. When anyone else came in the room it would fluff up, make itself look huge, show signs of aggression. Soon it was taking short flights from its perch to land with talons firmly fixed in my scalp, from where it would lean round, gently chew my ear-lobes, and shit down my back. By now it was about eighteen inches tall and weighed over a pound – a big bird, albeit still downy. Those hypnotic, fathomless eyes kept a continual focus on me, the lateral movements of the head establishing distance, the bird's confidence and strength growing by the day. I never intended keeping this wild creature as a pet, though I grew very fond of it, and enjoyed the communication between us. I wanted to integrate it safely back into the wild. Also, keeping it indoors was dangerous for other members of my family. It attacked them if they came in the room where I worked, and owls carry dangerous weapons. Remember how the photographer Eric Hosking lost an eye? It seemed to thrive on its diet of cat food. As it grew larger I traded extra rations with my cats for the mice and voles they brought in, which I'd cut up and feed to the owl. I was soon taking it outside, perching it on the picnic table, tying cotton to the front legs of dead mice, and pulling them past the owl to teach it to swoop, catch, and dismember for itself. The intensity with which it sighted

---

[14] Needed to produce the pellets for regurgitation.

the prey by lateral movement of the head was hypnotic. My good friend and then-neighbour the sculptor Jonah Jones came round sometimes to watch. He was the only other person the owl tolerated. For strangers, those savage talons and the hooked beak were ever ready.

I loved this bird, communicated with it at some level, and it with me. I wanted it to be free, to be safe and independent in the wild, to mate and procreate. I was glad when it started to roost in the high ash tree by the house instead of indoors. It still came down to perch on my arm and be fed. The cats – always wary of the bird, as it of them – continued to provide mice, even a grey squirrel or two, which were ripped apart and swallowed down, the pellets of fur and bone regurgitated within an hour or two. When I went for walks down to the estuary or up to Jonah's house of Tyddyn Heulyn, I'd be aware of it following me through the trees. Sometimes it would fly down to perch on my shoulder, pick my pockets and nuzzle my ear, but all the while it was clearly becoming wilder. There would be days when I didn't see it, or when it refused food from me. I felt it was healthy and feeding well, and was glad. But I saw it less and less often, which was a sadness to me. Jonah said that he encountered it from time to time in the woods along the estuary, watchful, communicative still, but no longer prepared to socialize with humans. Which was as it should have been. Recently, at sunset and back on a brief visit, I went down to the rocks by the estuary where all this took place over thirty years ago. In the last glow of the light, and on impulse, though it was not the season for owls' calling I hooted gently into the gathering night. There came an answer, then more of them. Not from "my" owl – its lifespan most probably would have been over years ago – but conceivably from one of his or her descendants, still in this lovely territory. When I was back in the house, I took down a book I'd bought from Powell's City of Books in Portland, Oregon, whilst on a Harley ride round the American West years ago. I'd never read it before. It's called *"One Man's Owl"*, and is by the great American wildlife biologist Bernd Heinrich. It recounts Heinrich's rearing of a Great Horned Owl in the woods of Maine – Thoreau country, and Heinrich is steeped in Thoreau. I read it through with exhilarated recognition. Somehow, by instinct and the firm repression of the instinct to own, I had got it right with "my" tawny as Heinrich – far more knowledgeable and expert than I am – had got it right with his formidable Great Horned Owl. We can interact with the wild, and occasionally assist – but only so long as we do so not from egotistical need but with loving attention and respect, all the while dismissing any desire to own or control. I recommend anything by Bernd Heinrich to you. He's as mad as I am, his human relationships quite as disastrous; but he knows where beauty and freedom lie. Here is one of those places.

When the tide ebbs from Traeth Bach, the estuary gathers the western light, resolves it into a pattern of interlocking curves, gleaming channels and draining sand that is beautiful to view. Look down on it from the foothills of the Rhinogydd in the evening light as you walk down from Bryn Cader Faner along the green path beneath Y Gyrn leading to Caerwych and it seems a huge, transcendent pattern of interlocking Celtic motifs, an embodiment and evanescence of light. Far out on shifting submarine sandbars along which I used cautiously to venture in the 1980s were natural riches. In winter, the estuary teemed with migrant ducks and waders. Scurrying sanderling animated the tideline. Wheeling clouds of Curlews descanted above; there were Golden plovers down from the moors, here in their winter retreat; Great crested grebes, Great northern and Red-throated divers. I came across the corpse of a diver one Sunday morning, cast aside on the saltings by Abergafren, its beautiful ruddy throat blown away by a local wildfowler I'd seen there that morning, the bird-brained dog badge of the British Association for Shooting and Conservation prominent on the rear window of his dark blue Fiesta van. That winter I'd often been within feet of this gorgeous bird. His death felt like a bereavement.

Now, where there *were* natural riches, in a twilight of the present day, what did I see? A couple of shelduck, a single curlew, a pair of ravens. The sense of desertion, of emptiness was overpowering. Around the time of this rare, precious bird's killing, a local shooting club secured leases from the Crown Estate to this foreshore. These were later extended right round Morfa Harlech National Nature Reserve. (Birds, I take it, are not aware of human territorial distinctions.) Notices along the foreshore advertise the availability of day-shooting permits to attract more "sportsmen" to this place of wonders to sate their bloodlust. My subjective impression of declining bird-numbers at Traeth Bach since organized shooting began is supported by statistical evidence. Mick Green of the pressure group *Ecology Matters* notes Welsh populations of golden plover – one of our most beautiful and redolent hill and coastal birds – have declined by over 80% in 30 years. Yet countrywide the *British Association for Shooting and Conservation* in alliance with local shooting clubs urgently seeks further foreshore leases with these birds on their quarry-lists. There's a disturbing lack of transparency in the granting of leases. The secretary to the body that advises Crown Estate – the body that grants shooting leases along British foreshores – is a paid officer of the BASC. Letters of objection by reputable conservation agencies and interested individuals seem often to disappear. The BASC lease applications list target species – Golden plover among them – that are red-list-endangered in Wales. The Crown Estate website insists on preservation of refuge areas to which species may fly to escape the shooters. It's well known locally that when the latter are active at Traeth Bach birds fly across the sands to Aberdwyfor – where a BASC lease-application was recently rejected after national press publicity given to a concerted local campaign of opposition. Will the Crown Estate be so callous as to deprive them of this place of safety? Surely it's time for a moratorium on all shooting of red and amber list species in the U.K? As I mused on that at dusk by Traeth Bach recently, a pair of little egrets – once shot to extinction[15] in Britain, their numbers here over the last forty years steadily increasing – drifted past like a glimmer of purity in the surrounding gloom. Now the local population shares the small heronry in the lee of Harlech Castle. Gales out of the south-west come hurling and roaring against the castle walls. They shudder against massive curved bastions, buffet past them, slip round to tear at a ragged copse of larch, cherry and sycamore in the northern lee. From the slope above, where great boles of beech and ash have snapped and splintered in the tempest-blast, I watched recently as a solitary heron struggled into the wind. Not for this bird the usual, paunchy amble along the breeze, neck retracted, wingspan larger than a golden eagle's propelling it with irregular beat. This heron strained with every muscle and pinion. Its neck outstretched, it looked huge, awkward, prehistoric, labouring. I saw him disappear into a density of branches. Moments later another heron followed into shelter. Even ravens and jackdaws had retired from the wind-fray. I marvelled at the herons' inelegant obduracy, remembered too the account Henry Williamson – of all writers on nature the most acutely and savagely descriptive, his perceptions brutalised by his Great War experiences – gave of a battle between a lone heron and a falcon family in *The Peregrine's Saga*.

---

[15] The loss of this species was the original impetus to the 1889 formation (initially as the Society for Protection of Birds) of the *Royal Society or the Protection of Birds*, by Emily Wilkinson in Manchester.

Finding a calm place, I took tripod and optic out of my rucksack and focussed on the copse. A glint of white led me to hope the little egrets from Traeth Bach were nesting here alongside their larger cousins. But it was no more than a Harlech holidaymaker's plastic bag caught on a branch. Through a haze of larch branches came a glimmer of incomparable grey, sable gleams, a flash of brilliant yellow. I zoomed in, and there, deep among the trees atop an ivy-strangled stump, two herons were grooming themselves, taking their ease on a sprawl of untidy nest. They spread wings, drew feathers through long beaks, preened meticulously at pale breast-plumage. There's a sense of delicacy, of spatial awareness, in the home actions of these gaunt, at times ungainly birds. The co-operation vouchsafed by this intimate glimpse was palpable. I thought of herons' ancient proximity to man; their still presence on shoreline or in city parks; their historic use as falconers' quarry; the Egyptians' sense of them as soul-symbol; and was glad for this pair's having found shelter from the storm. Mating occurred in storm-lashed February, the vast grey birds wheeling and soaring on measured wing-beats in graceful aerial dance, their harsh cries, tumbling aerobatics, strange contortions an ecstasy filling the wild air. The rough platform among the larches, half-concealed by a boss of ivy, was carefully renovated by both herons in a heart-warming display of mutual co-operation. There was remarkable spatial awareness as long twigs were passed bill-to-bill through dense branch-cover and woven into the nest-fabric. Eggs hatched before March was out. After weeks of patient sitting, it became successively nursery, kindergarten, then adolescent hang-out to a pair of scrawny young punks with black Mohicans and bedraggled breast-plumes. A noisier, smellier pair of offspring it's hard to imagine. When from their high vantage point they spied a returning adult, a phenomenal racket ensued – screeching and yelping, howling and grunting at solicitous parents who trail back and forth day-long between tidal pools of the estuary, woodland streams or hill-lakes. Jackdaws and rooks added their caw-cophony to the general din, harassing the huge birds, forcing them into further circuits as they parachuted down on arched wings, long legs extended, into the tree. Noticeably, the corvids kept distance from those orange dagger beaks; so that eventually the flustered herons could land, to regurgitate half-digested crop-contents of fish and frog, vole, rat and eel into the youngsters' maws in a frenzy of beak-snapping, neck-snaking and wing-stretching that culminated in long sessions of careful grooming, drawing out unruly breast-feathers, smoothing primaries, scratching for fleas, sun-dozing. Affronted maybe by the growing fishy stench around the larch-copse or fearful perhaps for their own offspring, the rooks migrated to a stand of sycamore a few hundred yards away. So the voices of the fledgling herons were now dominant over a snare-whisper of jackdaw calls. The young birds were watchful, curious. They tussled with their beaks, practiced the lightning-fast hunting-strike on leaves, probed the nest with grey juvenile beaks for overlooked scraps. More and more, they craned those long necks, stretched and flapped their wings, moved around in the tree, scrabbled back nestwards. Another few weeks later and I'd see one or other solitary along the estuary: the bird W.H. Hudson describes as "ghost-like … a haunter of lonely waters at the dim twilight hour; mysterious in its comings and goings"; sight of which for me always induces a mingling gladness and melancholy. This small heronry in the lee of the castle is of great antiquity. The bird whose activity Robert Graves, who spent much of his youth in the vicinity of Harlech, describes in a passage from his remarkable work of syncretism, *The White Goddess* (1948), surely hatched here:

A peculiarity of wading birds such as the crane and heron is that,

when they have speared a quantity of small fish in a river ready to
take home to their young, they arrange them on the bank with the tails
set together in the form of a wheel, which was formerly the symbol of
the sun... This must have astonished the ancients as it astonished me
as a boy when I saw a heron doing it in the Nantcoll River...

Back on the old embankment to the south-west of Pont Briwet, salt creeks were draining all along the margins of Traeth Bach. Canada geese bustled down in ragged, loud skeins from hill-tarns to alight in them. From the old mill in the hamlet of Ynys – the word means "island" and this ground was once just that – the footpath leads to Llanfihangel-y-traethau. A circular enclosure clearly apparent on both ground and map alerts you to the ancient foundation, its origin as a Celtic Christian *clas*[16] – of this "church of St. Michael of the sands". In the early medieval period pilgrims, bound for Ynys Enlli, gathered here to be guided – and guides they would have needed – across the perilous and ever-changing two-mile crossing of the Dwyryd and Glaslyn estuaries. This pilgrimage was sufficiently important for the twelfth-century Pope Callixtus II to decree that three Bardsey journeys equalled one to Rome. Looking down from the churchyard, ice-smoothed Ynys Gifftan just upstream, cloud-capped Cnicht and the Moelwynion beyond, a swirl of channels, shimmer of receding water, vast expanse of sand somehow encourages you to imagine back a millennium or more and see a straggling line of the halt, the diseased and the blind, dwarfed by emptiness, devoutly making for the distant shore. These sands are a dangerous place. At times I've made my way a little too far out for comfort, studied for a little too long waders scurrying by the water's edge at Harlech

---

[16] A *clas* was an early Christian religious community in which men and women had equal status. Their sites are scattered throughout Wales. One distinguishing feature which endures at many of them to the present day is the circular churchyard, such as you find at Llanfihangel-y-traethau.

Point, before the habitual headlong quicksand-avoiding rush as the water gathers and begins to surge. Often a solitary grey heron, heavy glide of which to his fishing station I'd watched in rapt admiration, registered my flight with a slight inclination of his head. When I drew breath and glanced back, he had returned to his poised and deadly concentration. I wonder sometimes if these adrenaline-laced experiences have intensified the sense of beauty I've taken away from this environment, which must have affected or even terrified so many over the centuries? Here's a description by Lord Lyttelton from the *Cambrian Travellers' Guide* of 1808:

> *"The view of these sands is terrible, as they are hemmed in on each side with very high hills, but broken into a thousand irregular shapes. At one end is the ocean, at the other the formidable mountains of Snowdon, black and naked rocks, which seem to be piled one above the other; the summits of some of them are covered with clouds, and cannot be ascended. The grandeur of the ocean corresponding with that of the mountain, formed a majestic and solemn scene; ideas of immensity swelled and exalted our minds at the sight; all lesser objects appeared mean and trifling so that we would scarcely do justice to the ruins of an old castle..."*

Mrs. Radclyffe could scarcely have expressed it better! Little more than two centuries ago, the sheaf of long and narrow rocky ridges between the great and the little strands would have been wild country indeed, capes and wave-battered promontories, tide-encircled, the low evening sun gleaming across a swirl of channels through the sand, gilding them into semblance of those interlocking spiral Celtic designs that have come down to us through artefacts surviving from the Hallstatt and La Tène cultures. However heroic a saga was the construction of Madocks' government-approved dark embankment from Aber Iâ to the foot of Moel y Gest, it banished mere beauty to reclaim profitable land from the sea. Shelley, who briefly lived here, left for Italy, in lines from his poem, "Love's Philosophy", so perfectly evokes this place:

"See the mountains kiss high heaven
And the waves clasp one another..."

In twilights "quiet as a nun", when a hush permeated the landscape, I walked the northern shore of this land by a complex of paths into which shifting routes across the *traethau* linked in. Tree-tops and hedgerows where wood-warblers had sung and fly-catchers danced through summer months were silent. Only my movement caused alarm – a pheasant hurtled away on a harsh chuckle of frantic wing-beats, jays screamed, the magpie roost chattered abuse and by the gate where I paused, a crouching hare, ears back, looked up in fear and accelerated smoothly away down the lane. Wrens chipped and scolded at a scuffling shrew. Pinions of a white raven – rare omen-bird of legend – and its black mate creaked across the sky. On Afon Glaslyn a heron rose from riparian shadows downstream of the empty ospreys' nest, passed me in lumbering flight. Light slipped under clouds massing to the west and blushed slopes high on the notched top of Moel Ddu – "the black hill", but dusted on this early spring evening with *eira bach yr ŵyn ifainc* – the small snow of the young lambs. It picked out in glinting silver filigree outcrops along the southern ridge. I looked up, and saw through bare branches a bright and slender moon. These two estuaries – y *traethau* – have given me over so many years such plenitude. I remember lying in bed at Stentir on a spring day over thirty years ago with the doctor peering at a thermometer he'd just plucked from my mouth. I was 40, and had caught chicken pox from my son Will.

"104 degrees! If it goes up any more we're going to have to whisk you into hospital, old chap…"

My mind had been on other things entirely. What doctors say is so predictable, so tediously conformist in terms of medical protocols their profession insists they observe. So I barely heard him. On this particular morning huge flock of curlews that had gathered over the winter months were wheeling above the sands, the bright air thick with their gliding forms, the whole congregation descanting up to that ecstatic crescendo from which it cascades plangently down in waterfalls of silvery sound.

"Are you listening..?"

His voice broke once more into my attentive reverie. I shook my head.

"Aren't the curlews glorious?" I responded.

He frowned down at me.

"Drink plenty of fluids. Check your temperature every couple of hours. Call me if it rises…"

I gave him a quick nod of thanks and turned back to the window, curlews being more to my taste than iatrogenic edicts. At this time of my life, when not bed-bound I walked daily on Traeth Bach with Jonah Jones. He was Director of Dublin's National College of Art and Design from 1974 to 1978. This Irish sojourn gave him material for a fine novel, *A Tree May Fall* (Bodley Head, 1980), that focuses on a little-known and tragic encounter during the Easter Rising. These walks of ours were glorious adventures. The Dwyryd estuary is not obviously "wild". Pont Briwet, beneath which the flooding tides boil and swirl, marks its eastern limit. The northern shore is Aber Iâ with its major tourist attraction, Portmeirion. The A496 to Harlech, burdened with holiday traffic, traces round southerly. Yet this estuary is as "wild" – whatever that fashionably posturing word so beloved of the *metro litterati* may mean – as any place I've been in sixty years of travelling marginal lands, initially around Britain, later of the globe. Differently wild, perhaps; diminishingly wild I fear: but there's a quality about Traeth Bach that has enthralled me for decades. It derives from intimate knowledge of place and its elemental affect. I'm not talking here of a landscape those eighteenth-century adherents steeped in Edmund Burke and the cult of the Sublime would have admired. Y Traeth Bach (literally "the little strand") is simpler than that. It has an absolute simplicity – sky, sea, sand, distant surrounding hills – that acts as magnet and *tabula rasa* for a mind seeking clarity. On my walks with Jonah we'd slip down on to the sands by the abandoned slate quay steps near Borthwen, where he had his workshop. We'd wade the inshore channel and head out towards the ancient pilgrims' church of Llanfihangel-y-traethau, a mile away above the farther shore. Emptiness accentuates distance. Within a hundred yards you're *"environ'd with a wilderness of sea"* (Titus Andronicus). We'd trek in a great arc to the wide channels where precise knowledge of tidal flow became crucial. The sea surges across these sands with astonishing velocity and force, channels become deep and flooding black torrents against which you could not swim. But that fear is adrenaline-inducing; decomposed adrenaline is chemically almost identical to LSD; our trips here were distinctly trippy. One clear St. David's Day, far out at slack water we waded knee-deep along sinuous, rippling submarine sand-bars in translucent turquoise water, heading for Clogwyn Melyn. It felt so remote – few places so isolated as on those sands between ebb and flow, senses attuned to sudden, perilous turn of tide. The channels teemed with birds. From draining sandbanks came the loud clamour of geese. There was plenitude, distance, a kind of solitude. Also immense fragility, to which selfish humanity pays scant regard. And there was the fascinating conversation of my good old friend and neighbour.

Jonah was a widely cultured, widely knowledgeable man. He had learnt his stone-carving from Laurence Cribb, who had been a student of Eric Gill in the latter's workshop at Piggotts in Buckinghamshire. He was a friend and confidant of Clough Williams-Ellis, of whom he wrote a respectful and entertaining memoir. Bill Condry was another friend, and the house where he and Penny lived for forty years on the Dyfi estuary now has a fine plaque carved by Jonah's apprentice Meic Watts. All this texture of friendship and tradition enriched and informed Jonah's conversation. I remember one talk we had, knee-deep in the draining tide as we splashed across towards the old *clas,* that centred on something I'd just read by Bill on the notion of global cooling that was prevalent at that time over thirty years ago before the evidence for anthropogenic global warming became incontrovertible.

My exposition of Bill's argument had led Jonah into a lucid account of Milankovich Cycles – named after Milutin Milankovich, a Serbian mathematician who provided the first quantitative description of them. Essentially these are phasal cycles prompted by earth's orbital eccentricities over a period of 100,000 years. Add in a few wobbles and variations in planetary tilt, and variation becomes the norm – but one to which anthropogenic global warming adds a frightening new dimension. I remembered this long-gone conversation, and pondered how it tied in with the undoubted and drastic species-loss from Traeth Bach that I've witnessed accelerating particularly in the last decade. Looking out from my window one evening, there was something about the light across the bay that prompted me to slip out and walk by the sea-defences, past the mill-pool at Ynys, to Llech Ollwyn, the point I'd often reached with Jonah from the northern side. There I sat on one of the benches looking over the estuary to Aber Iâ, took out the habitual flask and spy-glass, and awaited developments. The tide had drained from Traeth Bach. Westering sun added a dimension of luxuriance to the sensuality of curving sand-banks, an intensifying brilliance to rippled water and scalloped sand. Low hills along the Peninsula – Garn Fadryn, Garn Boduan, Yr Eifl, bulky little Moel y Gest in the foreground – were slipping behind a shimmering, pointilliste veil that was moving rapidly my way. Focusing the eyeglass, I scanned the estuary for bird life once so abundant at this season. On a sandbank where in previous years I'd seen major flocks of pintail, there was a single small group of birds far out, only three or four of them, clustered on a low ridge of sand above a sinuous deep channel. The retroussé bill of the largest bird, a suggestion of dove-grey and russet along the thick neck, identified it. Rain geese! Red-throated divers! A couple of juveniles, and one adult, still in his gorgeous summer plumage, down early from their breeding grounds on northern Scottish lochans. A dapper squad of oystercatchers flighted in to splash down alongside them. Somewhere far out on the estuary a lone curlew, having descended from nesting on wild moors above, insistently cried out the two notes from which its name derives. No response came, no plangently soaring counter-song. Today's solitary presence, unseen, set against the shimmery light, the memory of multitudes here, felt ghostly somehow. I watched as clouds hid the western hills. Swaying, mercury columns of rain detached and moved across the water. A double arc of rainbow was suddenly flung across high hills easterly, its end almost at my feet. Two redshank sped past, scolding out a warning. Heavy drops of rain fell. I fled for home before the deluge, thinking that the time had come to whisk our planet into hospital for urgent responsible treatment before its case became one for terminal care. Next morning a flight of redshank, wings elegantly barred and bent, clattered and yelped out of a draining channel as I circled Glastraeth. The redshank circled round, calls modulating to a plaintive diminuendo, and descended towards the reed-fringed former mill-pool at Ynys.

I trailed after them, noting as I went four egrets feeding across the saltings. From the footbridge over the channel (a legacy of the early land reclamation project on this part of the traeth and now a habitat for mink) that drains the fine northern lakes of the Rhinogydd, on a sandbank downstream I glimpsed a flash of colour. Focusing the glass, what leapt into view was the ruddy, wind-ruffled, punk hairstyle of a red-breasted merganser. Backlit by the lowering sun, it became a glorious, vibrant halo, visionary and intensely strange. I wandered close, interposing tufts of reeds for concealment. There were four of them, a male and three females, pearly-flanked, crested heads glowing among the muted sea-marsh tints. Mergansers are reliable presences on the estuary for much of the year. They saw me and took to the water, paddling quietly upstream in queenly convoy. Beyond Llechollwyn, where the saltings curve round to merge into Morfa Harlech nature reserve, I spotted a group of stooping figures, sallied over to them and recognized a woman among them as someone I'd once met at the house of Mrs. Lock, the Roma fortune-teller on Anglesey. I asked after her, and dropped a few words – probably shockingly mispronounced – conned years ago from George Borrow's *Romano Lavo-Lil* into my greeting, to reassure them of friendship and good intent. We talked of the samphire they were gathering. One of the men handed me a sprig, carefully pinched off rather than uprooted. I savoured its sharp, salt tang. This is rock samphire, a member of the carrot family, now a much-prized delicacy with which metro-foodies garnish their saltmarsh lamb. Only slim pickings here, so I told the Roma family of an unexpected rich source on the farther shore (in a very public place, but it's a secret between the Roma and myself now). We parted with goodwill on both sides, and a few curses on the head of Priti Patel for her political designs against the community of Roma and travellers. Imagine what Gipsy George Borrow's fate would have been were he alive today, at the hands of this termagant?

I've long been fascinated by the question of what were the routes taken in former centuries in making the crossing of these formidable *traethau*. The pilgrims on the Taith y Pererin (pilgrims' way) for Ynys Enlli supposedly gathered at Llanfihangel to meet guides who conducted them across the Great Traeth before they reassembled at the little church just north-west of Glan y Morfa. To look back across the sands they had traversed from Llanfihangel must have occasioned some tumult in their minds as incoming tide swept across the bay. Many, hearing of the dangers of this route, would opt for a longer but safer connection with a pilgrims' way that links up churches along the northern coast of Llŷn – Clynnog, Tudweiliog and Llangwnnadl – before arriving at Aberdaron. The link to this arrived at Llandanwg south of Harlech, its simple medieval church continually threatened by burial among the wind-blown sand dunes[17] in which it stands. From Harlech it continued along the coast to Talsarnau, before breaking off across Glastraeth, rounding the eastern tip of Ynys Gifftan and fording the channel, shallow at low tides along the northern shore of Aber Iâ, to reach Abergafren. Ynys Gifftan came up for sale in the 1980s for a price of around £30,000, which included the then-habitable house on the island and also a DUKW amphibious vehicle. I could have raised that amount at the time. What stopped me was the fact that my son Will was then at school in Penrhyndeudraeth. The regrets we trail in our wake on the voyage through life! The choices from Abergafren were to

---

[17] I remember being on Omey Island off the westernmost point of Connemara several years ago and seeing JCBs under the supervision of a local priest excavate the church there from sand dunes which had buried it – a very moving sight.

take old sunken ways round the western and northern sides of Penrhyndeudraeth before following the shores of Traeth Mawr inland past Garreg. There was at one time a mooring for boats plying the *traeth* at what's now the Brondanw Arms in Llanfrothen – hence its local name of *Y Ring*, after the mooring rings along its rear wall. Continuing across Afon Nanmor to Pont Aberglaslyn, a rough track south under wooded slopes leading up to Moel Ddu passed through Prenteg. Thereafter it arrived at what between 1805 and 1811 became the site of a model village, Tremadog, planned and promoted by that fascinating character and boldly attractive Regency buck and speculator William Alexander Madocks[18] (1773-1828) – the man who changed irrevocably (and for some controversially) the whole appearance and nature of this incomparable corner of Wales. In earlier centuries this route was viewed as being extremely hazardous, perhaps less on account of the physical obstacles of current and tide than from the banditry that characterised much of Welsh society in the century after the Wars of the Roses. Here's an incident described by Sir John Wynn, the most interesting chronicler of the period, in his *History of the Gwydir Family*, written some time during the last two decades of the Sixteenth Century:

> *"Ieuan ap Robert, on his return from Chirkland, riding home to his house by Gallt y Morfa Hir by moonlight (the tide in Traeth Mawr giving him no sooner passage), talking with his men carelessly and out*

---

[18] The essential reading on Madocks is Elizabeth Beazley's *Madocks and the Wonder of Wales* (Faber, 1967) – an entrancing, lively biography which is as charming as it is unfailingly well informed and elegantly written. It's a classic of modern Anglo-Welsh biographical, historical and topographical writing. If it were published today, it would deservedly walk away with a plethora of literary awards. Madocks, son of a wealthy London barrister, spent several fortunes on the construction of the cob – the embankment that runs from where Porthmadog now stands to Boston Lodge close to the north-western tip of Aber Iâ. The construction of this monumental work of civil engineering between 1808 and 1813, the disastrous breaches during the time of its being built, and the eventual success are an enthralling saga related by Mrs. Beazley in all their dramatic detail.

of danger, as he imagined, suddenly lighted[19] an arrow shot among them from the hillside which was then full of wood. Whereupon, they made a stand and shot wholly all seven towards the place from which the other arrow came. With one of which arrows of theirs shot so at random they killed him who shot at them...

Sir John Wynn continues with his tortuous account of the attempted murder of Ieuan ap Roberts and its repercussions:

"Hywel ap Rhys, understanding that Ieuan ap Robert and his people had occasion to go to Caernarfon for the assizes, thought it a fit time by force to enter upon his house in his absence and to apprehend all these [i.e. the members of Ieuan's household] *and to bring them to Caernarfon to be hanged, for there was none of them but was outlawed of murder and felony in the country where he dwelt. To this end, to strengthen himself in this purpose, he sent for his trustiest friends about him, and among the rest procured Dafydd ap Siencyn, his cousin german, then a famous outlaw in the rock of Carreg-y-gwalch[20], with his crew and followers to assist him. And so suddenly came in a morning to the hall of Ieuan ap Robert's house where there were not many men to be seen for the outlaws were in outhouses about and upper chambers in the lower end of the hall stowed and none to be seen."*

The apparent peace soon gave way to one of the recurrent bouts of mayhem that are a distinguishing feature of Sir John Wynn's text:

"Those people of Ieuan ap Robert that were in the hall raised a cry and took themselves to their weapons whereupon the outlaws awakened, arose, betook themselves to their weapons and bestirred themselves handsomely. It happened the same time that Ieuan ap Robert's wife

---

[19] In the old sense of "alighted" – i.e. descended among them.

[20] "The rock of the falcon", in the escarpment above Gwydir Castle, from which the publisher of this book takes its name. Both the outlaws' cave and the peregrines who gave the rock its name are still to be seen.

stood at the fireside looking on her maid boiling of wort to make metheglin[21], which seething wort was bestowed liberally among the assailants and did help the defendants to thrust back them that were entered and afterwards to defend the house.

The house was assaulted with all force and pierced in diverse places, and was well defended by those who were within, for having made diverse breaches, they dared not enter, few resolute men being able to make a breach good against many. Upon the cry the country did rise and Ieuan ap Robert's tenants and friends assembled in great numbers, whereof Robin ap Inco was captain who fought with the besiegers who, in the end, with their arrows did drive the besiegers from the one side of the house who continually assaulted the other side. After they had continued all day and all night in that manner, the next morning, seeing they could prevail little to enter the house, they came to a parley with Robin ap Inco who advised them to be gone in time for, said he, 'as soon as the water at Traeth Mawr will give leave Ieuan Grach, my master's kinsman, will be here with Ardudwy men, and then you shall all be slain.'"

After that resounding statement of *Realpolitik*, Sir John Wynn reaches the following palliative conclusion to skirmishings around the two estuaries:

Daily bickerings too long to be written passed between so near and hateful neighbours. In the end the plague, which commonly follows war and desolation after the earl of Pembroke's expedition, took away Ieuan ap Robert at his house in Gesail Gyfarch in the flower of his age being but one and thirty years old. Whose death ended the strife of those houses for his three eldest sons were sister sons to Hywel ap Rhys ap Hywel Fychan.

Enough of clan warfare and feuding in late-medieval Wales, fascinating topic though that may be. We need to consider the history of the structure that has irrevocably changed the nature

---

[21] A spiced mead.

of these two magnificent estuaries of Dwyryd and Glaslyn. If we were to follow downriver from Pont Aberglaslyn to the now-stopped mouth of Afon Glaslyn, we might choose to continue past the thunderous sluice gates. (The manner in which the river scoured away foundation for the cob in its construction was a contributory factor to recurrent serious breaches in the embankment during 1812-1813 – disasters which it took all Madocks' considerable strength of purpose and rather more than his equally impressive family wealth to overcome.) As the Glaslyn spreads out across the sands once beyond Porthmadog's harbour and Cei Ballast, and passes the little cove of Borth-y-gest (another of the former harbours for Traeth Mawr in pre-Cob days), if you follow the coastal path round from the latter towards Ynys Cyngar and Morfa Bychan, you look down from low slatey cliffs on to a clear channel of relatively clear and unpolluted water flowing across golden sand. We could do that, and in all probability in the spring and summer we'd witness one of the spectacular sights of nature in Eryri. This is one of the favourite hunting grounds for the ospreys which come from Africa each year and nest on the stretch of river above Pont Croesor (under 24-hour video surveillance, thank heavens, otherwise the chicks might fall prey to the unscrupulous operators who, in exchange for a substantial wad of cash, provided the subject, in the form of a young Goshawk, for a prodigiously popular and to my mind odious recent book within the idiom of "New Nature Writing" – bad examples don't come much worse than this). Here you may witness the untidy flounce for fish in the shallows of these majestic fish-eagles – a wonderful sight, steel-like talons on great feet appended to feathery pantaloons coming up gripping a mullet or even a grilse to carry back to the constantly-monitored young in their platform nest three miles upriver, with a volunteer-staffed visitor centre at the roadside which is now one of the major tourist attractions of Eryri, where visitors can park and sit indoors to watch on a bank of monitor screens every cute gobble and screech of the ungainly chicks, whatever the weather. If that's your thing, then I recommend it. But to watch the ospreys in unmonitored, unsupervised habitat, though it may be less reliable, and might even involve getting cold and wet at times, is surely a more genuine, thrilling, adventitious experience than the simulacra available on the banked screens in the hut. I leave the choice with you, and would like to tell you of my finest osprey moment. This took place on the quay at Saint Simeon, on the north bank of the Saint Lawrence Seaway 120 miles east of Quebec City, where I was waiting for the boat to take me across to the Gaspé Peninsula. Out from a beach of clean sand an osprey was circling above shallows just like the ones at the outflow of the Glaslyn. It stooped suddenly, there was an untidy detonation of long wings and water, and the bird rose with a large fish – a sea trout – in its talons. It flapped leisurely back to the shore, perched on a post to feed, pausing only briefly to glance across at the arrival of the dapper little ferry in sky blue for which I was waiting, before it commenced ripping at the sea trout's flesh and swallowing it down in large strips torn off by that wickedly curved and powerful beak. The great bird was at most twenty feet from me whilst this was taking place, and wholly unconcerned by my presence as spectator. Get along to Carreg Goch, keep still and quiet, and the same happy chance might befall you (though there are no perching posts for the ospreys available there).

Having visited its outflow, let's now follow the Afon Glaslyn upstream to its source. We can start at Pont Aberglaslyn, reputedly constructed by the Devil. He could thus claim the soul of the first creature to cross the bridge after its completion[22]. The Devil was

---

[22] You'll find many examples of this folk-tale motif if you look it up in Stith Thompson's Motif Index of Folk Literature: A Classification of Narrative Elements in Folk-tales etc.,

foiled by a magician, Robin Ddu, who was drinking in *Y Dafarn Delyn* – a pub in the village of a dozen houses that used to stand, before the Enclosure Acts, by the quay the remains of which are faintly discernible on the Glaslyn's eastern bank, along with the footings of the pub and houses close by its confluence with the Afon Cwm Bychan. This quay and Borth-y-gest were the main ports for Traeth Mawr during the period before construction of the Cob at Porthmadog. The brutal fate of the village by Pont Aberglaslyn is recounted as follows in D.E. Jenkins' 1899 book, *Bedd Gelert: Its Facts, Fairies, and Folklore*:

> *"...three men and a bailiff drove up to the village and told the occupants ... that they must quit at once, that their houses were to be unroofed. The helpless women began to weep and pleaded for some explanation. The only one they got was to see their furniture hurled out through the door. One poor fellow, Cadwaladr Roberts, was lying ill in bed; he was dragged down the ladder which connected the ground floor and his tiny bedroom, and left in the hands of houseless neighbours until he found shelter in the Union of Penrhyndeudraeth[23]. After this*

published in six volumes in 1955-1958 and an invaluable research tool for folklorists. The soul/bridge motif is ubiquitous. In Wales you'll also find it at Devil's Bridge. In Scotland it underpins Burns's 1791 poem Tam o'Shanter. It is, of course, anti-Pelagian, since a fundamental tenet of Pelagianism was that animals have souls. My suspicion is that it may have its origin in clerical anti-Pelagian sermonising. In the Pont Aberglaslyn story Robyn Ddu lures a terrier from *Y Dafarn Delyn* in the village at Aberglaslyn to follow him by throwing it scraps of bread. When they arrive at the newly-built bridge he rolls the loaf across and the terrier chases it, but not having a soul it is safe from damnation. Anyone who has ever cared for a terrier will appreciate the inherent contradiction here. Terriers are the most magnanimous and loyal of dogs! But to enable this one to escape the devil, let's allow the theological orthodoxy to stand.

[23] Later the Minffordd Hospital – the grim and semi-derelict building on the left heading south just beyond the roundabout at the end of the Porthmadog by-pass. Many of the old workhouses ("Unions") were put to this use. My maternal grandfather, who had been an agricultural labourer in Cheshire, had fought in the Boer War at the Siege of Ladysmith and the Relief of Mafeking, ended up living in Manchester, and in later life was in absolute fear of dying in the workhouse. After my grandmother's death he was taken into an old

*piece of daylight robbery, the property passed into the hands of David
Williams, esq., for some time M.P. for Merionethshire."*

The way onwards is now up the Pass of Aberglaslyn[24], by way of
the road which was, according to D.E. Jenkins, another of W.A.
Madocks' contributions to the network of communications in
Eryri. "One of the gentlemen who had most to do with the
opening up of the present road was W. A. Madocks, Esq., who
connected Llanrwst and Porth Dinllaen with the intention of
getting the Irish mail-boat to land its mail and cargo there, instead
of at Holyhead." Thomas Pennant, in his account of *A Tour in
Wales* from 1784, extolled Aberglaslyn. In its then-roadless state,
it must have been a tremendous defile leading down to the
impressive sea-inlet of Traeth Mawr:

*The mountains approach so close, as to leave only room for the furious
river to roll over its stony bed; above which is a narrow road, formed
with incredible labour, impending over the water... The scenery is the
most magnificent that can be imagined.*

people's home in south Manchester. As he became increasingly frail in his mid-eighties,
he was transferred from there to a geriatric ward, where I last saw him, hopeless and barely
alive, just before his death. He had turned his face to the wall, and was waiting for the end.
This geriatric ward was part of Withington Hospital – another grim Victorian building
which had, in its time, been a place of consuming dread for him as the south Manchester
workhouse.

[24] Unless, of course, you choose to circle round from just below Aberglaslyn into Cwm
Ystradllyn by way of Oerddrws – a route rich in interest and association which begins with
a moss-grown, beautiful, narrow and abandoned lane down through the woods above
Aberglaslyn Hall. There's a favourite poem of mine called Oerddwr by the great poet of
the Welsh hills, Sir T.H. Parry-Williams:

> *"Nid daear mo'r ddaear yno, nid haen o bridd;*
> *Mae ansylweddoldeb dan donnen pob cae a ffridd...*
> *O feudy'r Cwm hyd at feudy'r Hendre draw*
> *Y mae llwybrau'n arwain i leoedd a fu neu ddaw.*

(Earth is not earth there, no mere crust of soil;/There is insubstantiality under each
calloused field and sheepwalk.../From the cowshed at Cwm to Hendre beyond/Paths lead
to places past or unborn.")

The anxious register of that passage from Pennant chimes well with the National Trust's posting of contemporary warnings about the dangers of this selfsame "fishermen's path" as it's now termed. If you're heading on foot for Beddgelert or Nant Gwynen[25] you don't need to join the procession along the desperately tourist-crowded path through the gorge and thence into the thronging, traffic-jammed streets of Beddgelert. There is an alternative loop that will take you round to the southern end of Llyn Dinas. It goes by way of mine-scarred Cwm Bychan to descend to the shore of this beautiful lake. I used to live in a leaking caravan half-a-mile away and would walk to the lakeside daily, strolling along riverside paths through high bracken wet with dew. Sometimes the rocks and oakwoods of Dinas Emrys were sun-gilded, and I wiled away the mile to Llyn Dinas by rehearsing the story from Nennius[26] of the first appearance of Ambrosius (who was later to become famous as that mysterious presence in the *Matter of Britain*, Merlin the Magician) – a story of which modern archaeologists have vindicated much of the context at this site. Dinas Emrys itself is very well worth a visit. It's right at the centre of an exceptional concentration of sites connected to folk stories. The main legend that locates here, of the red and white dragon locked in mortal and destructive combat under the walls of the fort, is strongly redolent of the native tale of *Lludd and Llefelys*, which first appears in a Welsh translation inserted into the *Historia Regum Britanniae*. (One of the great imaginative source-texts of early British historiography, Geoffrey of Monmouth's bizarre and fanciful tales have been the subject of derision and amused wonderment ever since their first appearance in 1136. The lack of an authoritative recent edition has not helped in this dismissive response to a work that had enormous influence on

---

[25] I shall be using this older correct form rather than the OS's tautological version throughout, so get used to it.

[26] Ninth-century Welsh monk and author of the useful source-text *Historia Brittonum*.

generations of later writers, poets and dramatists.)

There is another story of less magical provenance that also finds a place in this landscape. This story concerns two chieftains from the time of Macsen Wledig (late fourth century). One of them, Brynach Wyddel, an Irishman who was first king of Gwynedd (we are not in the realms of reliable history here), and first of that position to be baptised into the Christian faith, fought with Owain Finddu (Owain the black-lipped), one of three sons of Macsen Wledig and Elen Lueddog. He is mentioned in the Welsh triads as one of the Three Monarchs of the Isle of Britain chosen by a national convention, and by repute was the battle-chief who restored Britain's independence and freed it from the burden of an annual financial tribute to Rome. A local tradition recounts how he fought with steel balls the giant of prodigious strength who dwelt at Dinas Emrys. The great antiquarian Edward Lhwyd (1660-1709) gives this version of their encounter:

"Between Dinas Emrys and the lake is the grave of Sir Owen ab Maxen, who had been fighting against the giant with steel balls. There are depressions in the ground where each stood, to be seen still. Others say it is with arrows that they fought, and that the depressions now seen were places dug by them to defend themselves. Neither of them, however, got over the affair. When the knight perceived that there was no hope of his living much longer, he was asked where he wished to be buried; he requested that an arrow should be shot skyward, and where it fell, they should make his grave there."

In D.E. Jenkins' time, the grave of Owain was still to be seen, and Beudy Bedd Owain ('the cowshed of Owain's grave') is still marked on the map at the foot of Llyn Dinas, whilst on the opposite side of Afon Glaslyn "an immense stone on the hillock beyond the river … was called Maen y Cawr ("the giant's stone"). It was broken up to construct the dam for carrying water to the copper mill below [at Sygun Fawr]". There is another presence haunting Dinas Emrys, and one we've met before in this wandering narrative. It's that of Vortigern (a title, perhaps, meaning "warlord", rather than a specific name). It was he, we learn from Nennius, that had the child Ambrosius brought to the fortress of Dinas Emrys to be sacrificed as suggested by his three magicians. They'd been commanded to establish the reason why every night the days' work on fortifications being built around the fort would collapse. Ambrosius discovered that the newly-built walls collapsed each night because underneath the fort a red and a white dragon fought in an underground lake. The king's men dug beneath the fort, confirmed the truth of Ambrosius's vision, and Vortigern's three magicians were hence executed and interred nearby, close to the track up to Hafod y Porth, where their tombs, naturally enough, were still visible not long before the time of our estimable local historian, D.E. Jenkins. Vortigern, of course, had particular opprobrium reserved for him by Gildas – a Breton monk from Rhuys who lived perhaps between 500 and 570 AD. In his *De Excidio et Conquestu Britanniae* Gildas laid the blame for inviting the dastardly heathen Saxons on to British soil firmly at the door of Vortigern, for which he has been viewed as forever damned by Welsh storytellers and historians. He turns up here and there throughout the country. In the north, apart from his association with Dinas Emrys, he's also connected with Nant Gwrtheyrn, near Llithfaen on the northern coast of Llŷn. The old quarrying village of Porth y Nant in this surprisingly remote valley was deserted in the Second World War, the population leaving as the surrounding granite-sett quarries were closed. When I first knew it in the early 1960s, it was known as 'the deserted village', and was an interesting place to go in fine weather, to sleep out and gather driftwood for fires, then sit round them telling stories in the approved fashion of the *cyfarwyddion* (the itinerant story-tellers of medieval Wales). Later in the 1960s a travelling band of hippies, the "Friendship Family", who'd been squatting the old quarry buildings of Dorothea in Dyffryn Nantlle and selling off pitch pine baulks used in construction of the roofs, moved in. It became a venue for acid-head parties, dancing to the Grateful Dead with music provided by speakers powered by car batteries carried down there from travellers' vans parked at the top end of the then-undrivable track. They didn't disturb anyone, were too remote for the police to disturb them, the place was derelict anyway so that little damage could be done, and a high old time was had by all, from Sefton Park LSD suppliers who were, with others from west London, eventually rounded up and given draconian prison sentences at Bristol Crown Court in 1978, to the alternative climbing community of Llanberis and Dinorwig, (termed by one strait-laced commentator as "the psychiatrists' paradise of Llanberis and Deiniolen"), student populations of Bangor, Aberystwyth and Lampeter, and the long-established hippy communities of Ceredigion. The police might have been better advised to let them continue with their micro-tab manufacture, in the hope that some of the remarkable drug would find its way into the brains of Tory politicians, and stimulate a little imagination, spirituality and kindness there, to alleviate the brutally corrupt materialism of the Thatcher, May and Johnson years that were to follow. But this is a heterodox viewpoint, so I'll not pursue it in this context. Instead we'll consider Vortigern.

There's a marvellous modern folk-tale I first heard from Alun Jones Pontypridd – one of the best teachers and storytellers I ever met: a mild-mannered, brown-eyed, soft-voiced Welshman and teacher at the Welsh-medium school in Aberystwyth who inducted thousands into the mysteries of *yr heniaith* through Wlpan summer schools and courses in places like Coleg Harlech and Coleg Prifysgol Bangor. He came once with his wife, and with John and

Gwenno Hywyn, who were also inspired Wlpan teachers, to a meal of jugged hare, baked salmon fresh from the Dwyfor, and potatoes and greens from my garden, all cooked in or on a calor gas cooker in my rented farmhouse in Cwm Pennant. But the company was the soul of forbearance, I had ample assistance from the highly competent distaff side, and afterwards, over brandy in front of a roaring log fire, Alun told this version of the folk tale that locates at Nant Gwrtheyrn. It hinges on that traditional Celtic device of the triple curse. (We came across this briefly in the story of Lleu Llaw Gyffes.) In Alun's story, the triple curse was placed not upon an individual, but on a place associated with an individual – Nant Gwrtheyrn! In mellow South Walian tones, those gently amused brown eyes fixing on each of his audience in turn, he told of the three (that number again!) seafaring monks in the Age of the Saints who were cast ashore on this rough and windswept coast, and received no hospitality – gravest of transgressions! – in these early days of Celtic Christianity from the valley community Vortigern/Gwrtheyrn had founded here after he had fled from Dinas Emrys. As the monks paused before beginning their arduous ascent out of the valley, one by one they turned on those who had refused them assistance and sustenance, and pronounced the following curses: that no church would ever be consecrated here; that no marriages could ever take place from here between relatives however distant; that the village would fail three times, and have no future.

Alun related how, two hundred years ago, there were three farms in the valley. Tŷ Uchaf was occupied by two orphans, Rhys Maredydd and his sister, Angharad. At Tŷ Hen dwelt Meinir and her father. The three children were cousins, but the bond between Rhys and Meinir was always the closest. Rhys and Meinir duly fell in love, a marriage was arranged for June at St. Beuno's church in Clynnog Fawr. In those days in Nant Gwrtheyrn there was an ancient tradition called the wedding quest. After their return from church the bride would hide and the groom would have to hunt for her. So Meinir left her father's house and ran for the hills. Rhys searched the valleys and mountains. There had been a trysting place at an ancient oak they had often shared. He went there, and found no sign. It was as though she had disappeared into the air. Years passed. Rhys, desolate, grew old. Fifty years beyond their marriage, at twilight, he was once more at the trysting oak. A violent storm rolled in from the sea, lightning flashed and thunder rolled. A jagged bolt of lightning struck the trunk of the ancient oak, splitting it apart. Another flash of lightning revealed the secret the tree's hollow heart had concealed for half a century. The skeleton of his bride, in her faded bridal gown, fell out of it and into his arms. He kissed the blanched skull and died, on the turf where years before he and Meinir had dreamed and loved together. Other residents of the valley found their remains entwined next morning, and buried them together in St. Beuno's churchyard, and so, concluded Alun, did the triple curse placed upon Gwrtheyrn finally work itself through. Nant Gwrtheyrn is now the Welsh Language and Heritage Centre, the compact village's buildings restored, a road built down to them, the whole place now a fitting milieu in which to take courses to teach you Welsh. Long may it be spared more tragedies, folkloric or otherwise, and its future, as well as that of the language, endure.

Back by the riverside below Dinas Emrys, on my walks from the caravan I'd stop at the footbridge below the craggy old fortress. Tint and texture of weed in the outfall from the lake, wavy russet and vivid, mottled green, and the unpolluted clarity of the water, always held me gazing for minutes in delight. Sometimes canoeists or children in rubber boats floated by as I stood by the river, splashing me playfully, and though that was sweet and innocent and pleasing too, the smooth-running silence was fractured and my reverie with it, so I'd go on my way. One evening I encountered a picnic party, their MPV parked in a nearby lay-by – half-a-dozen friendly men and women from the Black Country with a store of tinnies cooling in the lake, foil barbecues on the turf sizzling with steaks and sausages, and plates with buttered baps on them at the ready. When I went back next morning, the turf was scorched, the lake-shallows desecrated with plastic bags, lager cans and the barbecue trays. Litter was spread all around. I trailed back to my caravan for a couple of bin bags to clear it all up, and scarcely knew what to think. They had seemed such amiable people. Lack of empathy? The example set in cities? The Thatcherite Diseducation Project and her wicked precept that "there is no such thing as society"? So why should people have any regard or concern for the feelings and values of others, for their differing perceptions of utility and beauty? All I could do practically was to clean up in the hope that the lowered standard would not be emulated, the to-me holy ground not further defiled. For the climbing community of Eryri, one of the most redolent sites lies among the *ponticum* thickets that line the path rising from Llyn Dinas's south-eastern shore. Within a little over a quarter of a mile, it leads to a tiny cottage called Hafod Owen. This house is indelibly associated with the lives of two major rock-climbing pioneers of 1930s Eryri: Colin Kirkus (1910-1942)[27] and John Menlove Edwards (1910-1958). Edwards's association with Hafod Owen is the more potent. He was a psychiatrist, and by far the finest and most incisive writer, in a small corpus of essays, on the strange sport of rock-climbing. During the Second World War,

---

[27] For biographies of these two see Kirkus, *Hands of a Climber* by Steve Dean (Ernest Press, 1993); and my own *Menlove: The Life of John Menlove Edwards*, with an appendix of his writings (Gollancz, 1985 and subsequent editions). In the context of a book about rivers, it would be remiss of me not to mention Menlove's exploits on water. He swam the Linn of Dee near Braemar when in spate, rowed alone in a heavy wooden boat in midwinter across the Minch, made the first solo Greater Cuillin traverse on Skye.

after appearing before a brutal tribunal which initially rejected his application to be registered as a Conscientious Objector, he closed his psychiatric practice on Rodney Street in Liverpool, moved to London during the Blitz, and worked at the Tavistock Clinic and at Great Ormond Street Children's Hospital. In 1941 he ceased even that work, and – believing that as a non-combatant in the fight against fascism he should in no way be dependent on society, he took over Kirkus's lease on Hafod Owen and went to live there. As a statement of self-isolation in a crucial time, it was a radical move, and its negative aspects were exacerbated by his involvement with Wilfrid Noyce, who was Kirkus's cousin. Male homosexual practices at the time, pre-Beveridge, were illegal, and carried both social stigma to a degree (though widespread particularly at certain Cambridge University colleges, including King's, the one where Noyce was a student), the threat of heavy prison sentences, and the possibility of very damaging medical interventions in order to "cure" the patient of his condition (the existence of lesbianism was not officially recognised at the time). The absolute isolation at Hafod Owen, the profound unhappiness in his emotional life, the impossibility of pursuing his psychiatric research, the lack of any understanding context in his life, and the extreme tension of German rocket attacks upon London when he moved back there in 1942 all precipitated an ultimate mental collapse which was to end, after many years of confusion and suffering, in his suicide in 1958, by swallowing cyanide at a cottage in the garden of his sister Nowell's husband, Hewlett Johnson, the "Red Dean of Canterbury". His ashes were scattered on Bryn Castell, the prominent tree-crowned knoll just above Hafod Owen.

I've already given you a brief footnote detour through Beddgelert – a charming-enough village built upon a fabricated story which David Prichard, the former landlord of the Royal

Goat Hotel, derived from Rhys Goch Eryri (he of the chair by Pont Aberglaslyn) to bring custom his way. Prichard later even constructed a dog's grave in the water meadows in front of his establishment, which has now been further embellished by a remarkable dog sculpture. Now I must hurry you on along the course of the Afon Glaslyn to Pont Bethania, though we can stop briefly along the riverside path to hear the Nightjars churring and wheeling from the *ponticum* (rhododendron) thickets around Sygun Fawr. If we walk the riverside path at dusk, chances are that "the dewfall hawk" (Hardy) will brush past us on its mouth-agape pursuit of moths. Most times of the year, Welsh weather being what it is, the southern flanks of Snowdon will be braided with white threads of rushing streams; the water spirits will be garrulous in every cwm. On so many days of the year, rain here will be drenching down. I remember one year, 1966, when I was working as a rock-climbing instructor at Plas y Brenin, the National Centre for Mountain Activities, in Capel Curig. It rained every day between April and August. Each and every day boots and outdoor clothing had to be hung up or stowed away in the drying room ready to be dubbined and donned again still damp the following morning. There were no indoor climbing walls to offer respite from the relentless onslaught of the rain in those days. And yet, somehow, in some form, enjoyment was distilled from the experience (and arthritis stored up for our maturer years?).

Time to hurry along now to the shrine of the water-sprites – a haunting and atmospheric place. I had a description of it committed to memory from the rare and wonderful book of 1899 mentioned above: D.E. Jenkins' *Bedd Gelert: Its Facts, Fairies and Folklore*. It took me to Cwm Merch above Hafod y Llan, and I went there looking for Ogof y Gŵr Blewog – the cave of the hairy man. The story Jenkins relates to explain the name is a garbled mix of folk-tale motifs familiar from other Welsh, Scottish and Irish sources: pregnant women, stolen food, severed hands. Anything that would enhance the effect went into the mix, as it does with story-tellers to this day. I mused on it as I clambered up a faint path beside torrents and cataracts. Ash and holly cloaked the slopes, the ground was soft with vivid mosses, and the branches of the trees too were a luminous green. The gnarled wood had its own sense of enchantment, regardless of what I might find. A rocky scramble past a sidelong, broken fall of Afon Merch brought me to a long, narrow pool between steep walls that exactly matched Jenkins' description. Down to its swift green water a veil of ivy, leaves glistening, hung to conceal the farthest dark recesses into which a water-spout thundered. All the old mystery gathered about the place. To arrive here solitary on a winter's afternoon is to find yourself in the presence of the *Uruisg* – the water-sprite, stories of whom recur throughout the Celtic countries – who "haunts lonely places and waterfalls and, according to his mood, helps or harms the wayfarer. His appearance is that of a man with shaggy hair and beard…" I shuddered past the hairy man's lair and climbed on up the stream. Wild goats watched me from the old mine-track into the cwm – original inhabitants of these hills whose existence is recurrently threatened by authority and a cull. Even though I'm on their side and against officialdom, the goats were not to know this, and sagaciously shunned my human presence as I descended the winding green way, through stands of Scots pine where Crossbills whirr around among the topmost branches, into the valley again. Afon Merch, which drains this cwm throughout its short course, in its lower reaches is one of the loveliest of Welsh hill streams: winding, boisterous, jewelled with pools and brilliant falls. It flounces about, headlong and impetuous, in a series of torrents and cataracts through open woodland of ash and holly, the more open places shimmering with bluebells before the bracken croziers out across them in spring and cloaks them in summer verdure or autumn fire. This gnarled wood has a strong sense of enchantment. If Merlin were to appear here, I think it would scarcely be a surprise. But our path doesn't take us up Cwm Merch, interesting approach to Snowdon's alternative horseshoe[28] though that sequestered valley is. I ought to tell you something about it whilst we're here and before we head back into the main valley. The name means "woman's cwm", and Jenkins has a tale to explain that, which is a horror story with a happy ending. In brief, it begins with a *noson lawen* (a social evening of music and story-telling when the young people of a neighbourhood gathered to meet and to plot what young people have always done to ensure the survival of the human race). The noson lawen in question was held at the farmhouse of Bwlch Mwrchan, now in ruins but formerly on what's now Hafod y Llan land close to the sheep-folds at the southern end of Llyn Gwynant. The night for the assembly was during an equinoctial gale. It was one of violent storm and drenching rain, a wind roaring from the north-east down the valley, hurling the waves it raised on the lake against the house, the chimney smoking and the night outside pitch-dark and moonless. Wind whistled in the casements, and squalls of rain rattled down on the roof. The dire scene outside lent its mood to the orations within, and with the spirits of the company failing by the minute with the prospect facing them of a walk home through the tempest, it was decided to put an early end to the proceedings. Though not before the man of the house, disappointed with the depressed tenor of the evening's entertainment, had issued a sardonic challenge to the young men present. Which of them, he asked, would dare venture through the storm to the *hafod* in Cwm Merch, and bring from there the halter hanging on the wall

---

[28] Snowdon's southern horseshoe, starting from Pont Bethania, taking the old green mine track up Cwm Merch from beyond the clapper bridge at the foot of Cwm Llan to reach abandoned copper mine workings high on Lliwedd Bach, gaining the ridge above these – wonderful views into Cwm Dyli and up to Yr Wyddfa – then following round over Y Lliwedd to Bwlch y Saethau before climbing to Yr Wyddfa and descending over Bwlch Main and Yr Aran back to Pont Bethania is as good in its way as the circuit from Gorffwysfa by way of Crib Goch and Garnedd Ugain.

farthest from the door, which he needed to ride to Llanrwst market the following day?

The *hafod* was not much more than a mile from Bwlch Mwrchan, but the path to it was rugged and tortuous. The men sat on their hands, eyes downcast to avoid the challenge. The women smiled and taunted. Eventually one young man with no *cariad* there to puncture his manly pride rose to his feet and ventured out into the wind and rain, perhaps in the hope that by doing so he might change his single state. He managed to thread his way through the woods, across the flooding streams, up the outcropping rocks, into the cwm and forced his way across the bouldery ground until he was within sight of his objective. Where a light was showing! Was it a will o'the wisp, a *cannwyll corff*, hob's lantern? The one thing he knew for certain was that at that time of year none of the valley people would be there with their flocks. The hair on his scalp prickling, he moved closer. Were the anguished groans he thought he could hear no more than the gale whistling through cracks and crevices in the rock? He arrived at the door of the *hafod* and peered through cracks in the weathered, worm-eaten timber. What he saw was a roaring fire, on the ground in front of which a woman lay bound and scorching before the leaping flames, two men standing by to use whatever means might increase her pain. He tried the door but it was barred. He stepped back, charged at it with his shoulder, and sent it along with its rotten frame flying into the centre of the room. Startled by the intrusion, the two oppressors fled. The young man picked up the woman, moved her away from the fire, and with a knife he carried for his shepherding he slit her bonds, took her hand, and having had the presence of mind to pick up the halter from the wall farthest from the door, led her back along the treacherous path to Bwlch Mwrchan, where the woman was warmed in front of a friendlier fire, given a clean nightgown, and put to bed with the daughter of the house for the night.

Next morning, perfectly blue-skied and calm as so often after a storm, the people of Nant Gwynen assembled to search for the monsters who had been torturing the young woman. They found their corpses at the foot of Clogwyn y Barcud, over which, blinded by the rain and leaning on each other, they had stumbled in the darkness and fallen a hundred feet to their deaths. Those early risers the ravens had already breakfasted on their tongues and eyes. What was left of them was buried under a cairn of rocks where they were found. The only mystery that remained to its protagonists from this episode was that of love itself, as the woman – fully recovered from her experience – and her rescuer found favour in each others' eyes, were soon married in Beddgelert church, raised many children in their home place, and most of the native inhabitants of Nant Gwynen, it is said, are descended from them. As a corollary and perhaps an objection to this strange love story from long ago, which is probably at root another example of the onomastic element at play in the Welsh folk-imagination, we need to mention that the antiquary Edward Lhuyd refers to Cwm Merch as Cwm Ierch or Iwrch – the valley of the roe bucks, which would surely have been numerous here at one time. He also calls the river of Cwm Llan the Afon Cwm Llem – the leaping river, which is not only entirely appropriate in its lower reaches, but also has historical authority, having been rendered thus in an old charter of Aberconwy from the time of Longshanks. And on that thought, I take my leave of the southern *cymoedd* of Yr Wyddfa, and head for the footbridge at the south-western end of Llyn Gwynant, which takes us initially through woodland clothing the lower slopes of Gallt y Wenallt before descending to riparian pastureland along the banks of the Afon Glaslyn. If we were to follow the path all the way to its destination, it would take us to Gorffwysfa at the head of the Pass of Llanberis, but our present objective is only the source of the Glaslyn.

These woodlands in Nant Gwynen are a glorious feature, the long strip on the north-western bank of Llyn Gwynen particularly so. The bird-life here in spring (both varieties of flycatcher in particular, along with redstarts, all of them feasting on the caterpillars that devour the new leaves) is one of the joyful sights of Eryri. The contrast with bare slopes of Gallt y Wenallt is particularly delightful. That 2,000 ft. grass slope might look innocuous, but I remember being part of a rescue team called out from Plas y Brenin to search for a missing walker in the area. He'd become separated from his party in the mist near the summit of Gallt y Wenallt. We found him very quickly. He'd been wearing an orange Helly Hansen PVC suit that were standard outdoor wear at the time, and decided to try sliding down the steep, wet grass. He was soon out of control, speeding head-first through thick mist towards the drystone wall above the wood. In the collision his skull was crushed. He died instantly from massive head injuries. You could see the line he'd gouged into the turf as he desperately tried to control his slide for weeks afterwards. On a dry day you wouldn't give this slope a second thought as a place of potential hazard. The little cliff of Clogwyn y Wenallt, above the "Roman" footbridge just up-valley from where he died, has long been one of my favourites. There are a couple of classic Joe Brown[29] routes here that he did in his south-of-Snowdon

[29] Joe Brown (1930-2019) was the outstanding British all-round climber of his time, and one of the sport's most likeable characters. A jobbing builder in his youth, from a poor Manchester Catholic background, his climbing career led him from the gritstone outcrops of Derbyshire, where he made first ascents of a roll-call of what are now the difficult classics of the region, to Wales, where again many of the outstanding lines on the great cliffs fell to this lithe, humorous, phlegmatic master of movement on rock. He made the first ascent of Kanchenjunga on a small, lightweight reconnaissance expedition led by a Welsh surgeon, Charles Evans. It was the third-highest mountain in the world, and a far more difficult one than Chomolungma ("Mount Everest"), which had been climbed by Tenzing and Hillary on a large siege expedition two years before. Joe carried on putting up major new climbs on British cliffs well into his seventies, and is universally revered in the world

exploratory phase in the late 1950s, as well as an excellent climb by Brian Wright of Dolwyddelan called *Bovine*, which is by no means extreme but has one of the best medium grade wall pitches in Eryri, at a perfectly vertical angle on enormous holds, and with its most difficult moves low down near the starting ledge. One damp Sunday morning, after a party in a climbing club cottage at the head of Crafnant, I took a friend of mine from Manchester, Al Bevan, up this. Al had done very little climbing and wanted to try his hand at the sport. I thought the top pitch of *Bovine* was ideal for his first experience. He was several years older than me, and weighed several stone more. At the top you attach yourself to a good spike and take a stance on steep grass. After twenty feet Al swung off and came on the rope. I was turned upside down and dragged to the edge, my feet in smooth-soled rock-shoes slipping on wet grass. Lowering him to the big ledge burnt the skin off my palms. Al and I remained good friends until his death from cancer in July 2021 (he was buried on a flawless August day in the churchyard of Trelystan, on the Long Mountain above Y Trallwng). There is a very popular campsite in the meadow below Clogwyn y Wenallt, with a beautifully clear and deep stretch of the Glaslyn running through it into the lake. On the little knoll looking down on it from the north-east is a barn which has a prominent place in climbing folklore. During the 1960s this was the headquarters of the Wallasey Climbing Club. It had been fitted out with *matratzenläger*[30], a cast-iron stove in the centre, cooking facilities and chemical toilets in an outhouse. The Wallasey members had a reputation as one of the climbing ginger groups of the day, spurring each other on to daredevil feats and

---

of climbing, not only for the monumental scale of his achievements, but also for his modesty, down-to-earth attitudes, and slyly humorous outlook on life. From 1966 onwards he lived in Llanberis, where he ran an outdoor equipment store and became a regular and starring performer on BBC live outside broadcasts.

[30] Sleeping platforms of the kind found in alpine huts.

outrageous behaviour. Their members included mountaineers like
"Mo" Anthoine (1939-1989), about whom Al Alvarez wrote a fine
memoir called *Feeding the Rat*; the mountain painter Anthony
"Ginger" Cain, who has a gallery in Llanberis, and an amused,
steely, equable red-haired character always known simply as Fox,
who was a former Derbyshire miner, a one-time professional
boxer, and who now lives in a former Iron Curtain country and
relishes the freedoms of life there after the authoritarianism of
Britain. Their parties in the Gwynant barn were the stuff of
Rabelaisian legend. I remember the first one I went to as a sixteen-
year-old, on a Saturday night in Brian Greenall's ancient A40
Devon estate car with bits falling off it as we careered down the
old road to park near Hafod y Rhisgl and waded the ford to the
barn. Inside all was mayhem, illuminated by flickering firelight
from the stove. There were rough boys' games like British Bulldog
and Jousting; there was much drinking, and more intimate activity
taking place on the bunks. I glimpsed Joe Brown closely engaged
with a woman whose garments seemed to be self-divesting; but
they were old friends and it was innocent fun, I suppose. Or so
the grins on their faces suggested. The finale of these evenings
was always an outrageous ritual, legendary in Welsh climbing
circles, that became known as "the dance of the flaming arsehole".
All the men present (I don't remember any prohibition on women
participating, but nor do I recall any doing so) stripped off and,
with a spill of burning newspaper clenched between their buttocks,
they performed a frenzied dance around the stove. The older and
cannier ones made sure the newspaper spills were rolled tight and
merely smouldered. The women perched on the top bunk, peering
down attentively, studying form, and passing loud, ribald
comments. I draw a discreet veil over the rest of the proceedings.

When no party was taking place, the club members would
generally head down to Beddgelert, crowd into the bar of the

Royal Goat, wind up the locals and the farmers, and end up around closing time having a mighty fracas in the car park to which every gwas from every farm in the vicinity would feel duty bound to join in and kick the living daylight out of whichever insolent Sais crossed his path. They were strong and tough, those local farm boys, out on the hillsides in all weathers, and this, in the absence of any *Noson Lawen*, was the best entertainment they had to look forward to all week. I remember seeing Mo one Saturday night roll underneath a Land Rover to escape the brutal kicking then being administered. They couldn't get at him, were battering their shins against the vehicle's sills to no avail, so they rushed back into the bar to get the keys. By the time they were back Mo had crawled out, leapt over the wall, forded the river, melted away into the dark, and was halfway back to the barn by Hafod y Rhisgl to party the rest of the night away. I don't think behaviour like this is remotely normative or socially acceptable in the current time, and have to admit to a degree of ambivalence on that score. But maybe that's because I'm too old, frail and respectable these days even to consider taking part? To return to the peaceful environment of Nant Gwynen, in medieval times it was said that a squirrel (red, of course) could make its way from Bwlch y Gwyddel to Beddgelert Priory without ever touching the ground. With the navy's perpetual demand for oak, particularly throughout the eighteenth century and the Napoleonic Wars, the woods of Nant Gwynen were sorely depleted, to the extent that by the beginning of the nineteenth century concern was being expressed at the sustainability of supply. A very clear statement of this comes through in a paper read by a Reverend Wynne Jones to the Caernarvonshire Agricultural Society in 1814, and afterwards reprinted as a pamphlet with the title *Planting in Mountainous Situations*. The following is an extract which goes a long way towards explaining the exceptional arboreal richness and variety of Nant Gwynen to this day:

*"In the month of May, 1809, I took possession of the farm of
Penybryn, in the parish of Beddgelert, consisting of about 550 acres.
By the month of March, 1810, I had enclosed about sixty acres with
a wall six feet high, and 218 roods in length, and immediately planted
a considerable part of it with 50,000 Scotch fir, and 10,000 oak and
ash. In the year 1811 I enclosed 30 acres more, with a wall the same
height as the former, 120 roods in length: and in this and the two
following years I planted 103,000 trees in these enclosures: 97,000
of these were oak, and 8,000 ash, all of which were raised by myself;
the remainder were Scotch fir and larch, which I purchased as two-
year-old seedlings..."*

For what we see in the valley at the present day, we have to thank
the Reverend Jones (as well as forgetful jays and squirrels). This
gentlemen for once put a positive construction on what was
happening to the Welsh landscape during the period of the
Enclosures Acts. Apart from Hafod y Llan, there are two
historically important farms in this upper part of Nant Gwynen,
and another a little higher up near the Cwm Dyli hydro-electric
power station[31]. The two farms nearest Llyn Gwynen are Hafod
Lwyfog and Hafod y Rhisgl. The last time I called at the former
I had the patron saint of the access movement in Britain, Benny
Rothman[32], staying with me for a few days. Benny wanted to re-

---

[31] Built in 1905, this is the world's oldest operative power station. Its electricity used to
provide power to several important slate quarries in the area, including Dinorwig at
Llanberis, and Pen yr Orsedd and Oakeley in Blaenau Ffestiniog. The architecture of the
building housing the turbines might best be described as Welsh ecclesiastical. Built of local
stone, it is far less environmentally intrusive than, say, the nuclear power station at
Trawsfynydd.

[32] Benny Rothman (1911-2002) was prime mover in the most important event in the
movement for access to open country in Britain – the 1932 Kinder Scout Mass Trespass.
At the time he was a 20-year-old Manchester communist working in the motor trade –
Jewish by descent, tiny in stature and fiery in rhetoric. The middle of five children of
Romanian-Jewish parents, his father ran hardware stalls at Glossop and Shaw markets.

visit Hafod Lwyfog, where he'd experienced hospitality 62 years before. None of the family he'd met were still living. The ancient farmhouse was now base to a team of itinerant New Zealand sheep-shearers. They invited us in for tea and cake, and were enthralled to hear Benny's stories of the 1932 Kinder Mass Trespass (for his role in which he received four months in Leicester Gaol after the judge had delivered a biased summing-up which drew attention to his politics and his Jewish ancestry); of his anti-fascist activity at Oswald Mosley rallies; of his union activity during the depression years in the Lancashire cotton industry and after the war in Trafford Park industries. On the platforms we shared, his steely presence would enforce my own mild radicalism. Afterwards he'd invariably come up to me beaming, thump me in the ribs, laugh quietly, and proclaim indulgently that "yer'll 'ave us flung in't Tower, lad, if yer carry on like that." I took that as a compliment, and conscientiously accepted my pile of *Soviet Weeklies* from him to distribute and sell wherever I could. Strapping antipodean sheep-shearers aside, the most notable former inhabitant of Hafod Lwyfog was a particularly active poltergeist which hurled beds around, dragged covers off those sleeping in

---

The family were very poor, so that, although Benny won a scholarship to Manchester's Central High school for boys, he had to leave at 14 when an errand boy's job came up. In the summer of 1925, he cycled on a home-made bicycle to north Wales and climbed Snowdon with a sixpenny map from Woolworths: "I was the only person up there. It just hit me, that great open view with the sea all around." He and I were comrades in the CPGB and became close friends during the 1980s when I was working in Manchester and frequently speaking at rallies against the latest Thatcherite atrocity, whether it was the sinking of the Belgrano, the handling of the Miners' Strike, or the criminal privatisation of water utilities. I'd frequently call on him and his wife Lil at their house on Crofton Avenue, Timperley (number 86 – there's now a blue plaque on the wall in commemoration of him). I picked him up from here in 1987 and brought him to Eryri because he wanted to re-trace his memorable holiday in 1925. He was one of the great influences on my life, and his son Harry, a retired professor at Bristol University, is still a close friend and neighbour. For more on Benny and other stalwarts of the campaign for free access to Britain's moorland and mountains, see Roly Smith, *Walking Class Heroes* (2021).

them, frightened away guests and tradesman, and was only finally laid to rest by an exorcist from Pwllheli, who despatched the troubled spirit to the depths of Llyn Gwynen. As for Hafod y Rhisgl, this was an early centre for the Calvinistic Methodists in Eryri, who were so busy with Sunday schools, doctrinal dispute and rehearsing for their frequent *Cymanfeydd Pregethu* (preaching festivals) that it's to be doubted whether they would ever have registered the activity of poltergeists. One last point of interest about this part of Nant Gwynen is that here was Wenallt, the seat of Madog ap Owain Gwynedd. The old house where he lived has completely gone, and the stones from it in the usual Welsh fashion were recycled and used in the construction of outbuildings to Hafod y Rhisgl, including the barn that became for a decade or two the Wallasey climbers' base. Madog is famous as reputedly the first European discoverer[33] of America, having sailed away westwards from Traeth Mawr in 1170, returned briefly with stories of vast acres of fertility, rivers teeming with fish, plains with buffalo, peaceable indigenous people, and other such delights to tempt Welsh men and women away from their cloud-palled and sodden homeland. He assembled a fleet and sailed away into the west once more with a dozen ships constructed of Nant Gwynen oak, never to be seen again. There are still those who believe in the myth of a tribe of Welsh-speaking Indians on the Upper Missouri river. I recommend to them an attentive reading of Gwyn A. Williams' deconstruction of the story in his *Madoc: The Legend of the Welsh Discovery of America* (Oxford, 1987), which is as sensible and well-researched as it is a gloriously funny entertainment. There are those who wish that Dowlais's finest historian might have left us with our colonialist dreams. For my part, I enjoy the spectacle of a balloon being deftly and gently pricked.

---

[33] The Vikings certainly preceded him, as excavations at L'Anse aux Meadows in Newfoundland have proven.

From the farmyard of Hafod y Rhisgl, a path climbs steeply to the main road through the valley, crosses it and continues beyond towards Bwlch y Rhediad. In my early visits to Wales this was known as the ancient trackway between Nant Gwynen and Dolwyddelen. It takes you over a shoulder of Moel Siabod into the watershed of Afon Conwy, which fine river we do not have space to deal with adequately in the present volume[34]. I remember taking this route between the youth hostels of Lledr House and Bryn Gwynant on a misty, wet Easter in 1960 and unexpectedly coming across the tailplane of a large aircraft protruding from the

---

[34] It will have to wait for volume two, along with the Usk, the Rheidol, the Arrow, the Alun, the Cleddau, the Serw, Afon Dyfi and many other such delights. But to whet your appetite, and since it's so close, here's a glimpse into one of the fine, secret places on Eryri's rivers – the Lledr Gorge below Pont y Pant, and more particularly its unique fishermens' walk: "Above deep green pools in the Lledr Gorge, a rickety-looking structure traverses mossy, primrose-and-anemone-starred rock walls rising from the water. I've been using this fishermen's walk for fifty years as approach to one of my favourite rock-climbing venues in Eryri – the esoteric, 30-metre-high Craig Rhiw Goch. A notice tacked to a tree where the access path starts its descent towards the river reads: 'Warning. Dangerous structure. The owner accepts no liability for any loss, damage or injury, however caused.' Rescue from this location would be problematical. It's a fair precaution to alert the unwary to potential risks here, though I've always believed that instinctive awareness developed from personal experience is the best safeguard we possess against danger.

'The walkway's probably Victorian in origin, seems to have been built by local workmen using the materials you see abandoned throughout the slate quarrying region. If you're of timid disposition, or if the river's in spate and the noise and flooding motion is disorientating, you'd be well advised to keep away, or use the harness-and-sling security techniques appropriate to an Alpine *via ferrata*. That's the closest analogy to this remarkable structure I can cite. I skittered down the steep path to the river-bank, scrambled downstream across slippery rocks, and stepped gingerly across to its start.

It had been repaired since I was last here: planks with wire-mesh tacked to them for grip laid across the horizontal ladders; a rope handrail strung between bolts and spikes at head level. Being as dilapidated and worn in body as the walkway itself, I moved along it cautiously, preferring to rely on balance and holds in the rock wall. The ladders take you into a wonderland. Dappling light's reflected on to ivied green walls. A yellow wagtail dipped and flitted after the biplane cruise of a sage-green dragonfly. On mauve and ochre boulders rising from the water, slender shoots of wild chives sprouted, and the first feathery hints of hemlock water dropwort's sinister, umbelliferous presence. Just round the corner the steep cliff held memories of difficult, youthful climbs. I looked across wistfully from ramshackle ladders to memories of silken bodily ease. "

bog. It belonged to an ex-military DC3 Dakota, the *Saint Kevin*, which had been flying passengers from Northolt to Dublin in 1952. Caught in severe turbulence, it crashed in Cwm Edno very close to the ancient trackway, killing all 23 people on board. Twelve corpses were recovered from the scene and buried in Llanbeblig churchyard, Caernarfon. The remaining eleven were never found, and presumably are preserved deep within the bog. The site of the crash is a doleful pool on the moor with a gaunt alder growing at its margin. I shuddered as I passed by that day, alone, a thirteen-year-old schoolboy, glad to be descending into the less brutal landscape of upper Nant Gwynen. Once there I hurried on past the power station and nearby medieval settlement, and decided against taking the path into Cwm Dyli with its eyesore pipelines. It's a very interesting place in its own way, and Pennant's detailed description of his visit here is a *locus classicus* for anyone interested in the practice of transhumance in Wales, but if you want to read that, you can find the details in my *Snowdon: The Story of a Welsh Mountain*, onto the territory of which we're now intruding. So let me hurry you along the path as it rises gently across the hillside below Bwlch y Gwyddel to the car-park at Gorffwysfa, where you would have needed to have pre-booked on your credit card and incurred a considerable charge had you arrived by car or minibus. From here the Miners' Track takes you in quick succession to the three feeder lakes for the upper Glaslyn. The first of them is little Llyn Teyrn. Before I'd ever seen a stoat in ermine, I asked Evan Roberts, the naturalist, former quarryman, member of the Gorsedd y Beirdd, world expert on arctic-alpine flora and first Warden of Cwm Idwal National Nature Reserve, where on Snowdon gave the best chance to see one (upland stoats being the likeliest to turn white in winter)? "I saw one just the other day by Llyn Teyrn", he responded over tea in his house of Gelli, up the track beyond Joe Brown's Shop in Capel Curig. "It was crossing the slope above the Miners' Track by Llyn Teyrn. I watched him for ten minutes. Plenty of voles in that scree. Best after the morning sun's been on it, I'd think." I was soon able to follow up Evan's hint at the right time of day and year. I trudged along the Miners' Track in an icy winter dawn, glanced across the Llyn Teyrn scree, saw nothing, hastened on to Glaslyn where the usual verdigris coloration of the lake was strikingly darkened by gleaming slopes all around. Then I contoured round to the foot of Clogwyn y Garnedd. The Trinity Face gullies were banked out with snow. I strapped crampons to my boots, took a pair of ice-axes from my rucksack, and set to, front-points and picks biting securely into firm névé for a thousand feet to the summit ridge, beyond which the mountain's morning shadow stretched out mauve across the Eifionydd hills. Yr Wyddfa was deserted. I sheltered on the station platform from a cold east wind (never follow the railway track down in these conditions – it's a notorious death-trap that has claimed many lives over the years), then descended to Bwlch y Saethau, climbed over the crest of Y Lliwedd and down to the Miners' Track – a perfect winter's morning excursion. Its perfection was soon complete. I caught a flash of movement in the screes above Llyn Teyrn. With a glass I followed the stuttering progress of a stoat, brilliant white and conspicuous as it darted across grey rocks coroneted with golden sun-reflecting ice where they had melted through the snow. Moments like this last a lifetime. Thomas Pennant, the indefatigable Welsh traveller and pioneering early naturalist, can introduce us to the magnificent lake under Clogwyn y Garnedd which is the source of the Afon Glaslyn. Here's his description of it:

This brought us into the horrible crater, immediately beneath the great precipice of the Wyddfa, in which is lodged Ffynnon Las[35]. Its

---

[35] The old name for Glaslyn – the green lake – was Llyn Ffynnon Las – lake of the green spring. For folk-tales and legends associated with it, particularly that of the *afanc* which was dragged here by the oxen of Hu Gadarn from Llyn yr Afanc ("beaver pool") at the confluence of Afonydd Conwy and Lledr, see the appropriate chapter in my Snowdon book.

situation is the most dreadful... the waters had a greenish cast; but what is very singular, the rocks reflected into them seemed varied with stripes of the richest colours, like the most beautiful lute-strings; and changed almost to infinity. Here we observed the Wheat-ear, a small and seemingly tender bird; and yet it is almost the only small one... that frequents these heights: the reason evidently is the want of food.

To connect that passage to the present day, there've been many times over more than half a century when I've sat on rocks by the outflow from Llyn Ffynnon Las or on the close turf all around – by the actual source of the Glaslyn, therefore – and had my gaze drawn to the constant flitting and breathless trilling of a Wheatear. I love these little dancing birds of the hills with their abrupt cascades of song and bowdlerised name. (The original and accurate "whitearse" was too robust for Victorian ornithological taste, so they changed it to the present inaccurate but respectable nonsense.) Their return is one of the true signs of spring. Formerly it coincided with that of the Curlew to its breeding grounds across the damp and rushy hollows, where its haunting soft crescendos are one of the defining sounds of the Welsh uplands. But curlews are now in such sad decline. All the more cause, then, for celebration that this exquisite little passerine, the Wheatear/Whitearse, is still present in Wales – though "For how much longer?" is a question that haunts us with regard to all the wild creatures encounters with which enhance our lives. I remember a day by this lake, at this exact place, when I kept very still and watched as the male Wheatear returned continually to a small cleft in tumbled rocks above. Derek Ratcliffe – as great authority on mountain birds as Evan Roberts was on arctic-alpine flora – in one of his books talks of the frequent disappointment when a small pale passerine proves to be not a snow bunting but "only a wheatear". For once I'd disagree with him. At close quarters the wheatear is astonishingly beautiful, its pied markings perfectly set off by overall pale hues of cinnamon and grey. The commonplace is often marvellous, *"could we but look with seeing eyes"[36]*. If I've helped readers towards that end in the course of these wandering journeys alongside the lovely rivers of this little country of ours, then I will have done what I set out to do.

---

[36] Christina Rossetti (1830-1894). The whole couplet runs thus: "Could we but look with seeing eyes,/This very spot might be Paradise."

PART FOUR:

Conflicting Demands: Dyfi & Dysynni

There is a word in Welsh, *bro*, which translates literally as region, but the resonance of which transcends that literal meaning. The earliest recorded Welsh poet, Taliesin from the sixth century, gives us the clue when he writes of his home country as being *"bro sêr hefin"* – land of summer stars. Wherever I travel among the hills and valleys of this inexhaustibly rich old country of Wales, I'm conscious of nuance, demarcation, shading local difference that fascinates. Maybe the textures are those of history, or settlement, or the defining tones of geology. But always there is the sense of boundaries, of a continual moving through into the country that is beyond. Even the names of the hill-groups that divide these regions reflect this: *Berwyn, the white barrier; Rhinogydd, the thresholds.* Nowhere is this sense of moving from one region to another more pronounced than on the great hill-scarp that dominates the westerly view along Llyn Tegid from its Bala shore, from the western slopes of which Afon Dyfi rises. Aran's two main summits, along a ten-mile ridge that stretches from Llanuwchllyn to Dinas Mawddwy, are separated by a bare twenty metres in height. View them as you drive up the wild pass of Bwlch y Groes, and these tops seem virtually a level gable. The higher and westernmost of the two, Aran Fawddwy, at 905 metres, may be the highest summit in Wales outside the heartland of Eryri, yet in no sense does it queen it over the marginally lower Aran Benllyn (885m.) The curious thing about these main summits of Aran – despite obvious unanimity in their rising from a common base, on which Thomas Pennant commented in 1781 – is how contrasted they are in character. The two high points of the ridge may only be separated by a short mile and descent of a few metres, yet they inhabit different countries. Bro Aran has always been a place of contradictions, a troublesome land fought over and apart. To reinforce distinction, each peak is named for a different *cantref* of medieval Wales. To grasp the sense of their mutual belonging, walk over them. They're like an old couple, utterly different, utterly dependent, their grey crowns speckled with white quartz, their marriage as strikingly obvious as their independence of character.

Aran Benllyn is the presiding peak of Penllyn – a region echoey with myth and legend, sheaved with poets, preachers, educators who made their marks on Welsh cultural life. Its bro stretches around Llyn Tegid ("Bala Lake"). Aran Fawddwy more closely belongs to the high, riven moorland heights above Llyn Efyrnwy. Those wastes, stronghold of the hen harrier – our most beautiful raptor, and also the most persecuted, its presence being perceived as inimical to the shooting interest who destroy it and its nests mercilessly – are as inhospitable, rough and trackless, apart from the odd forestry or shooters' incursion, as any in Wales. The western Aran's *bro* encompasses the headwaters of Afon Dyfi,. The outlook from the highest Welsh peak south of Yr Wyddfa is of the whole of western Wales: of moorland; of nearby Cader Idris against the westering sun; of Pumlumon to the south and all the rolling little hills and patchwork valleys of Radnor and Montgomery along the Welsh Marches. The traverse of these two hills, from Llanuwchllyn to Dinas Mawddwy and descending through rocky, beautiful Cwm Cywarch, is one of the great Welsh hill-walks. It has loftiness and spaciousness, a sense of crossing watersheds both physical and cultural – for this ridge is the east-west watershed of Wales, and the north-south divide of language and history: *"Mangre dawel fynyddig ydyw, lle ardderchog i enaid ddal cymundeb a Duw"* (This is a silent, mountainous retreat, an excellent place for communion with God), O.M. Edwards wrote about *Bro Aran*. This eminent Welsh educator, tutor at Oxford to Edward Thomas, had his home in Cwm Cynllwyd above Llanuchllyn. There is a fine memorial to him in that village by Jonah Jones. I wonder if O.M. would feel that his motto as an educator, *"Codi'r hen Wlad yn ei hôl"* ("raise the Old Country to its former glory"), had something of an ironic ring to it if he could have viewed what has happened to his *bro* in the last fifty or sixty years: the marring, fencing, afforesting, turbining of wild hill-country, which is so precious, of which we have so little? However that may be, the rocky character of the Aran summits is still something to rejoice in. If you set off on a summer's day after a pint of good beer in *The Eagles* at Llanuwchllyn, and enjoy another in the twilight sitting outside the Red Lion in Dinas Mawddwy, you'll be stretched of leg and more content of mind. And unlikely these days to find in the latter place, as George Borrow did in 1854, "a collection of filthy huts", from which "fierce-looking red-haired men, who seemed as if they might be descendants of the red-haired *banditti* of old, were staggering about, and the sounds of drunken revelry echoed from the huts".

This was an outlaw region still suffering from Wars of the Roses consequence in in the sixteenth century. It was stronghold of *Gwylliaid Cochion Mawddwy* – the red robbers of Mawddwy, more on whom later in this chapter. I look back fondly to a summer's day years ago when I first completed this traverse of Aran, setting out early in the morning from the former youth hostel in the ancient house of Plas Rhiwaedog at Rhosygwaliau, and finally sleeping by a small fire in a hazel wood in gorgeous Cwm Cywarch as the dew fell. Sweet though the memory is, good though this straightforward traverse of Aran may be, sometimes I think that our hill-walking itineraries can be a little too linear, a little too unimaginative, inclined at times to miss out on some of the less obvious delights of a region. If you want to enjoy the best that Aran has to offer, including a visit to what's arguably the source of Afon Dyfi, consider approaching its main summit by a considerably more circuitous route. Take the footpath that winds through the *ffriddoedd* of farms in lower Cwm Cynllwyd to Plas Morgan and on into Cwm Croes. You'll meet men and women of the farms of these hills along the way. Despite their aggressive and hostile reputation within outdoor spheres – access problems were recurrent over years, but are now diplomatically resolved through diplomacy by the Snowdonia National Park, the British Mountaineering Council and local community representatives – I would vouch for their friendliness, helpfulness, interest, especially when you talk with them in their own language (and have your dogs under control). When you enter Cwm Croes, there is a little diversion to be taken that shouldn't be missed – to a place celebrated as of interest to visitors to these hills since the seventeenth century. Here's the great Welsh naturalist Edward Lhuyd, writing to his cousin David Lloyd in 1686:

"Aran Benllyn is I hear too far from you, else I am sure you might find there twice as many plants as on [the Berwyn]. Divers gentlemen have gone from London, Oxford and Cambridge to Snowdon, Cader Idris and Flinlimmon in search of plants... to my knowledge [Aran Benllyn] produces as many rareties as Cader Idris [in] ye rivulets that run through ye rocks above Llyn Llymbran."

Llyn Llymbran, courtesy of the Ordnance Survey down in Southampton, now appears on the map as Llyn Lliwbran, which translates as "crow-coloured lake" – pleasantly descriptive enough, but it may conceal an older, mythological allusion. What is not in doubt is the exceptional quality of the lake, famous for its golden-coloured trout, and its dramatic surrounding cwm. It has a magnificent columnar cliff, Gist Ddu, with soaring, angular aretes of clean, firm rock which give delectable rock-climbing[1]. They lead your eye up to the summit ridge of Aran. This is one of the great mountain places in Wales, and the chances of your sharing it with anyone other than a very occasional angler, botanist or climber are remote indeed. Don't climb to the summit ridge yet, however enticing a scramble it looks to be up the back wall of the cwm alongside the cliff. Descend instead into Cwm Croes, follow the ancient way that runs from Nant y Barcud to Dinas Mawddwy by Bwlch Sirddyn, but branch off at Gors Llwyd and contour round the spur of Foel Hafod Fynydd to Creiglyn Dyfi. Here, you are in another of the untrodden places of the Welsh mountains, by another jewel of a lake – a round pool under dark and broken crags that's the clear, deep source of Afon Dyfi. Savour it, the rich natural life of the place, and its undespoiled beauty. There were reports of Pine Martens – perhaps the most beautiful and certainly the most elusive of British *mustellidae*[2] – here in the 1930s, but none recently to my knowledge. If your urge is for the summits after all, climb up loose scree and broken crags on the flank called Erw y Ddafad Ddu (black sheep acre). It brings you out equidistant between the two Aran summits. Choice of which of them to visit all yours, and fixed in your mind there will be the memory of the country beyond what's normally seen as we pass through on our way to our hills.

The way on from Creiglyn Dyfi can be to descend back alongside Afon Llaethnant, though that brings to my mind advice from *Safety on Mountains*, a booklet written by John Disley and published by the Central Council for Physical Recreation in the

---

[1] Sir Charles Evans (1918-1995), deputy leader of the successful 1953 expedition that claimed the first ascent of Chomolungma ("Mount Everest") pioneered the earliest rock-climbs here in the late 1930s.

[2] The weasel family, that includes weasels, stoats, martens, otters and badgers in Great Britain.

1950s[3], which tersely advised you, with accompanying cartoons by Gordon Mansell illustrating dire consequence, that "In the mountains, good routes seldom follow streams!" The name of this stream gives a clue as to why not. "Milk stream" is how it translates. There are two-and-a-half miles of white water and cataracts before it reaches the main valley and flows on more sedately, as Afon Dyfi now, to reach Llanymawddwy. But I'd not go that way, for to do so would be to miss out on the most delectable of Dyfi's headwater tributaries, Afon Cywarch, to reach which you must climb to Aran Mawddwy then head south-west into the afternoon sun to a wild little stream called Camddwr – "crooked water" – which spills into Blaen Cywarch with views of the line of dark and vegetated buttresses to impress, and plenty of waterslides, screes and cascades to ensure attention on where to place your feet. I climbed on those crags in my youth, made the first ascent of what must surely be the worst climb on them. It was on the north buttress. Rock-climb is perhaps a misnomer. Ninety per cent of its several hundred feet was on heather at an uncomfortably steep angle. Near the top, it found a neat little gangway up an impendent wall to a pulpit ledge above hundreds of feet of space, with a severely overhanging short wall above to more heather and release. We turned tail and retreated, to face admonishment from greybeard members in the Staffordshire Mountain Club cottage where we were staying for the weekend. But how we had laughed! Once you're in delectable Cwm Cywarch, a stroll down-valley lane with meadowsweet[4] frothing

---

[3] Now in its fifth edition, published by the British Mountaineering Council, and much changed from the original.

[4] Every verge, every marshy field-corner hereabouts billows in summer with creamy blossom of meadowsweet (*Filipendula ulmaria*). The air's heavy with its honeyed astringency – the defining smell of summer and Wales, lingering into autumn, carrying a powerful synaesthetic charge. Salicylic acid was first identified from meadowsweet root, and synthesized as aspirin in 1897. Far back beyond that date the plant's alternative name – "meadwort" – suggests its old usage. Traces of it have been found at Beaker burials and

across the fields in season and scenting the air with honey brings you to Aber Cywarch and into George Borrow's company once more. He passed through this hamlet on his 1854 tour, seized on the connection with Ellis Wynne, author of the early eighteenth-century prose classic, *Gweledigaethau y Bardd Cwsg* ("Visions of the Sleeping Bard", recently republished by Cockatrice Books in a fluent translation by T. Gwynn Jones), and left one of those dramatic vignettes that characterise his work from his first success with *The Bible in Spain* right through to the last book he published:

> ' "*What is the name of this place?" I shouted to a man on horseback, who came dashing through a brook with a woman in Welsh dress behind him.*
>
> *'Aber Cowarch, Saxon!' said the man in a deep guttural voice, and lashing his horse disappeared rapidly into the shades of the night." Aber Cywarch!' I cried, springing half a yard in the air. 'Why, that's the place where Ellis Wynn composed his immortal Sleeping Bard, the book which I translated in the blessed days of my youth. Oh, no wonder that the Sleeping Bard is a wild and wondrous work, seeing that it was composed among the wild and wonderful scenes which I here behold.' "*

In fact, Ellis Wynne (1671-1734) composed his *Gweledigaethau y Bardd Cwsg*[5] at Y Lasynys Fawr, at the northern end of Morfa Harlech where it curves round into Traeth Bach, the estuary of the Afon Dwyryd. So the remarkable fact emerges of the two

---

in Bronze Age tombs. It's present too in *Math fab Mathonwy* – a redaction, transcribed in the late fourteenth-century, of much older folk-tale motifs that's one of the masterpieces of medieval Welsh literature. In the story the enchanter Gwydion creates a wife for his nephew Lleu from the flowers of the oak, the meadowsweet and the broom. She's called "*Blodeuwedd*" – "of flowers" – and it ends badly. She betrays him, in punishment for which Gwydion turns her into an owl – "*Blodeuwedd*" – "flower-faced".

[5] At the time of writing, a new edition with an introduction by Rob Mimpriss from his excellent Cockatrice imprint is in prospect, to which I look forward intensely.

major Welsh religious classics – *Y Bardd Cwsg* of the first decade of the eighteenth century, and Morgan Llwyd's *Llyfr y Tri Aderyn* of 1653 – having been written by the same river, Afon Dwyryd, or its headwater tributary Afon Cynfal, within half a century of each other over three hundred years ago[6]. Llanymawddwy's little church is dedicated to the Celtic Christian Saint Tydecho, who was probably Breton and had a long-running feud with Maelgwn, founder of the royal dynasty of Gwynedd. Little is known about Tydecho apart from a few charming generic saint stories that recount how kings came to be miraculously chained to rocks, and horses turning into oxen into stags and eventually back again when the nuisance-value point had been made. Kings needed to know their place, in the view of these determined old saints of the seaways and settlements. From Llanymawddwy, Afon Dyfi, augmented by Afon Cerist which rushes down from the Dyfi hills, swirls round the outskirts of Dinas Mawddwy and seems not much to like what it sees (it should have paused a while to listen to the Saturday night singing in the Red Lion – the *ffermwyr* in these parts have developed mighty lungs from the surrounding hill slopes and used to delight in exercising them in the pub on Saturday nights. Perhaps they still do, though I've not been in at that time for a few decades now). Afon Cerist hastens on past Mallwyd. The burial mound where the *Gwylliaid Cochion* were interred after their hangings is in the water meadows close to Pont y Cleifion, and still clearly visible. Here's the account from Thomas Pennant:

> *To put a stop to their ravages, a commission was granted to John Wynn ap Meredydd, of Gwedyr, and this gentleman, in order to settle the peace of the country, and to punish all offenders against its government.*

---

[6] A branch of Ellis Wynne's family certainly had a house at Aber Cywarch, but it seems more likely that Y Bardd Cwsg was written at Y Lasynys Fawr, where there is now a museum dedicated to Wynne's life and work.

In pursuance of their orders, they raised a body of stout men, and on a Christmas-eve seized above four score outlaws and felons, on whom they held a gaol delivery, and punished them according to their deserts. Among them were the two sons of a woman, who very earnestly applied to Owen for the pardon of one: he refused: when the mother, in a rage, told him (baring her neck) These yellow breasts have given suck to those, who shall wash their hands in your blood.

Revenge was determined by the surviving villains. They watched their opportunity, when he was passing through these parts from Montgomeryshire assizes, to way-lay him, in the thick woods of Mawddwy, at a place now called, from the deed, Llydiart y Barwn; where they had cut down several long trees, to cross the road, and impede the passage. They then discharged on him a shower of arrows, one of which, sticking in his face, he took out and broke. After this, they attacked him with bills and javelins, and left him slain, with above thirty wounds. His son-in-law, John Llwyd of Ceisgwyn, defended him to the last; but his cowardly attendants fled on the first onset. His death gave peace to the country; for most rigorous justice ensued; and the whole nest of banditti was extirpated, many by the hand of justice; and the rest fled, never to return.

The traditions of the country respecting these banditti, are still extremely strong. I was told that they were so feared, that travellers did not dare to go the common road to Shrewsbury, but passed over the summits of the mountains, to avoid their haunts. The inhabitants placed scythes in the chimneys of their houses, to prevent the felons coming down to surprise them in the night; some of which are to be seen to this day. This race was distinguished by the titles Gwyllied y Dugoed and Gwylliaid Cochion Mawddwy.

At Mallwyd is another of the Dyfi valley's trinity of churches dedicated to Tydecho. The river hereabouts enters its mature phase, passes Aberangell where in autumn and winter months you'll encounter fleets of up-market 4WDs brimming with portly loud gentlemen who've been refreshing themselves in Mallwyd's *Brigands' Inn* between morning and afternoon sessions dedicated to slaughtering a few score pheasants on one of the driven shoots hereabouts. The river ignores them and saunters away westwards, passing yet another church dedicated to Tydecho in Cemaes before arriving in the local metropolis of Machynlleth. Just before it arrives there it's augmented by two rivers of the same name, flowing in from different directions. The northern version of Afon Dulas (black and blue river) surges in from the valley coming down from the former slate-quarrying region around Corris and Aberllefenni, whilst the southern drains moorland around the eastern end of Pumlumon. This branch powered machinery in Machynlleth's former industrial satellite village of Forge. The northern one has a more tragic story to tell. Two witnesses driving along the A487 where the river runs alongside the Dolgellau road one torrentially wet early October night in 2012 saw a man throwing black plastic bin bags into the flooding water. He was later identified as Mark Bridger, a 46-year-old policeman's son from Surrey who'd moved to Wales and worked as slaughterman in an abbatoir near Machynlleth. He had abducted five-year-old April Jones, the daughter of a neighbour of his ex-partner, as she was playing outside her home on the Bryn y Gog estate in Machynlleth. Bridger drove her to his rented house in Ceinws two miles up-river. Once there, what happened to April does not bear thinking about. Small fragments of the bones of her skull were recovered by a police forensic team from Bridger's fireplace. Traces of her blood were everywhere. After his arrest, police examining his computer found an extensive collection of the most extreme child sexual abuse material. Huge community searches were mounted around Machynlleth in the days immediately after her disappearance. Bridger's explanation was that he had run her over by accident, had panicked, and could not remember what he had done with her body. The flooding Afonnydd Dulas and Dyfi and the wide sandbanks of the Dyfi's long estuary are surely April's unmarked grave. As to Bridger, he received a full life sentence with the recommendation that he never be released. He has offered no account to the police, the court or her grieving parents of what atrocities he committed on that dreadful night. I remember driving into Machynlleth in the lashing rain the following night in connection with the Condry Memorial Lecture I ran annually at Tabernacl/MoMA from 2008 until Covid rendered it unsafe for our elderly core audience. Everywhere you looked on that night in 2012 there were police cars. Pink ribbons and bouquets were fastened to every lamp-post in the town. For day after day in terrible weather the people of the town had been out searching, until the police finally made the announcement, from the evidence they'd gathered, that the little girl must be presumed dead. I've never known a community in such a state of collective shock. Raymond Jones, a neighbour of April's family on Bryn y Gog, was the manager of Y Tabernacl, and the man with whom I co-ordinated each year. He'd been out searching throughout the downpours for long hours in the early days of her disappearance. "Should we cancel?" I asked. "Please don't," was his response, "We need every scrap of normality we can muster to cling on to in the face of this horror." A police spokeswoman gave me the same advice when consulted. The lecture that year was by Ray Woods, the bryologist. It was on lichens, and was masterful, intense, comprehensively knowledgeable. Beforehand we'd held a two-minute silence for April and her parents. Looking round from the rostrum, there was not a face in which tears were not starting to the eyes. After Bridger's conviction, April's mother Coral co-ordinated a campaign to have removed from the internet the kind of debased material – snuff movies and the like – which had fuelled Bridger's appalling appetites and subsequent actions, and from which apparently there is much money to be made. There are many kinds of pollution covered glancingly in this book, all of them with their malign effects. This incident was the grimmest reminder of the brutal depths. Just as the faded scraps of pink ribbon I still see here and there when I drive through Machynlleth remind me of humanity's capacity for collective decency and mutual support.

Simon Jenkins, former editor of *The Times*, knighted for his services to journalism in 2004, sometime spouse to the glamorous American film star and model Gayle Hunnicutt, and long-time inhabitant (when not in Primrose Hill) of Aberdyfi, used to refer to Bill Condry as "the man who put Machynlleth on the map" – a reasonable point of view, given the Welsh nature dispatches by him that appeared every other Saturday in *The Guardian* between 1957 and 1998, and were headed by the town's name. Bill was certainly associated with Afon Dyfi for a very long time. When he and his wife Penny of fifty-two years first married, just after the Second World War, they went to live in a cottage called Glygyrog Ddu, below the Panorama Walk at the top edge of woodland in Pant Eidal. Redstarts nested each spring in the walls. Green woodpeckers called. Bill rode off on his bicycle each morning to teach Classics in Lapley Grange school at Ffwrnais. He and Penny were centrally involved in Welsh nature conservation in those hopeful years, and in the regeneration of the small surviving Red kite population in the upper Tywi valley.

The Dyfi estuary had long been a centre for boat-building in West Wales. The river was navigable up to Derwen Las, where a shipwright, John Jones, had a yard that built from local oak small schooners and sloops, handy and agile, that best suited the rough waters and narrow creeks of this coast. They brought in lime for the acid pastureland, and corn. They carried out timber, slate, hides, oak bark for their tanning, lanolin from sheep fleeces to render them flexible, lead ore from the hinterland's mines. Between 1780 and 1880 thirty-six sea-going vessels were built at various wharves along the Dyfi estuary, and chapels and alehouses sprang up to service all this activity. *The Black Lion* in Derwen Las – a characterful little community pub – is the last remaining between Machynlleth and Tal-y-bont. The tenor of life here has changed. Now, in the village hall on regular Saturday nights, communitarian-minded, rainbow-skirted, long-haired "hippy" women who began to colonise these hills in the 1960s, who raised their children here and integrated them into Welsh cultural life, pursue their own brand of alternative cultural tradition with circle dancing to music from local musicians. This apart, the chief attraction of the Dyfi shoreline is its natural life, particularly its birdlife. *"The years have gone since Penny and I came to live at Ynys Edwin and there have been many changes, especially after the death of Hubert Mappin who had owned Ynys-hir estate (which includes Ynys Edwin) since 1929."* The thought of what Ynys-las might have become, and of how this opportunity for a conservation enterprise which is now of world renown might have gone to waste, is very troubling. Bill Condry's amiable character and indefatigable persuasiveness on behalf of the natural world ultimately saved it from harm, though at times it was a heart-in-the-mouth progress towards safety:

> "[Hubert's] *death was the start of an anxious period. What would now happen to Ynys-hir? We knew that his widow, Patricia, wanted if at all possible to keep the estate just as he had made it, retaining its quiet beauty and its status as a wildlife refuge. Further, we were consoled by the knowledge that with his dying hand he had signed a covenant empowering the National Trust to safeguard [it] against the worst forms of commercial exploitation. … The decision came at last: the estate was to be sold. … if possible to someone sympathetic to conservation. … Too often when wildlife-rich estates come on to the*

market their value is far beyond the resources of the local naturalists' trust. So it was with Ynys-hir. But, we wondered, what about the Royal Society for the Protection of Birds? Patricia Mappin proved sympathetic to this idea. And in due course the R.S.P.B.'s director, Peter Conder, arrived on a March day of raw east wind. The world was grey and shriveled; there was no sky; the oakwoods were black and lifeless; a dismal haze hid the estuary...

The world of nature, as though sensing the need, provided its own corroborating, alluring testimony:

As we got near their clump of Scots pines our pair of ravens rose and circled impressively, proudly trumpeting their ownership of the site, for after eight years they were still using their old nest. We watched them as they flew across the sky at speed to chivvy off a buzzard that had floated too near. Beyond the pines, as we walked along the ridge of Ynys Feurig, a lovely pale hen harrier sailed closely past.

The purchase of Ynys-hir by an RSPB-headed consortium was one of the most heartening conservation victories ever to have been achieved in Wales. Yet the battles between conflicting interests still go on. The next estuary to the north is that of Afon Dysynni, a remarkable river that begins life as Nant Cadair, spilling down from the southern slopes of Cadair Idris into Llyn Cau of Richard Wilson's famous painting[7], flows into Llyn Myngul ("Tal-y-llyn lake"), heads west along the great fault that cuts through the whole of North Wales and then, in one of the classic examples of river capture, at Abergynolwyn it changes direction, slips under the formidable slope of Gamallt, joins its sibling Cader stream from the western slopes, the Afon Cader, and together they curl round the astonishing bastion of Craig yr

---

[7] Richard Wilson's small (45x60cms), glowing canvas of 1765, Cader Idris, Llyn- y Cau of 1765 is in the Tate Gallery. If you take the trouble to seek out the point from which it was painted, it is very realistic, and is of the satellite peak of Mynydd Pencoed.

Aderyn, where cormorants nest inland, before gentling along through valley grazing, ever more serpentine as the Dysynni approaches the sea, and finally merging gently into the inland lagoon that was formerly known as Broad Water and is now properly called Morlyn. From source to sea the Dysynni is sixteen miles long. It has otters, of course; the rare, shy bittern booms out its cow-like call from extensive phragmites beds. Between Crynllwyn and the old farmstead of Rhydygarnedd, red-breasted mergansers bob on waves sent lapping upriver by the wind. I was invited here recently by Marged Tudor-Turner, whose family have farmed on this land for generations as well as supplying a lineage of rural veterinary surgeons to the region. She's a voluble, articulate, red-haired woman, formidable in presence – an Ellen Wilkinson for our time. You quickly come to know that she'd be as doughty a friend as she is a formidable adversary. Certain groups of men – the shooting interest, the Crown Estate commissioners who lease rights along the foreshore, even the Ordnance Survey – have done just that. And they have met with spirited opposition and been forced to retreat!

Rhydygarnedd is a marvellous place, right on the river and looking out across the phragmites beds of Morlyn which are important cattle grazing for Bro Dysynni farmers. But the enemy of peace, tranquillity and properly unharmful traditional usage has infiltrated here as part of the *British Association of Shooting and Conservation*'s intense drive in recent years to sign up Crown Estate leases to foreshore around the British Isles. There have been times, when Marged has been in her garden with her two young sons, or when her neighbour Robert Allen at Crynllwyn has been in his with grandchildren, when shot from wildfowlers has pattered down around them. Enquiry into these episodes finally revealed a secret shooting map for trespassing gunmen. Locals say otters have been affected by what shooters term "predator control". The

Crown Estate, which leases British foreshore, finally called for suspension of shooting here. The Ordnance Survey early in 2021 sent an aeroplane along the river to establish its tidal (hence foreshore) limits. A team from Bangor University has endorsed its findings. The river through Morlyn is barely tidal except for a very brief section in its extreme lower reaches below Rhydygarnedd, thanks to nineteenth-century works by the Corbett family, one of two major landholders on the Dysynni. The wildlife-slaughtering interest at one of the crucial places around Wales for winter migrant birds (sea eagles included – and the sight of one of those huge birds is welcome indeed on the Dysynni!) is now facing, thanks to one bright, brave, resourceful woman, a humiliating defeat and climb-down. In 2022 the Ordnance Survey agreed to re-draw of its master map to show tidal limits (on which Crown Estate land and shooting rights across it depends. Marged had won the battle. She had another formidable ally upriver in William Williams-Wynne, representative of the other old landowner of the area. He's proprietor of the Peniarth Estate. William's land runs for six miles along the river. He's now fighting to reclaim its riparian frontage from the grasp of the Crown Estate who hold it under the false pretence that it's "foreshore", which you cannot have on a non-tidal river. His land runs all the way down to Ynysmaengwyn, alongside Marged's Rhydygarnedd. Marged and William have won this fight, and rightly so. The Dyfi estuary and its surrounding area will soon have another nature reserve – a working one too, and not a debased "sporting" one trespassed over by murderous thugs. All this coast should be a wildlife reserve. Thanks to Maggie's forensic presentation of the case against wildfowling here, it will now be preserved as such, her ancestral patch, her *milltir sgwâr*, protected once again. On that sobering note, we'll let the Afon Dysynni slip out under the Cambrian Coast line a little over a mile north of Tywyn and add its relatively pure tribute to the Irish Sea. Broad Water, the Afon Dysynni, the area's teeming wildlife will be safe under the watchful guardianship of Marged.

Pam, Arglwydd, y gwnaethost
Gwm Pennant mor dlws,
A bywyd hen fugail mor fyr?[1]

Perhaps we all have a favourite river? Mine has its source at the head of Cwm Pennant, and runs into Tremadog Bay a mile west of Cricieth: Afon Dwyfor. Through the most educative years of my life sound of water, pulsing after storms, trickling even through droughts, came in at my window day and night from a tributary the source of which is high on the western flank of Moel yr Ogof. One late afternoon in 1976, in a pool yards from my house, I saw a sea trout, slipped a cord round its tail and flipped it out onto the bank. It graced my dinner table that night. I'd not do that now, my diet having changed. It's something I regret – *agenbite of inwit* and all that. Empathy and respect for all earth's living forms (apart from Johnson's Tories, though I suspect them of being zombies and therefore not to be included among the forms of life) has grown in me over the years. In my twenties, I had less conscience, less awareness, though I was still appreciative of and receptive to natural and landscape beauty. There are few valleys in Eryri as beautiful as Cwm Pennant.

Beauty's hard to quantify. Surely the lesser part has to do with surface appearance? When I think of Cwm Pennant, two things leap to mind: the people I knew there – the valley's community. And the clear water of Afon Dwyfor, unsullied, unpolluted. I was

[1] "Why, Lord, did you make Cwm Pennant so beautiful,/And life of the old shepherd so short?" (Eifion Wyn)

277

fortunate to live there at that time. It was a hard, solitary life. Everything had to be brought down to the house on my back across a stream and along a muddy track, or down a steep and slippery grass slope (the late Tony Conran, poet and translator, slipped here and broke his thumb when visiting, for which I've felt guilty for many years). Water came from the stream. It was my good fortune to encounter and enter into the valley community when it was on the cusp.

Old respectful co-existent ways before the modern exploitative modes of being in a landscape still held sway. No barbed wire in Cwm Pennant in those years! The cure the Morus brothers at Gilfach used for sheep suffering from y *bendro*[2] was to wait for it to die, cut off its head, and hang the head from an alder branch (it had to be alder) above the stream that ran alongside the track up to their house. I asked once how the cure worked? *"Blowfly come, lay eggs in sheeps' brains, maggots hatch out, eat brain, drop off into stream, and the sickness is washed from the land."* Biblical! So much about the living in this valley resonated with what I'd heard from my grandparents, with whom I lived in Manchester until the age of seven, all through my earliest years. They had been country people. Most of their early lives were spent as agricultural labourers within sight of the hills of Wales. They were rich repositories of stories and beliefs. They reminisced continually. My grandmother believed in the existence of fairies. *"Their bodies of congealed air are sometimes carried aloft, otherwhiles grovel in different shapes, and enter in any cranny or cleft of the earth (where air enters) to their ordinary dwellings, the earth being full of cavities and cells and there being no place or creature but is supposed to have other animals (greater or lesser) living in or upon it as inhabitants and no such thing as a pure wilderness in the whole universe."*[3]

---

[2] *Y Bendro*, otherwise known as the staggers, is a condition in sheep caused by a mineral deficiency, hence the sheep-licks you find on Welsh hill grazing.

[3] From *The Secret Commonwealth of Elves, Fauns, and Fairies* (late seventeenth century) by Robert Kirk.

My grandmother Gertrude Sproson could easily have come out with an explanation like that to me on the occasions when, as a child, a little mystified, I queried her too closely about what fairies were like and where I might meet them – particularly when her readings of the tea-leaves had induced in her a fit of the divine afflatus. At such times my grandfather, Arthur, would peer over the top of his newspaper, smile fondly, roll his eyes heavenwards, and I, following his gaze to the blankness of the ceiling, would remain perplexed.

Half a century later, after my son's and partner's deaths, when I moved to a remote hill hamlet of Ariège in the French Pyrenees, once again I encountered the same point of change I'd met in Cwm Pennant. The Ariègeois were another old peasant community, with traditional beliefs and magical practices giving way to newer, more thrusting ways of land-utilisation. I felt at home – and would still, but for the political perturbations of Britain's asinine and self-harming EU secession. The rivers – the feminine principle of landscape – are crucial within this gorgeous physical framework of Cwm Pennant. They were always associated with lines of communication – itself a feminine principle. Roads and paths followed their courses. Fields and houses were close to them, the cleared land was in the valley bottoms. Every *bro* centred on its own river. My friends in Cwm Pennant were farmers. At dipping and shearing, at hay-making and lambing, I would help them. The valley ethos was co-operative, communitarian, civilised. I remember the first social event I went to in nearby Garn Dolbenmaen – a concert by a local singer, Eleri Llwyd. What registered with me most strongly were the themes and preoccupations of her songs. They were about mist on the hills, swallows building their nests, swimming in the river during the high days of summer. The visions they evoked were simple, rural, eternal, and framed by the exquisite environment in which I had found a home. My summer nights were spent on the river, catching salmon in deep pools with one of my two closest friends there, Owen John "Now" Owen, youngest of three brothers from Cwrt Isaf farm. Through the years I lived there, few days passed without my seeing Now at some point of the day. He was dark-haired, his brown eyes luminous. He struggled with English but in Welsh could talk volubly, passionately and for hours on the life he knew, the things that mattered to him – among which Afon Dwyfor figured large. He knew its every inch from source to sea. In summer, after foxglove had come into bloom, which was a sign that salmon would be coming up-river, every night with *tryfar* in his hand and a car spotlight wired up to a battery in a cut-down plastic container that had held sheep drench, which I carried slung by rope across my shoulder, we would be out on the river.

We earned our living from it on those summer nights. On a good night we'd catch a dozen salmon, averaging eight to ten pounds each. Whatever we didn't keep for our own consumption would be taken next morning to the back door of a pub, the landlord of which always had fresh salmon steaks on his menu. He paid us generously. Now reckoned he earned more from our nights on the river than he did from raising sheep, even when the practice, prevalent at that time, of transporting large numbers of sheep to a farm miles away with the same ear-markings in order to increase headage payments (which would be split between the two farms) was taken into account. Not long after I left the valley, he gave up farming and worked as linesman for the electricity board, and after that in his wife Glenys's family hardware shop in Pwllheli, where I'd see him from time to time, and always with the greatest pleasure. He fell ill of a wasting disease in his fifties, and it carried him off with merciful speed. I still miss the wholehearted enthusiasm, the playfulness, the rural skills, the openness that were such hallmarks of his character. In memory's eye I see him standing in the Dwyfor up to his waist in a deep pool near Pont Llan, eyes fiercely intent on following swift progress of a salmon up-river, directing me where to shine the light, the *tryfar* on its long pole slowly raised, held still as he gauged refraction in the water. Then he plunged down with unerring accuracy and force. I'd be beckoned urgently into the river to hook the stricken fish by its gills onto the bank – a primitive and brutal scene that had been enacted and re-enacted for centuries, perhaps millennia, along this very river. We re-lived it nightly. Sometimes we'd stop off at the topmost farm, Braich y Dinas, and give old Wil Braichdinas a salmon. He'd been farming there for generations, ran a small café for the tourists. Everyone in the valley knew he was descended from the *Tylwyth Teg* – the beautiful folk, which was the propitiatory name by which those tricksters the fairies were known. Their other name hereabouts was the *Belisiaid*, and the story to explain that came from beyond Bwlch y Ddwy Elor at the head of the valley.

This "pass of the two biers" led over to Bwlch Gylfin close to Llyn y Dywarchen, which had been famous since the time of Giraldus for its floating island (under which the Astronomer Royal, Edmund Halley – he of the comet fame – had swum to check that it really did float). Bwlch Gylfin has a dramatic, quartz-seamed rocky knoll, Clogwyn y Garreg. It's a bare three miles from Braich y Dinas in Cwm Pennant. Welsh folklore identifies this knoll as a portal to fairyland. Beyond it are Cwellyn and the Gwyrfai valley, which also abound in associations with *Y Tylwyth Teg*. Early Ordnance Survey maps show two dammed lakes at Bwlch Gylfin. Llyn Bwlch y Moch is now no more than a sedgy bottom. Sluices ran from its now-breached dam to power machinery for the Drwsycoed copper mines down-valley towards Nantlle. The dam of Llyn y Dywarchen is, however, still intact.

For centuries the lake's floating island was a major attraction. In 1188 Giraldus noted how it was "driven from one side to the other by the force of the wind". Thomas Pennant in 1784 reported that cattle occasionally wandered onto it and were carried away from the shore. Better still was the experience one evening of a young man from nearby Drws-y-coed farm who found a fairy woman of great beauty reclining there. She agreed to be his servant if he could discover her name, which he did by eavesdropping on a fairy conversation as he returned from market one evening. It was Bela (hence the Belisiaid to which family Wil Braichdinas belonged), and she proved expert at animal husbandry. Their flocks thrived. She agreed to take the lad from the farm as husband on condition he never touched her with iron. Children were born. (It was their descendants who migrated beyond the "ridge of the red cairns" by way of the "pass of the two biers" into Cwm Pennant, where even in my time they were still known as "Belisiaid".) Inevitably, the catastrophic day came when he carelessly tossed her a bridle and she vanished instantly into the lake. In one version of the story, Bela's mother enabled her nightly return to the floating island for as long as her husband lived. He and the island are long gone into the realm where folklore, travellers' tales and prehistory all mingle. Only a summer-resident teal up from the estuaries, or an occasional angler there for the small brown trout, bobs on its lapping waves now.

As to the fairies, even a shallow acquaintance with the scholarly writings of Kathleen Raine, Principal Rhys, Lady Gregory, W.B. Yeats, Marie-Louise von Franz, Marina Warner and W.Y. Evans-Wentz will leave you with the impression of a certain maziness about them, *"for these are the Hosts of the Air"*. To join their merry dance leads to abandonment on forlorn hillsides, to waking suddenly old and in a country from which all past certainties have fled. The Fair Folk are tricksters. At this strange lake you're right by their front door. And they'll be laughing, as Wil Braichdinas used to laugh at Now and myself years ago, wet from the lovely river that runs through his land, holding out a salmon for him to feast upon. The Welsh scholar W.J. Gruffydd believed that the fairy lore that lingered long into the twentieth century among the Welsh hills was a distant tribal memory from waves of invaders during the bronze and iron ages who displaced earlier settlers in these mountains, driving them into the most remote places (as Blaen Pennant certainly would have been then) or even crannog habitations in lakes, intermarrying with them occasionally. I like the theory. It feels right when you sit in these places and ponder the what-must-have-beens of their long histories. The stories are sounding boards to their atmosphere, and as to their historicity, only lost time can vouch for that, and speaks few words of witness, except within the oral tradition. I remember spending time with the Inuit in their homeland of Nunavut, that at the time of my sojourn among them had recently seceded from Canada's North West Territories. The coherence and underlying factual reliability of their oral traditions were remarkable[4]. Why should they not also be thus in a quite remote valley of western Eryri that had seen very little change of population until the post-war period?

* * *

Walking upriver recently from Aberdwyfor there was the usual seethe of grey mullet by the drain from Aberkin farm. I left behind the splashy and flotsam-littered saltings, scrambled over the railway crossing, passed the small island with its purling rapids on either side where Jan and Elizabeth Morris – whose home ground

---

[4] Inuit folk memory of meeting survivors from the Franklin expedition boats and even taking part in joint hunting was crucial in the recent locating of the wrecks of the Erebus and the Terror. For more on this fascinating topic see *"All Well": Narrating the Third Franklin Expedition*, by Edward Parkinson in *Echoing Silence: Essays on Arctic Narrative*, ed. John Moss (University of Ottawa Press, 1997).

this is – will lie buried together, and took the muddy path beyond the village through beech copses alongside the river. Rare sunshine after a cold spring had brought tight clumps of small and delicately-frilled native daffodils into flower. The clear water swelled slick between mossy boulders, as though unwilling to ruffle the surface of the long pools behind. A half-mile upstream from the Lloyd George memorial I stood on a green bank of bladed bluebell leaves still weeks from their flowering and looked down into a shadowed eddy, where something odd had caught my eye. On the silty bottom, a black and writhing knot the size of my fist rolled around in rippling bankside eddies, slowly uncurling to thread itself ragged and disjointed along the river margin. I knelt down and peered more closely at something I've never seen before – not in this river, stretches of which I've known intimately for fifty years, nor in any other. In fading light I finally made out that it was a mass of tiny eels – elvers the length and thickness of my little finger, here too early surely, possessed of a frantic and relentless energy which split into separate creatures and surged forward in procession against the force of swift water. Chastened somehow, bemused at witnessing a natural wonder, I watched ball become line and swim on in formation towards the shallow mountain headwaters. To see it felt like a precious gift. But it also reminded me of what I'd read in Tom Fort's masterful study, *The Book of Eels* – a classic of 21st-century nature-writing, and the most lucid and persuasive illustration I know of climate-change and our profligacy towards natural resources – about the drastic decline in population of a species the life-history of which is as extraordinary as any on this planet. Memory chastened of the profligacy Now and I had shown toward the salmon in this selfsame river, at a time in our lives when everything seemed boundless, limitless, there for our taking.

A wind had sprung up from the west as I knelt there musing,

a passage from Thoreau's rivers book was running in my mind:

The wind, rustling the oaks and hazels, impressed us like a wakeful and inconsiderate person up at midnight, moving about and putting things to rights, occasionally stirring up whole drawers of leaves at a puff. There seemed to be a great haste and preparation throughout nature, as for a distinguished visitor ...

That passage is preceded by one where Thoreau the Transcendentalist is reaching out toward the sense of oneness that is the mystical experience:

...all things seemed with us to flow; the shore itself, and the distant cliffs, were dissolved by the undiluted air. The hardest material seemed to obey the same law with the most fluid, and so indeed in the long run it does. Trees were but rivers of sap and woody fibre, flowing from the atmosphere, and emptying into the earth by their trunks, as their roots flowed upward to the surface. And in the heavens there were rivers of stars, and milky-ways, already beginning to gleam and ripple over our heads.[5]

That sense of the interconnectedness that continually teases and excites and reassures in closeness to nature was strongly with me throughout my time in Cwm Pennant. "Now" led me to innumerable instances of it, and I found it for myself in the seasonal round of shepherding. Sometimes it takes years to understand what we've learnt from people who've been important in our lives. Both my close friends from the Pennant years are gone, "Now" from sudden-onset motor neurone disease. Welsh of the Welsh, he taught me much about these hills. The lesson of my other friend from those magical years was more fundamental, how he came by it historically fascinating. Bob Rickford was a London

---

[5] From "Thursday" in Thoreau's *A Week on the Concord and Merrimack Rivers* (Volume five in the Princeton edition of *The Writings of Henry D. Thoreau*).

boy, born at King's Cross in 1922, so when I first met him in the summer of 1973 he was 51.

He was brought up in Essex. At school his only aptitudes were for English and woodwork. When the family moved back to London he was apprenticed to an uncle who ran a confectionery shop on the Bayswater Road. The Second World War broke out, Bob enlisted in the Merchant Navy, and was serving as assistant cook on a tanker *en route* for Cuba in 194??. It was attacked and sunk by the German battle cruiser Scharnhorst, which picked up the survivors – Bob among them – and conveyed them to Brest. They were transferred by train from there to a PoW camp near Hamburg, where he spent the rest of the war. He occupied his time as prisoner-of-war in studying navigation, hoping to become a Merchant Navy officer once hostilities were at an end. Back in Britain, with the war, over he passed his exams with flying colours, but failed on eyesight requirement, which demanded 20/20 vision without spectacles. That didn't apply in the fishing fleet. Bob headed for Wales and signed on as crew on a trawler sailing out of Milford Haven. Some of the stories he told me were hair-raising. In one Atlantic storm his boat put in to Castletownbere on the Beara peninsula of Co. Kerry for shelter.

The skipper detailed Bob to shovel coal away from the side of the hold. As he did so he found the whole side of the boat was laced and fretted by rust. A single powerful wave at sea would have sent them to the bottom. He quit, married, took a local government job in Chelsea; he and his wife had a daughter (the former *Guardian* social services correspondent Frankie Rickford) before they separated. His captive years had unfitted him for domesticity. He lived in a cabin cruiser moored on the Thames at Walton. After a few years he married Jeannie, and in 1972 moved with her to a smallholding without road access above Llanllyfni. He worked as warden, storesman and handyman at the Cwm

Pennant Mountain Centre in the former stable blocks to Bryncir Hall, where he charmed and entertained the hundreds each year who encountered him, myself included.

"Bee-swarming, wasp-exterminating and bird-stuffing.
There was nothing he did not know; there was nothing, nothing"[6]

Over the next four years I saw him most days. He was the most sociable of men, with a fund of stories and a lively interest in all that went on around him. We climbed together on at least a couple of occasions. He'd had a particular desire to do the Cyfrwy Arête on Cader Idris, and the Upper Slab route on Craig yr Ogof in Cwm Silyn. He was short and heavy, but immensely strong and competent, encouraging, genial. And – this is the defining characteristic of his which distinguishes all my memories of him – utterly appreciative of every dimension of the experiences in which he was engaged. I remember one holiday he took when he and Jeannie walked up to little Llyn Clyd below Y Garn, set up camp, and simply imbibed the atmosphere of the place for a fortnight, swam, fished, made an occasional foray down to Bethesda to stock up on whiskey and food. This quality of deep absorption, quietistic almost, in experiences no matter how apparently limited, caused my own pleasure in them to be amplified. That was as true of an evening round of Pennant after rabbits for the pot as it was of an evening in some local pub in Garn, Bryncir or Llanllyfni, or even a pot of tea and piece of cake in a Betws-y-coed café. The deprivations he'd known had taught him to value what he had. By his warmly celebratory responses; by his valuing of things, whether they be the solid length of yew cut from dead sections of an ancient tree (it played havoc with my

---

[6] Ivor Gurney, "The Lock Keeper". This fine autobiographical poem always puts me in mind of Bob, who had amassed an impressive amount of country lore for a city boy, and who added to and refined it continually.

chain saw – yew wood is of exceptional hardness), which I gave him so that he might make Jeannie a spinning wheel; or the fly-rod I passed on to him that he delighted in carrying up to high tarns, he made sure that I learnt that lesson from him. I still thank him for it, still hold his memory dear.

As life-tutors, Now and Bob could scarcely have been bettered. But the valley and the river, as well as the community we lived in, were their tutors, instilling in them the ways in which they both, differently, brought the same out for me. I reach again for my refrain from Thoreau:

"The life in us is like the water in the river."

The same sense permeates Matthew Arnold's Victorian lyric, "The Scholar Gipsy", with its melancholic harking-back from the height (depths?) of the Industrial Revolution to a time when:

"...wits were fresh and clear,
And life ran gaily as the sparkling Thames;"

Pastoral idylls, you might well point out, are all very well, but on this over-crowded island of Britain very few are fortunate to be able to live them. That depends on how much you have, or how much you're prepared to give up. A naturalist will return time and again to his or her favourite places. In Wales there's a term for this ritual of habituation: *"dyn ei filltir sgwâr"* – someone of their own square mile. Being thus brings rewards. This precious landscape, between where Afon Dwyfor sidles into the sea and its headwaters at Blaen Pennant has brought gifts to me that have been glorious: a marsh harrier hunting across the saltings; monochrome flicker of knot scouring like smoke across a sunset sky; soft whistlings and purrings of pintail and wigeon at pre-dawn; swirl of otters in pursuit of salmon; reed-buntings and bearded tits among phragmites beds; the Glaslyn osprey flouncing down on a solitary mullet or a dab sighted in the river's shallows; goosander and merganser arrowing upstream; gleam of little egrets in the tide-flow; even a great skua – all these are now assimilated into perpetual memory. Yet this quiet estuary of Aberdwyfor a very few years ago was the target of an attempted land-grab by the British Association for Shooting and Conservation, which supported an application by a local wildfowling club to lease for shooting Crown Estate land all along the tidal river. This is land traversed by the Wales Coastal Path. The farmer, Peredur Parry, a concerned and decent man who died in 2019, kept his fields in good heart through unstinting labour. He didn't want shooters here. Nor do walkers who exercise here throughout day and year. Nor do I. But don't imagine that will stop those whose idea of recreation is the slaughter of wildlife that others intensely value. The BASC application included a form that listed species of goose, duck and wader permissible to shoot. It included wigeon, pintail, golden plover, snipe, woodcock. Look up current status of those species and you'll find a recurrent vocabulary: rare, declining, irregular visitor, threatened…

When will we learn? The BASC application outlined plans to breed and introduce more mallard as quarry. They would have become the dominant species, had the BASC's application succeeded, excluding others from this habitat. Extinction's tipping points? Shooting and conservation? That structure is oxymoronic. The lease application was made last-minute, in the hope of slipping it through unnoticed before imminent new gun legislation. Local naturalists along the Dwyfor have keen eyes. It was noticed, a concerted local campaign of opposition was mounted. For once the shooters' designs were frustrated and blocked. But their power and wealth is immense. If we are to continue in our enjoyment of Welsh rivers and their wildlife, we not only have to hold the polluters to task. We also need to take guard and fight when necessary those who seek to destroy all that we hold dear. Public opinion is strongly on our side – that of real conservation, not the cynical and mendacious adoption of that tag as concealment for destructive motives. It's a fight that we can and must win. For Nature's sake...

Select Bibliography

Footnotes throughout the text will direct you to useful sources of further information. For more general further reading around the subject area, I would recommend the following titles:

George Borrow, *Wild Wales* (1862 – many editions).
One of the major classics of British travel writing – eccentric, humorous and quirkily knowledgable.

W.M. Condry, *The Snowdonia National Park* (Collins New Naturalist 1966)
A better and more useful volume than its North, Campbell and Scott precursor of 1951.

W.M. Condry, *The Natural History of Wales* (Collins New Naturalist 1981)
A marvel of compression and lucidity by the foremost Welsh-based field naturalist of his era.

W.M. Condry, *A William Condry Reader*, ed. Jim Perrin (Gwasg Gomer, 2015)

Gerald of Wales, *The Journey Through Wales/The Description of Wales* (Penguin 1978). Medieval perspectives from this opinionated and ambitious cleric.

Robert Gibbings, *Coming Down the Wye* (Dent 1942)
A delightful period piece with exquisite woodcuts.

Francis Kilvert, *Kilvert's Diary* (three volumes, Cape 1938-40, revised edition 1961)
An invaluable insight into Victorian rural life. The boxed set is rare and expensive.

Keith Kissack, *The River Wye* (Terence Dalton 1978)
As well informed as you could expect from a former curator of Monmouth museum.

The Mabiniogion, translated by Gwyn Jones & Thomas Jones (Dent 1949)
Still by far the best translation, its register ideally suited to the subject-matter.

Jan Morris, *The Matter of Wales: Epic Views of a Small Country* (Oxford 1984)
Deliciously redolent and vastly informative from our late *grande dame* of Welsh letters.

Thomas Pennant, *The Tour Through Wales* (1778-1783)
Invaluable, plagiarised by Wordsworth, praised by Dr. Johnson. Bridge Books of Wrexham published a two-volume edition in 1991 with a useful introduction by R. Paul Evans.

Gwyn Alf Williams, *When Was Wales?* (Penguin, 1985)
An exhilarating ride through Welsh history with Wales's pre-eminent modern historian.

The Ordnance Survey 1:25,000 scale maps are indispensable and by no means always to be trusted in matters of toponymy. If you've ever seen a production of Brian Friel's great play *Translations* (1980), about the colonialist project of mapping 1840s Donegal, you'll have a sense of what's been going on here.

Finally, the Welsh language series *Crwydro*, issued in the 1950s and 1960s by Christopher Davies Llandybie, set a standard for Welsh topographical writing that its counterparts in English have seldom approached. If you have no Welsh, book yourself in for a course at Nant Gwrtheyrn right away!

Acknowledgements

There are so many people to whom I'm indebted for any richness, variety and insight this text may possess. You'll find them credited in footnotes throughout the text, and I hope you'll follow those leads to the sources cited there. I'm also immensely grateful to those with whom I've shared these journeys and riparian explorations. I owe a particular debt of gratitude to Mrs. Penny Condry, widow of my great friend and mentor William Moreton Condry, for her permission to use long extracts from a lengthy and vibrant 1946 letter to his friend Reg Perry, and other excerpts from his writings. Other friends and acquaintances to whom I'm grateful for offerings, advice, help, companionship and other support are: Muammar Akhtar, Robert Allen, the late Al Alvarez, Roselle Angwin, Kenny Atmadji, Iwan Bala, Sally Baker, John Beatty, the late Alan Bevan, Bill and Honor Bowker, the late Joe Brown, Browsers' Bookshop in Porthmadog, Cochybonddu bookshop in Machynlleth, Donald Campbell, Ian Cartledge ("Fox"), Mark Cocker and Mary Muir, Fiona Collins, Sam Cooke, Jim Crumley, the late Bill Curtin, Iestyn Daniel, Siân Melangell Dafydd, Charles Dark of the Wynnstay Arms Machynlleth, Bill Davidson, Carey Davies at TGO magazine, Rhian Davies, Paul and Nancy Evans, James Friel, Rosemary Grant, Sarah Gregory, Dai Hawkins, Jeremy Hooker, the artists Maria Hayes and Mary Hill, Eric Hoole, Siôn Ilar for the latest in his sequence of delectable cover illustrations (those ghostly white shapes exactly capture what's happening on our Welsh rivers!), Simon Jenkins, the late Jonah Jones, R. Merfyn Jones, Raymond Jones, Pauline Frederica Kiernan, Jonathan Keates, Dewi Lewis of Siop Dewi Penrhyndeudraeth, Gwyneth Lewis, the painter Isobel Macleod, Cameron and Gina McNeish, Rob Mimpriss (to whom special thanks for the foreword and also for editorial assistance and extracts from the introduction to his masterful Cockatrice Books translation of

Morgan Llwyd's *Llyfr y Tri Aderyn*), the late Jan Morris, Sian Northey, Fiona Owen, the late Owen Wyn Owen ("Now Cwrt Isaf"), the late Will Perrin, Dean Powell, the late Ioan Bowen Rees, the late John Pledge, Sam Roberts, David Rose, Hilary Rowlands, Harry and Ann Rothman, Antony Shaw, Lorna Siggins, Cathal O'Searcaigh for friendship and an excerpt from his poem "An Tobar", the late Gwyn Thomas ("Yr Athro"), Soames John Whittingham, M. Wynn Thomas, Marged Tudor-Turner, Susie White, Ben and Susie Wildsmith, Neil Wilson, William Williams-Wynne, Jan Wolf, Ray Wood, Ray Wood. To the estate of Robert Gibbing I give thanks for extracts from *Coming Down the Wye*, and to that of T.S. Eliot for a brief extract in the chapter on Afon Teifi from Four Quartets; to the editors at the *Guardian* and *Cambrian News* for extracts from environmental articles credited along with their authors in footnotes, and my Country Diary editors at the *Guardian* newspaper over the last fifteen years, most especially to Celia Locks, Anne-Marie Conway and Paul Fleckney, who deserve a special vote of thanks from me for their diligence, enthusiasm, and careful expertise. The intelligent good humour and bantering impudence of my sons Conor Gregory and Lewis Perrin Williams have been an unfailing source of stimulus and delight for which I love them all the more dearly. Last but not least, my heartfelt thanks to Myrddin ap Dafydd of Gwasg Carreg Gwalch for taking on this book and other of my titles that were on the list of Gwasg Gomer Llandysul when that admirable old Welsh institution ceased book publishing; to the Welsh Books Council for grant aid that gave me breathing space to write; Dylan Williams read through the text and saved me from embarrassment here and there. Inevitably, I'll have missed many names out from this list. It I plead your forbearance until the matter can be corrected.